D1112108

Douglas Smith Anderson
Joan Terpstra Anderson
5-22-97

Survival of the

Spirit

* * * * * * * * *

Survival of the Spirit

✳ ✳ ✳ ✳ ✳ ✳ ✳ ✳ ✳ ✳ ✳

Chiricahua Apaches in Captivity

H. Henrietta Stockel

University of Nevada Press ▲▲ Reno LasVegas London

OTHER BOOKS BY THE AUTHOR

Women of the Apache Nation:
Voices of Truth

Medicine Women, Curanderas, and
Women Doctors
    with Bobette Perrone and
    Victoria Krueger

The paper used in this book meets
the requirements of American
National Standard for Information
Sciences—Permanence of Paper for
Printed Library Materials,
ANSI Z39.48-1984. Binding materials
were selected for strength and
durability.

University of Nevada Press,
Reno, Nevada 89557 USA

Copyright © 1993
University of Nevada Press
All rights reserved

Book design by Richard Hendel
Printed in the United States of
America

9 8 7 6 5 4 3 2 1

Library of Congress
Cataloging-in-Publication Data
Stockel, H. Henrietta, 1938–
    Survival of the spirit : Chiricahua
Apaches in captivity / H. Henrietta
Stockel.
        p.   cm.
    Includes bibliographical references
and index.
    ISBN 0-87417-208-X (cloth :
acid-free paper)
    1. Apache Indians—History.
2. Apache Indians—Diseases.
3. Apache Indians—Health and
hygiene.   4. Folk medicine—
Southwest, New.   5. Shamanism—
Southwest, New.   6. Prisoners of
war—Southwest, New—History.
I. Title.
E99.A6S75   1993
355.4'1—dc20   92-39772
                                         CIP

FRONTISPIECE
Unidentified young Chiricahua
Apache warriors in shackles, prior
to 1886. Note ration tags around
their necks, indicating that they
once had been on a reservation.
(Frisco Native American Museum)

*   *   *   *

To the Chiricahua Apache children who died

as prisoners of war.

This is the tragic story they didn't live to tell.

*   *   *   *

Once I moved about like the wind. Now I

surrender to you and that is all.

    —Geronimo to General George Crook, *1886*

*   *   *   *

The only good Indians I ever saw were dead.

    —General Philip Henry Sheridan, *1869*

*   *   *   *

Thou shalt love thy neighbor as thyself.

    —Leviticus *19:18*

CONTENTS

✴ ✴ ✴ ✴

✳   ✳   ✳   ✳

Chiricahua Apache campfires blazed through the blackness, scattered across a mountain range on the Mescalero Apache Reservation in New Mexico, and men called to each other in deep voices, canyon to canyon. Seen by firelight, the campsites were busy with visitors, all greeting each other as if they hadn't been together for years. All were attending a private puberty ceremony and had spent the last twenty-four hours participating in a ritual that helped celebrate a young maiden's passage to womanhood. Now it was, at long last, time to rest.

Louise Fairchild and I had left the sacred dance grounds earlier and had slowly picked our way up the long, heavily wooded route to our chosen campsite, being very careful not to stumble. We had forgotten to take our flashlight from the van earlier in the day, when the sun was still shining on the ceremony. Now, gingerly stepping along the narrow, rutted road, we finally found our vehicle in the moonlight. After fussing a bit, we hunkered down under zipped-open sleeping bags for the night. Early the next morning we were to begin the long journey to the East Coast sites of the former Chiricahua Apache prison camps, where the ancestors of the folks surrounding us had been incarcerated.

We opened the windows to let in the cool air. Although it was June, no bugs buzzed overhead. The seven-thousand-foot altitude acted as the best air-conditioner and flying insect deterrent we could hope for. Still, there was something moving outside; a large shadow had come and gone between our van and the neighboring campfire. A heavy voice asked, "You alright in there?" It was Dan Kanseah, a Chiricahua friend whose grandfather was Geronimo's nephew. He was just checking on us. "You don't have to be worried up here," he added. "You're safe, and my camp is right below you. If you get scared, just come on over." For an instant I knew how Apache women felt more than a hundred years ago, protected by their men.

At first light some of the fires were still smoldering, but other than that, most of the sleeping or whispering Apaches around us were quiet. The only sounds we heard were the wings of birds whooshing high above, a good omen. The top branches of lodgepole pines waved from side to side in the clean morning air. It wasn't hard to believe that they were bidding us *adieu* and wishing us a safe journey.

As we traveled from New Mexico across Texas, Louisiana, Mississippi, Alabama, and into Florida, we passed fields of wildflowers breathtaking in their blooming beauty. It was obvious that spring had been wet in the southern states and Mother Nature was really proud of herself. The sight of such lovely landscapes diminished the tediousness of seemingly unending roads and eased my worries about whether the journey would be successful.

Crossing Louisiana, the heat and humidity were nearly unbearable each time we stepped out of the air-conditioned vehicle. Yet the mysterious bayous held a murky attraction that was mesmerizing, and we had to have a closer look. In Pass Christian, Mississippi, we were excited to see shrimp boats lined up on either side of a boardwalk jutting out into the water. It was a rare sight for desert dwellers, so we stopped for more than an hour to take photos. A bit farther east, near Biloxi, we gave up—couldn't resist any longer the temptation to take our shoes off and rush into the Gulf of Mexico, clothes and all. When we reached our destination in Florida after traveling across many Alabama bridges, we camped beside a pond and took the time to watch a large family of ducks serenely float by as squirrels peeked from the limbs of trees right behind us. We were surprised one morning when we awakened to find a tiny toad sleeping beside us in the van.

And then it was time to begin.

ACKNOWLEDGMENTS

✳ ✳ ✳ ✳

My companion in these journeys was Louise d'Avignon Fairchild, a close friend who helped with the research required to write this book—including copying by hand the thirteen years of medical records pertaining to the Chiricahuas available at Fort Sill, Oklahoma, and helping to review the archival material in fifteen boxes at the Frisco Native American Museum in North Carolina. I cannot credit her enough, nor can I pay her adequate tribute for all of her support. Through her constant presence she has become a sustaining factor in my life and has, in many generous ways, enabled me to fulfill my lifelong ambition of being a writer. From the bottom of my heart, thank you, Louise.

After our research in Florida was completed, we visited my sister Teressa S. Matousek in central Florida, who lives with her daughter, Lorrie B. Stone. Spending time with my family, no matter how short the visit, is pleasant and rejuvenating, and we had a heartwarming time, even though I complained mightily about the weather. Loving thanks to them for their kindnesses and understanding that I've made a total adaptation to the dry southwestern climate.

Another niece, Erika T. Polhamus, lives in New Jersey, and for a while I thought I would have to travel there to further my investigation of all possible sources of information. Thanks to Erika for her enthusiastic anticipation of the trip that never happened.

Stopping in Pensacola, I met Woody Skinner for the first time and spent two hours listening to his remarkable tales of the events that happened during the imprisonment of the Chiricahua Apaches in his neck of the woods. His knowledge of the details about the way the prisoners of war were treated is extensive, and his outrage is genuine. I was struck by his sincerity.

In Mobile, I was reunited with my spirit sisters, Paula Taylor and Pam Witt, and we have continued a close relationship since then. I appreciate their hospitality and am thankful for the proof of my beliefs about another time, another place. I look forward to a long and happy friendship with these two southern belles and further exploration of our common heritage.

Still in Alabama, Arthur Capell and Belinda Jones, both information specialists at Searcy Hospital, were of inestimable assistance in my research activities. For three days they provided access to valuable documents held in their trust and answered many, many questions about the years of Apache incarceration on the hospital's grounds in Mount Vernon. Arthur drove us around and was patient and accommodating when we asked him to drive us around once more. Belinda made innumerable trips to the photocopy machine outside the building, and went back again and again, even to reproduce just one sheet of paper.

During the next trip, we met Carl and Joyce Bornfriend in North Carolina. They cook the best shrimp dinners I have ever eaten. Along with feeding us, Carl and Joyce made us feel like longtime friends who were just coming to call for a few days. The materials about the Chiricahua Apaches and their years of imprisonment that are housed at the Frisco Native American Museum were of so much importance to this book that it would not have been the same document without the Bornfriends' assistance. L'chaim!

In Oklahoma, William Welge and Judith Michener at the Oklahoma Historical Society devoted time and attention to our research needs. Thanks to them for their expertise and able assistance. Judy Crowder, the late Linda Roper, and Towana Spivey at the Fort Sill Museum offered their extensive files and expertise to us. As in the past, we took advantage of the donation, but I now want to express my appreciation to this team who are always available to cheerfully provide material needed in my field of research.

Another helpful professional was Lori Davisson at the Arizona

Historical Society (AHS), who sent along suggestions and provided important materials. Lori helped me make contact with Allan Radbourne, an Englishman who identified several women in one of the photos I had ordered from the AHS. His thoroughness in explaining his methods to me resulted in correcting an error I had made regarding that particular photo.

At home, Ed and Lee Tracy allowed me to travel because they watched the house and the cats each time I asked. Jane Cotter kept the tennis balls coming across the net and kept me away from the word processor long enough to be refreshed.

Dan Thrapp continues to inspire me. I hope my writings will some day be considered as important to knowledge about the Chiricahua Apaches as his works are today. And I must not forget Ed Sweeney, whose definitive biography of Cochise will undoubtedly stand alone for many, many years.

Tom Radko and his group of experts at the University of Nevada Press impress me with their sincerity and dedication to producing quality books. I look forward to a long and successful association with them.

Two physicians profoundly influenced me when I was a younger woman, and more than likely I still carry the effects of our long associations. Cardiologist Simon Dack, M.D., set standards of excellence in the practice of medicine that continue to command my respect. And Lillian Batlin, M.D., a family practitioner, is in the fullest sense a dear and glorious physician and truly an extraordinary woman. Thank you, Lillian, for not forgetting.

To the many friends and acquaintances who helped by their enthusiasm and willingness to contribute in many appreciated ways, especially to authors such as the late Eve Ball, Angie Debo, and "Doc" Sonnischen, and to others with an abiding interest in the same topic, thanks so much for beckoning, supporting, and clearing the path.

Lastly, I want to acknowledge the descendants of the Chiricahua Apache prisoners of war. Knowing that they still hold in their hearts the fire around which the Mountain Spirits dance has caused me to write this book.

INTRODUCTION

✳   ✳   ✳   ✳

Good health is a natural state desired by everyone. If you have your health, some say, you have everything; just ask someone who has been ill. When illness strikes and disease becomes the dominant condition, every aspect of a smoothly flowing life is disrupted. In a family, for example, children may be so frightened by a parent's illness that schoolwork is neglected, appetites suffer, and insecurity becomes a constant companion. If the situation continues over a long period, the entire family may be shattered, financially as well as physically and emotionally. Fortunately, if the ailments are not serious, a person's natural healing abilities or modern medical science and pharmaceuticals come to the rescue. In a short period, most maladies are under control. It wasn't always this simple.

Viewed from today's perspective of high-tech diagnostic machines and complex antidotes, medical treatments were once extremely limited. Many remedies were unscientific and were, in the West and Southwest particularly, based in Hispanic religious concepts, the folk medicine tradition, or in the frontier mythology that was growing along with the Anglo pioneer population. But hundreds of years before Europeans and their descendants settled this region of the nation, Native American shamans practiced their healing arts in ceremonies given to them by the sacred spiritual world, utilizing only rituals and naturally growing medicinal herbs to offset the effects of injuries and minor ailments. America's indigenous peoples were more than likely free from contagious diseases. However, after the first *conquistador* sneezed and the droplets sailed across Indian country, nothing was ever the same again. Epidemic diseases had arrived, and they spread indiscriminately, cafeteria-style, among all the Native American tribes and peoples. The Indians were virtual sitting ducks.

At first the Chiricahua Apaches were able to avoid much of the contagion because of their limited contact with the newcomers. As interactions became more frequent and more necessary, diseases such as measles and smallpox affected them, but still not to the degree that more sedentary Native American groups experienced them. It was not until the nearly three decades of incarceration by the United States government that the full, deadly medical assault on the Apaches occurred. In confinement the prisoners could not protect themselves by changing locations, essentially running away from the diseases, as they had done when they were free. So they were attacked head-on by killers they could neither see, nor do battle with, nor escape.

Imprisonment began with the surrender of Chiricahua chief Chihuahua. By the time the Naiche/Geronimo band capitulated six months later, almost five hundred Apaches were already incarcerated. Geronimo surrendered voluntarily, convinced that if his small group of thirty-five men, women, and children kept fighting, they would eventually be annihilated by a combination of the United States Army's manpower and weapons. None of the Chiricahuas, nor anyone else for that matter, had any way of knowing at the time that the threat of extinction would take another form, just as deadly. The fierce Apaches believed and trusted the military when they promised that everyone would eventually be free to return to their beloved homelands in Arizona and New Mexico. It would take almost thirty years to happen, a period that no one could have predicted during the surrender negotiations. Mildred Cleghorn, born a prisoner of war in 1910 and today chairperson of the Fort Sill Chiricahua/Warm Springs Apache tribe in Oklahoma, believes that her ancestors were promised only a two-year confinement, but confusion over this matter, as with other conflicts between official documents and oral history, still exists.

What is clear is that in the first two years of incarceration nearly fifty of the prisoners died from contagious diseases. The destruction of the mighty Chiricahua Apache nation was occurring, not honorably through the use of superior military strategy or deadly weaponry but unexpectedly, as a result of murderous germs run amok among prisoners who couldn't fight back.

For years this group of proud Native Americans fought encroachment frantically, even recklessly, and their techniques, seen as brutal from other cultures' perspectives, became increasingly barbaric. That they were fighting for their lives, for their land, for their children, for their future—as they imagined it—meant little or nothing to their enemy, the War Department of the United States of America. Land, land, and more land was most important to the growing nation, along with making sure the limited, precious minerals and water in the Southwest were available to miners and settlers.

The Chiricahua Apaches' expertise in guerilla warfare continually bested the army's customary methods of fighting. As more and more time passed without military success, officials grew increasingly frustrated. With the final surrender of the Naiche/Geronimo band in September 1886, the U.S. government finally had in hand the ferocious foe its army had fought again and again.

Now completely in charge, the government could have taken revenge immediately by ordering the Indians killed without further ado. Almost certainly this idea was debated but ruled out. Instead, the federal government showed "compassion" by imprisoning Geronimo's band and 484 other Apaches, most of whom were not guilty of any atrocities at all. Some had actually served as Indian scouts in the military, and quite a few were innocent children. The entire band was incarcerated first in Florida, then in Alabama, and finally at Fort Sill, Oklahoma. The medical disasters suffered by the Apaches during their imprisonment are the central theme of this book.

Because no other Indian groups, including other bands of Apaches, are relevant to this topic, with the exception of the Warm Springs Apaches, the terms "Chiricahua Apaches" and "Apaches" are used interchangeably and refer throughout to the people who were confined as prisoners of war. When discussed, specific tribes of other Indians are clearly named. Certain members of the Warm Springs Apache band were affiliated with the Chiricahuas and are considered to be part of them.

Spelling of the names of the prisoners varies somewhat throughout the text because I quote them as they were recorded in the historical documents cited. No doubt it was quite difficult for American soldiers to communicate with the prisoners, and often the Apache names were written down phonetically, based on a subjective interpretation by military personnel. Noting the names became so troublesome to officials that many prisoners were arbitrarily given Anglicized first names and surnames. For example, Cheez-le-teedley, which means "Helps Out Around the Camp," became Oswald Smith. Even today, many descendants of the survivors do not know who their ancestors were; all their lives they have carried the Anglo names given to their forebears just to make life easier for the soldiers who guarded them.

Compared with their wives and daughters, the Apache men were fortunate in having names at all. In most instances, Chiricahua women, excluding Warm Springs Apache chief Victorio's sister Lozen, weren't recognized as individuals. Lozen, because of her distinction as a mighty warrior, was mentioned by name on the census count dated the day she died. Ordinarily, in official records kept during the years of captivity, women were either referred to as "wife of So-and-so," or they were documented as "Number X."

In the Apache prisoner-of-war camps and in the Carlisle School where the Chiricahua children were sent, illness became the dominant condition. The social structure—disrupted initially because of the loss of freedom—was turned upside down and revolved around sickness and dying. Death was constantly present. Depression and melancholy were the predominant moods, followed by fear and confusion. Too, the oppressive conditions of confinement contributed psychologically to the Apaches' lowered physical and mental resistance to disease. In the first seven months in Florida, for example, 18 to 24 men, women, and children perished. In the next eight years, approximately 250 prisoners of war died in Alabama. In nearly twenty years in Oklahoma, more than 300 Chiricahua Apaches died.

This book describes that deplorable medical calamity and wonders whether the United States government could have done more, or better, for the prisoners. True, state-of-the-art medicine was nowhere near the level of sophistication we take for granted now, and not very much healing could be accomplished clinically during the late nineteenth and early twentieth centuries. But Indian advocacy organizations understood that and didn't petition the government for medical miracles. What they and others, including sympathetic military personnel, asked was that the dying Apaches be sent back to their homelands, into the healthful climate of Arizona and New Mexico, so that they might recover their vitality as individuals and as a group. After all, other people with tuberculosis were finding relief in the southwestern mountains and deserts. Why not the original inhabitants? For one reason or another, the government turned a deaf ear.

Especially poignant were the deaths of Chiricahua children in schools far from their families. In a misbegotten effort to demonstrate concern for these guiltless youngsters, the administration decreed that they would be forcibly removed from their parents during the first days, weeks, and months of incarceration in Florida and transported to a boarding school in Pennsylvania. There they were expected to learn the white man's ways, adapt, and become "good" Indians. No one bothered to consider that tuberculosis and other contagious ailments were running rampant in the school, and that the children, lacking natural immunities, would be doomed in the infected habitat. Horribly, more than 37 of 112 Chiricahua youngsters perished without seeing their parents again. When the school officials, initially reluctant to admit the problem, finally changed policies, dying Apache children were put on trains and sent back to the prison camps. Occasionally, corpses were gently lifted out of their seats by weakened, disease-ridden friends and handed to unknowing parents waiting at the depot.

As should be clear by now, this book is not just another dry academic recitation of regrettable events that happened to an Indian tribe more than one hundred years ago. Nor is it a variation on the well-known "smallpox blanket" horror that seems to be part of the collective unconscious of the American West. Instead, this is a sympathetic account of how contagion, little understood at the time, affected the Chiricahua Apaches while they were captives of the United States.

This story is told my way, not within any established academic framework. I start at the beginning, centuries ago in the Southwest, and then describe the harmony Native Americans achieved with the desert and mountain region. This includes, of course, their discovery of natural medicines growing in the earth, the ceremonies that evolved to promote healing, and developing cultural customs.

The next newcomers were the Spanish; and after that the Anglos arrived. A potpourri of information provides the reader with an ethnic clinical background embracing traditional Hispanic *curanderismo*, frontier home remedies, and Old West country doctoring. After setting the scene, the book takes a more specific turn, and the dreadful tale of Apache death and dying begins. It is not a pretty story. To some, it may seem as if this tragedy was the result of purposeful actions on the part of administration officials. However, I cannot prove willful genocide by the United States government through the existence of confirming documents or any other irrefutable evidence.

One of my history professors once claimed that no conclusive history of the American West could ever be written because history is always relative, is always characterized by change and continuity through successive generations, and is always shaped by an author's views and values. Given the fact that I did not expect to write another interpretation of Apache history, I selected the more warm-blooded "storytelling" format for this sad tale.

Consequently, this book may generate much criticism among bona fide scholars, or those who pretend to be, and others who may feel they are in a legitimate position to accuse me of telling the story in a biased manner or of any number of related shortcomings. These fault-finders may or may not be correct. No matter. To my judges I issue a simple challenge: do better than I have done, uncover more material of any kind about what actually happened to the prisoners during their years of captivity. Together we will help heal the painful broken circle that once held a whole, and healthy, Chiricahua Apache nation. Only then will more of the truth be released from its own century of imprisonment.

1

Peoples, Homelands, and Cultural Customs

✳ ✳ ✳

Like so many others, I am amazed by the scientific and medical miracles that characterize humankind's technological accomplishments as the millennium approaches. Yet, these scientific developments are really only the beginning. Surely not every enigma has been defined, not every secret has been discovered, and not every mystery cloaked in centuries of wonder has been solved. The spectacular achievements so much a part of our daily lives are only a baby step toward a future of unimaginable sophistication.

Instead of looking solely ahead, however, glance backward over your shoulder for a moment to gain perspective and to measure how far we, as a society and a nation, have come since our continent was first settled. If you are looking at the truth, it will be obvious that the Europeans were latecomers, and not, as so many history books have falsely taught us, the discoverers of America.

One widely accepted and popular belief holds that most pre-Columbian Americans arrived from Europe by tra-

Chiricahua Apache wickiup, ca. 1883. These traditional homes could be abandoned easily when seasons changed or other circumstances influenced migration. (Frisco Native American Museum)

versing a land bridge connecting their homelands with the unoccupied continent. It is believed that this natural passageway disappeared when immense glaciers melted at the end of the last ice age, and no scientific evidence has yet been produced to refute this theory. On the contrary, much circumstantial proof exists to support the premise.

One contemporary author, Edwin R. Sweeney, was able to place a specific group of travelers in Alaska and in the Mackenzie River valley of western Canada. From there these thousands of emigrants wandered southward until they reached and rested in what would become the American Southwest. In describing them, Sweeney pointed out their linguistic and social groupings and the origin of their name, Apache, as either from the Yuman word *e-patch* or from the Zuni word *apachu*, which means "enemy." [1]

Although the year when the newcomers first set foot in the desert and mountain country has never been firmly established, the Apaches arrived later than did other early Native American settlers —perhaps in the first years of the sixteenth century. One source claims that the first archeological evidence of an Apache-occupied site dates back to 1525,[2] but as with other matters of like genre, the issue is still being explored.

Through a gradual process of separation, many divisions emerged out of the mass migration. One of these smaller units was given the name Chiricahua, probably by the Opata Indians of Mexico, according to Sweeney. Further differentiation produced four bands of Chiricahuas: the Chihennes, the Nednis, the Chokonen, and the Bedonkohes.[3] The Chokonen are the band more familiarly known as the Chiricahuas. They are the focus of this book.

Scientific investigators, researchers, authors, and historians hold varying opinions about who the Chiricahuas actually were. Morris Opler[4] believed they were divided into three bands: (1) the eastern, who resided mainly in the territory west of the Rio Grande in New Mexico and were known variously as the Warm Springs, Mimbres, Coppermine, or Mogollon Apaches; (2) the central, who resided in the Dos Cabezas, Chiricahua, Dragoon, Mule, and Huachuca mountains of Arizona and a small territory of northern Mexico and were called the Cochise Apaches, in honor of one of their most famous leaders; and (3) the southern, who lived in a small portion of southwestern New Mexico and northern Mexico and were called the Nedni, Pinery, or Broncho Apaches.

William B. Griffen[5] wrote that in 1800 the Chiricahua Apaches comprised three groups: (1) the Chokonen, who lived primarily in the Chiricahua Mountains of Arizona; (2) the Bedonkohe, who lived north and east of the Chokonen; and (3) the Nednehi (same as Nedni above; spellings also vary), who lived in Mexico in the Sierra Madre mountain range.

Max Moorhead[6] concluded that at the close of the eighteenth century there were nine distinct Apache groups, including Navajos, Mimbreños, Gileños, Tontos, and Coyoteros, living west of the Rio Grande. To the east of the river there were Faraones, Mescaleros, Llaneros, and Lipanes.

As odd as it seems, all of these authors are partially or totally correct in their statements. The process of fission and fusion among the Apache bands was dynamic and continuous. People joined and left groups for reasons related to marriage, family matters, social events, the need for more food, and many other circumstances. Frequently, immediate family or extended family units and their various allegiances determined the size and nature of groups at any given time. This flow was common within the Apache units, not only when they arrived in their homelands but as time went on and the people became more and more involved with others who resided in the same region. By 1886, the end of liberty, the last free Chiricahua group contained members of other Apache bands who had survived years of warfare with Mexican and United States armies.

But long before that, one major aspect of the Apaches' early adaptation to the Southwest is clear: they had to develop a variety of techniques that would utilize the unfamiliar natural environment to its best advantage. For example, the southwestern plants were strange to the people from the north, and they had healing properties different from the natural remedies the people had left behind. After a period of experimentation, the Apache hunters and gatherers undoubtedly learned, identified, memorized, and then came to rely on the local medicinal flora to cure their ailments. Actually, however, application of the healing medicines was the second step in treating ailments. Initially, a consensus had to be reached regarding the causes of illnesses—those that were obvious and those that were not—in the new homeland.

Cultural patterns of the early southwesterners have been examined from many points of view, and most investigators agree, academically, that two basic beliefs explaining poor health prevailed: the world of spirits and the world of magic were both used to interpret and give meaning to mysterious reasons for sicknesses. Known formally as "theurgy" and "thaumaturgy," these concepts were described by Alex Hrdlicka, a physician and respected researcher of pre-European Native American customs. He wrote that

the fundamental and universal characteristics of Indian medicine in the Southwest and northern Mexico are the notions that all serious or protracted illness, the cause of which is not clearly appreciated by the senses, is due to occult evil influences of men, animate or inanimate objects, spirits, or deities, and that the influence is exercised by a magic or secret introduction into the body, particularly during sleep or through touch while awake, of a noxious object or objects, as poison, a worm, an insect, a hair, a thorn, a live coal, which produce and keep up the morbid manifestations.[7]

Simply said, death from unexplained causes was believed to be the work of the supernatural, and quite possibly the result of bewitchment.

No doubt beliefs varied, but these fundamental concepts were so well accepted that they remained unchallenged through time. Writing thirty years after Hrdlicka, Francis H. Elmore stated, "The belief that non-human agents are the causes of certain diseases is the prevailing thought,"[8] adding that religion and magic were two of the main techniques primitive peoples used to combat disease.

Traditional healers occupied exalted places within the societies of Native Americans and were consulted for specialized treatments and purposes. Routine maladies were treated by the ailing individuals themselves or their families with decoctions, poultices, and other applications of common plant medicines. Each group of Native Americans had its independent system of beliefs and rituals which included the ways healers were chosen and the treatments they trusted. Referring in a general way to shamans among prehistoric peoples, Benjamin Gordon wrote, "His position was usually achieved by performing an allegedly miraculous deed, by living a pious or eccentric life, by explaining a dream the interpretation of which later became a reality, or by foretelling successfully events during a state of ecstasy."[9] Famed ethnologist Ruth Underhill, an accomplished scientist and investigator, wrote about another aspect of Native American healing, one in which the healer was all-powerful: "The underlying idea is not that of a physician, searching for any means to combat disease. Rather, the curing agent [the shaman] has power over the disease for good or ill."[10]

Healing customs in many ancient societies consisted in part of a contest between the shaman and the evil responsible for the ailment and often took the form of an actual struggle or heated confrontation during a healing ceremony. In less competitive circumstances, which were the norm, a healer prescribed certain herbs that were well known for their curative properties when administered alone or during a healing ceremony.

In describing the conditions within the early societies in which male and female shamans had predominant roles, Gordon noted that

> the struggle for survival . . . and the long periods of fasting fol-
> lowed by gourmandism cut down . . . the span of life. Their
> women, who carried the main burden of their existence, matured
> young and died early. Child mortality was very high. . . . Animals
> were believed to cause diseases in man . . . it was held that ani-
> mals became so offended and outraged at the carelessness of man
> and the invasion of their rights . . . that they held council and
> determined to obtain revenge on each of them, inflicting disease
> upon their human oppressors.[11]

Whether the cause of illness was attributed to avenging animals, supernatural causes, or demonic possession, the first human inhabi-tants of the Southwest created systems to accommodate their medi-cal needs and to address many issues within their societies. And, more than likely, the cultural patterns that formed these support systems had their bases in a group's history and tradition. Creation myths are an example of a supporting structure that has endured from the earliest times when people tried to explain the earth's phe-nomena seen all around them—the plants, the animals, thunder and lightning, sunshine, the mammoth mountains, and running rivers, all leading to the concept of an omnipotent god or gods.

Many documents describe the forces generated, individually and collectively, when creation myths are repeated in traditional com-munities. In *Medicine Women, Curanderas, and Women Doctors* Bobette Perrone et al. explore the strength of these tales within Native American societies by portraying the general relationship among myths and the causes and cures of illnesses.[12] In *Women of the Apache Nation* I compiled renditions of the Apache creation myths.[13] At least one of the Chiricahua Apache creation myths starts in a familiar, time-honored way:

> In the beginning, when no human beings were alive, the flood
> subsided and clouds drew mountains up out of the water. Birds
> and animals moved into the mountains to find a good place to
> live. Child-of-the-Water, a supernatural being, stood in a certain
> place and caused a dark cloud to form above him, saying he was
> going back to the sky. The cloud encircled him and when it dis-

Unidentified Apache woman with tip of nose removed because she had committed adultery. This traditional form of punishment probably came to an end among the Chiricahua Apaches during incarceration. (Frisco Native American Museum)

appeared, Child-of-the-Water was gone. In his place were two human beings, one of whom was called Changing Woman and the other, suddenly reappearing, was Child-of-the-Water himself. From these, the Apache people have sprung.

Another example of a creation myth is a simple statement by an old Apache. "There was a world before this one according to the old Indians," he said, "and it was destroyed by water. All the people living before this world were washed out." [14] Geronimo never hesitated to tell his own version of his people's origin,[15] which included a battle to the death between birds and beasts.

The Apaches depended on the psychological support of these and other myths while they called on practical survival skills to live in an area Dan L. Thrapp described as "enormous in extent. It stretched from the willow thickets along the Colorado into the broken mountains beyond the Rio Grande, and from the great canyons of the north southward for a thousand miles into Mexico, excepting of course the agricultural empire of the peaceful Papagos and Maricopas along the Gila and other streams tributary to it. The tribes of Apacheria were a product of their habitat, harsh, cruel, and pitiless." [16]

Many groups of Native Americans in the area had experiences with the Apaches that affirmed Thrapp's characterizations. For example, the Pima of Arizona believed that "if a drop of blood of an Apache fell on a Pima it would cause sickness. If a Pima killed several Apaches, although the act was lauded, it was believed that some of the progeny of that man would become insane or otherwise injuriously affected. This result could be obviated by the use of Apache hair, a tuft of which, tied with a chicken-hawk feather and an owl feather and burned in a certain way with greasewood, would cure any sickness induced by contact with the Apache." [17]

It is a huge leap from the first unsophisticated tribal concepts about illness to today's futuristic medical equipment. Our longer lives as we enter the twenty-first century are certainly attributable to advanced medical technology, but we must not look back into the past without some respect. Our ancestors, Indian and non-Indian, were as "modern" in their uses of plant medicines and the faith they placed in them as we think we are presently.

Without being specific as to tribe, Elmore reported that the prehistoric peoples had classified plant remedies into three categories: (1) those which are absolutely noneffective and used only in a superstitious manner; (2) those which resemble a part of the body and are supposed to cure because of that similarity (e.g., plants with yellow flowers are effective against urinary ailments); and (3) those which are actually effective.[18]

For instance, one variety of the mesquite plant that clustered in dense thickets near arroyos was applied to wounds. The bark on its roots was smashed into a poultice and placed directly on the lesion, whether it was a bite, a laceration, or a more serious injury. As was the case with many plants, mesquite served several purposes. The plant's beans were ground into pinole meal for food, drinking a solution made from the roots boiled in water was the treatment of choice for nervousness and colic, and a fluid from the leaves served as an eyewash. The inner bark of the mesquite plant was so soft it was used as diapers for babies.[19]

Dozens, perhaps even hundreds, of natural medicines aided survival in the Southwest, and did a credible job. Occasionally, according to Hrdlicka, the southwestern Indians of old had ear infections, but they were not bothered by rickets, tuberculosis, typhus, cholera, smallpox, plague, or leprosy.[20] Cancer and skin diseases were rare. Gastrointestinal ailments, however, were quite common, the results of the hardships in obtaining food that beset early Native Americans. The erratic supply resulted in unavoidable patterns of gorging alternating with starvation, which in turn created internal havoc and resulted in abdominal disorders such as diarrhea, constipation, colic, gas, nausea, and vomiting.

Gordon identified one treatment for stomach ailments as the use of "emetics daily . . . [early man] produced emesis by inserting a feather at the back of the palate."[21] Also helpful in alleviating distress were roots and herbs that produced the same effect, such as decoctions of holly leaves, bloodwort, and butterfly weed. Teas made from wild verbena soothed stomach problems, especially when wild mint was added. External measures may also have been utilized for gastrointestinal problems, such as applying pounded ragweed to scratches or shallow cuts made in the abdominal area to absorb the remedy. Drinking water containing a high concentration of mineral salts was popular as a purgative. Teas made from cacti, the bark of the sycamore tree, or powdered jalap root were used in cases of obstinate constipation. If these remedies were unsuccessful, some tribes used a syringe made of an animal bladder attached to a hollow, long bone of a turkey as an enema.

Compounding the problems that resulted from organic disorders was the hazardous outdoor life-style of southwestern Indians. Ordinary accidents caused cuts, scratches, bruises, sprains and strains, broken bones, and other afflictions, many of which might be complicated by infections. The Chiricahua Apaches made their boots with an upturned toe to help them avoid the dangers of everyday life. For the uninitiated, however, walking across desert and mountain terrain wearing Chiricahua boots created its own perils. The upturned toe became more of an impediment than a facilitator by catching onto low-growing shrubs and causing the amateur to stumble, trip, and even fall.

Native Americans were also quite vulnerable to bites and stings from snakes, scorpions, and other creatures. "Among the southwestern tribes," Gordon reported, "snakebite was treated by applying to the wound a portion of the ventral surface of the snake that had done the damage. Crickets, lizards, spiders, and spider eggs were used by some tribes." [22]

Apaches took a cultural approach: avoidance of snakes and snakebites through taboos. Believing snakes and bears brought evil and sickness into their lives, the Chiricahuas developed customs that encouraged keeping a distance from anything having to do with either. If that was impossible, illness was a likely consequence of the contact. Snake sickness, which could result from any confrontation whatsoever with a snake—even stepping on its marks in the ground—showed itself in "loathsome sores that attack the face." [23] These lesions required the services of a shaman who specialized in curing the effects of snake sickness.

Bear sickness was caused by fright as a result of crossing a bear's tracks, touching bear fur, encountering a bear, or invading a bear's den, however accidentally. A physical attack by a bear was definitely one source of this ailment. Should the individual survive, physical deformities next appeared which could only be treated by a healer specializing in bear sickness.

Underhill generalized when she reported, "With [all Apaches], bear, instead of being a great curing shaman, is the symbol for all frightening experiences." [24] Her reference was to the esteemed position bears hold among many other Native American groups, particularly the Pueblo peoples, whose modern craftwork includes many varieties of bear fetishes which are believed to bring strength and power to the owner.

Ancient traditions are still alive in Apache society. Serious disruptions due to implied contact with a bear and a snake occurred in the recent past in two separate contemporary Chiricahua Apache households. The first experience began when a bear was killed by a stranger's car near one of the Apache houses. Shortly thereafter, a child from the household broke her arm, one adult broke her hip, and another had a terrible infection in his foot, all within a reasonably short period. The family concluded that these ailments were the direct result of the bear's death near their home, and no one would dare disagree.

In the second situation, less physically hurtful, several seemingly unrelated episodes of bad luck occurred after a rattlesnake entered a home. The owner quickly had the rattler removed by an expert in these matters. Later, the expert examined the home's exits and entrances and declared that the snake had wriggled in through a hole in the ceiling. Soon, the lady of the house had car trouble and broke her glasses, and a beloved relative became quite ill (but did eventually recover).

Were the bear and the snake the sources of the problems, the harbingers, or not involved at all? Many modern educated Chiricahua Apaches nod wisely when these situations are discussed but will go no further in offering an opinion about what many non-Apaches might conclude is coincidence.

One very important cultural custom was a prohibition against eating fish and reptiles. Traditional Apaches believed that "the departed spirit of a bad Apache entered a water animal, making these . . . taboo as food." Furthermore, "since hogs ate snakes and entered the water, pork was not eaten."[25] The power of this custom was so strong that nothing short of certain starvation would cause a traditional Apache to consume fish or pork.

While the ancient causes of many illnesses were attributable to dark, mysterious forces beyond control, the primitive peoples were also believers in deities, thus bringing balance to their world. Apaches developed ceremonies, based in spiritual beliefs, to offset the consequences of unexplained illnesses. Sacred rituals were directed by tribal members who had specific "powers" to cure certain ailments, but these people were not the same as "medicine men" or "medicine women," terms applied generally and indiscriminately to Native American healers. In the Apache way, there were no medicine men or medicine women. Apaches believed that all people were able to receive some sort of supernatural power, and so everyone could have a special ability. No one knew in advance what blessing would come along or when it would appear. Lightning might bring the power, or it might be revealed through animals, birds, or plants. The healing ceremonies were also diverse and could be as different as the individuals conducting them, depending on the specific power the healer had received. Curing snake sickness, for example, called for rituals distinct from those performed in a ceremony conducted to relieve stomach distress, and required a healer with powers specifically in the area of snake sickness.

Opler identified four common processes within Apache healing rites performed regardless of the illness: preliminary ceremonial smoking, the throwing of pollen to the four directions, prayer, and a set of songs.[26] In the Apache way, the power of the Creator, Ussen, is mentioned only in the opening prayers, if at all. Each curing rite has its own formalities, protocol, and procedures designed by the healer, including those that address illnesses derived from witchcraft, always considered by the Apaches to be among the major causes of ailments.

Perrone et al. described Apache witches and witchcraft:

Evil power can be obtained by (1) a person allowing evil powers to enter himself or herself and accepting the full knowledge of what such powers mean; or (2) a person having the power to do good and twisting it to wicked ends. . . . The degree of havoc that can be wrought is commensurate with the force of the power brandished . . . every Apache can twist power around. Consequently, Apache witches . . . [who are both male and female] keep their power and its source a secret in an effort to protect themselves, believing that if an enemy is unsure of the force of retaliation, chances are the enemy will not do anything foolish.[27]

Thus, an Apache can be a healer, a witch, or both simultaneously, depending on how his or her power is used.

Apaches had to protect themselves from their enemies, and occasionally from each other, while concentrating on surviving in one of the most desolate areas of the continent. "The land could not support many of them in one place," reported Donald Worcester, describing the Apache hunters and gatherers. "This hand to mouth existence in a begrudging land forced them to separate into small, closely knit groups of a few families who were always on the move."[28] Naturally, as the units got smaller, the risk of bewitchment by close colleagues diminished, but the size of the group was no guarantee of safety. A relative in the group might be a witch carrying a grudge and just waiting for the opportunity to avenge a wrong done recently or in the distant past. However, as compact bands of Apaches journeyed across the Southwest and into Mexico, often camping in one place for long periods, they continued to create a way of life for themselves that met their immediate needs and successfully adapted their life-styles to the terrain. The very important cultural processes and ceremonies related to healers and healing were a significant part of the developing customs.

2

Traditional
Apache Medicines
and Healing

✸   ✸   ✸   ✸

As the Apaches came to understand the value of the
plant and animal life around them, they developed beliefs
compatible with the new environment. For example, the
abundant sage (*Salvia* spp.) was thought to be powerful
enough to prevent an adult from being hit by lightning.[1]
No record exists of how the Apaches reached this conclusion, but the principle became so well entrenched that
traditional confidence in the plant still remains.

Sage should not be confused with the more medicinally
potent sagebrush (*Artemisia tridentata*), a favorite of traditional and contemporary Apaches. "The whole plant is
strongly antimicrobial," reported Michael Moore, "and
many people use or did use the smoke of burning leaves
or the steam rising from moist sagebrush on coals to clear
the air (as it were) of pestilence and spirits of the dead."[2]
This cleansing ritual is an example of an old cultural pattern of such importance that it continues to be practiced
in some contemporary Chiricahua Apache homes.

In September 1990, on a private tour of the sites of
former Apache prisoner-of-war villages at Fort Sill, Oklahoma, modern descendants of the first Apaches in the
Southwest eagerly gathered this plant from the fields,

roadsides, and the foot of sacred cliffs called Medicine Bluffs. As a matter of fact, about half a dozen young men bolted up the side of a hill, an almost forty-five-degree angle, when they saw sagebrush growing freely at the top of the incline. Their pleasure in harvesting this popular plant was obvious, as was the respect with which they tenderly placed it in their vehicles to take back home.

Among traditional Apaches, fumigation with sagebrush was essential to protect a home and its inhabitants from dreaded illnesses, especially those related to death in any form. The Apaches' fear of dead people and ghosts engendered elaborate procedures to negate any exposure to death—from the distant sight of a corpse to handling the possessions of the deceased.

To shield themselves, not only did the Apaches destroy the dead person's belongings, they burned his or her living quarters as well and then didn't return to the area for some time, if ever. The two customs—abandoning a death site and sterilizing with the heat of a fire—probably enabled the Apaches to avoid major medical devastations. Nonetheless, they still fell victim to European sicknesses, even though their cultural patterns provided some protection.[3]

Lost to history, unfortunately, is exactly why, when, and how the Apaches adopted their strong cultural taboos related to death, including prohibiting the name of any deceased person to be mentioned again by relatives and others. Opler reported that "nothing is more insulting, provocative, and certain to precipitate conflict than to call out the name of a dead man in the presence of relatives."[4] Although the passage of time has loosened the grip of these bans, some Apaches today are still influenced by the ancient customs. Elbys Naiche Hugar, a great-granddaughter of Cochise, has her own thoughts. "Your dead relative may be very busy doing something important where he is," she told me, "and when he hears you speak his name, he'll be interrupted. He might not like that."[5]

One of the reasons behind the constraints is an age-old fear of ghost sickness, thought to be caused by dead relatives and friends who are not permitted to rest in peace. The physical symptoms of this feared malady are similar to those of extreme fright: tachycardia, choking, weakness, vomiting, irrational fears, crying, and headaches. Though there were healers who specialized in curing ghost sickness through specific ceremonies, certain precautions were routinely taken by almost everyone to avoid becoming ill. For example, the members of a deceased person's family who prepared the body burned all the clothes they wore while doing this task. They bathed their bodies in the smoke of the sage plant and protected themselves while asleep by placing ashes near their beds. At the grave, they brushed their bodies with green grass and then left the grass on the ground in the form of a cross.[6]

A potent belief in the ability of ghosts to cause harm was a traditional Chiricahua custom. "Ghosts come around the Chiricahua all the time," reported the Apache who spoke with Opler. "That's why we believe in ghosts." One of the strongest forms a ghost could take to frighten the living was that of an owl, thought to be the spirit of an evil person. "Owls talk the Chiricahua language . . . when it [the owl] comes, it is a sign that someone is going to die. . . . When you are frightened by the owl, your heart begins to flutter; your heart gets weak and you fall down. . . . When you get scared you get sick," continued the Apache, and he went on to tell Opler a well-known tale about an owl.

> About two years ago [a man's wife] died and the husband continued to live at the same location, though he didn't use the place in which she had died. One night he heard a knocking at the door. Then something was calling him by name. He went to the door but could see no one. This happened for three nights. He was very frightened. He kept his gun ready.
>
> There was a full moon the fourth night. He had gone to bed. He thought he heard a rapping on the window. He looked and was pretty sure he saw his wife's face. He tried to talk to her. He said, "Come in at the door; if you have anything to say to me, let us see each other face to face." But no one came in.
>
> After a while he heard the rapping again. This time he shot, and he heard groans. He was afraid to go out until morning. When he went out the next morning, he found a dead owl lying by the window. The next day he told the story. He knew he wouldn't live long after that, and he didn't last long. He could have gone to an owl shaman, but he didn't care much about going on living after that.[7]

In a private conversation with a contemporary Chiricahua Apache woman I heard a long story about another woman, a survivor of the prisoner-of-war years. In her old age, the woman was brushing her long hair in the Oklahoma sunshine and humming a pleasant tune when her song turned to screams. An owl had landed on her head and was impervious to the blows she frantically rained on it with her hairbrush. Not too long after that, the old woman died of unknown causes. But the cause of death was no mystery to the Apaches. They knew what had really happened and that the owl was responsible. Incidentally, to the best of everyone's recollections, this elder never returned as a ghost, and no one found it necessary to speak her name, not even my storyteller friend.

Ghosts also appeared in dreams; if the image was of a dead relative, or if the dream recurred, the Apache was well advised to immediately seek the services of a ghost shaman whose power and ceremonial performances could chase the ghost away before it caused insanity, suicide, or sickness. While ghost sickness is only one example of a consequential illness among the Chiricahua that required the services of a special healer, there were many other afflictions, including minor ailments that, left to nature, would disappear without curing rituals. Given certain healthy attributes, every human body is remarkably able to heal itself although such processes may take time. The Apaches had these physical assets: they were in superb physical shape and were, for the most part, in relatively good health. Weaker individuals, including children and the elderly, couldn't long survive the rigors of outdoor life; hardiness became a highly desirable and necessary trait most Apaches shared.

Ordinary medical distresses such as constipation, with its attendant stomach and bowel side effects, were seldom considered serious enough to seek a shaman's assistance. With the passage of time, a healthy body, and the use of appropriate plant remedies, a temporary ailment usually abated. It was when any medical condition persisted or became complex that a healer was approached.

Apache shamans, male and female, attained their powers through contact with supernatural authorities, either animate or inanimate. The encounter often occurred in dreams when a force such as lightning would appear and offer its assistance and power along with songs and rituals to be used in conjunction with prayers. If the individual agreed to accept the gift of power, he or she was then thought to "own" the power and could perform shamanistic ceremonies, the majority of which were related to healing.

Accepting and having a power was an awesome responsibility and one that was never adopted frivolously. Coming with the authority was an attitude of humility; the power holder always feared that he or she was unworthy and unfit to be a shaman. Having power caused the shaman to exercise caution at all times, for power may easily be misused by mortals. Being only human, individuals might deliberately or inadvertently offend the power, and it might turn against the shaman, causing untold grief, misery, and illness. Importantly, if the healer cured a patient suffering from the effects of witchcraft, he or she could have incurred the wrath of the witch in the process and might become the target of revenge. The witch might cast a spell and cause the healer to become ill, possibly to die. And so it was not unusual for the individual approached by the power to refuse to accept it.

L. Bryce Boyer et al. stated that "in the aboriginal Apache conceptualization, all illnesses and misfortunes are caused by one of three agencies: (1) supernatural power which has been affronted, (2) the use of power for witchcraft purposes, and (3) the actions of ghosts."[8] In tabulating the reasons for which contemporary shamans were approached during the last thirty-five years, Boyer et al. determined that the most common cause was to perform a ghost-chasing ceremony, and the next was to treat the symptoms of ghost sickness.

A contemporary example of a reason other than ghost sickness for a woman to seek healing from a shaman concerns a Chiricahua friend of mine. She attempted to cope with a tragic family situation but could not rid herself of what might be labeled "depression" by Western scientific medicine. Despite her best efforts to control her dismal moods, she slipped deeper and deeper into the doldrums, almost to the point of being unable to function. This mature woman, living in both the old-fashioned Chiricahua Apache way and the fast-paced world outside the tribe, realized she needed professional help and contacted an Apache shaman. Sure enough, less than twenty-four hours later my friend was her usual bright and happy self, ready to catch up on weeks of overdue activities. What had happened? "Just realized certain truths," was all my friend would tell me and then requested anonymity.

This situation shows the stability and force of traditional ways that are still respected and called upon by many Chiricahua Apaches. Imagine the powerful effects, then, of the healing ceremonies on less experienced people back in the days when cultural remedies had no alternatives. Just for a moment, think about the tremendous influence of the healers in the ancient culture.

Quite different from shamans were Apache herbalists, often members of a band whose knowledge of curative plants and herbs was not related to spirituality or to the world of the supernatural. General information about the flora growing all around was shared among everyone, but certain individuals became more adept at applying the knowledge than did others. These individuals, known as herbalists, were consulted when common remedies didn't work, or when, for example, an eye ailment resisted treatment by family members.

Less serious secondary ailments such as eye infections were treated with plant medicines derived from vegetation growing in the surrounding earth. The ubiquitous mesquite (*Prosopis pubescens, P. juliflora, P. glandulosa*), possibly the most common plant in the Southwest, is a good illustration. Mesquite was an all-purpose medicine for the Apaches and other southwestern Indians. After the leaves were "ground to a powder," stated Virgil Vogel, an authority on American Indian medicine, the Mescalero Apaches "placed [the mesquite] in a thin cloth, added water, and squeezed . . . on the eyes."[9] Michael Moore reported that "the pods, made as an eye-wash, help conjunctivitis of any type and work nicely for the pink-eye of children, household pets, and livestock."[10] There were other uses for mesquite as well: as a general disinfectant poured over open wounds, as a chewing gum to soothe sore throats, to combat gastrointestinal disorders,[11] and as a tasty food similar to syrup and molasses. *Osha* root (*Ligusticum porteri*), another favorite Native American cure-all and known among the Anglo culture in the modern Southwest as celery root, provided relief from stomachaches and gas when drunk in the form of tea. When rubbed on the outside of the nose or forehead, *osha* alleviated congestion and headache.

To treat persistent stomach disorders, a healer who was expert in the use of an enema tube was consulted. "Chiricahua shamans were noted for this especially," said James Haley. Treatment consisted of inserting the tube, and then, "herbal decoctions were forced by breath into the patient's body, after which poultices were applied and kept on with a mixture of ocher and grease. Hemorrhoids were believed amenable to this type of treatment. Blood in the stool could be treated this way." [12]

Aches and pains of sore muscles were treated with snakebroom (*Gutierrezia* spp.), a prolific, many-stemmed plant with yellow flower clusters that grows most everywhere in Apache country and was identified by James E. Officer and Edward F. Castetter as being utilized by the Apaches in ceremonial as well as general contexts. [13] These researchers also listed other medicinal and edible plants that were Apache favorites: mescal, a food and mild laxative; piñon nuts, eaten raw or roasted and mixed with yucca pulp to make a pudding, or ground and rolled into balls to be eaten as a delicacy; and milkweed juice, squeezed from leaves and stems and mixed with secretions from pine and cottonwood trees to make a chewing gum that soothes the inside of a sore mouth.

One very important use of mescal among the Chiricahua Apaches was to control the bleeding from wounds, especially arrow wounds. In an article written for the *Chicago Medical Examiner* in 1869, E. Andrews noted, "Their prime [belief] is that the chief danger of a wound is from the loss of blood. . . . They have no idea of a circulation of the blood, but suppose that each part of the body has its own permanent stock of that fluid; but they recognize that hemorrhage from the head, neck, and breast is more dangerous than that from the extremities." Therefore, concluded Andrews, "the chief surgical aim [is to] plug the wound and thus put a stop to the hemorrhage." To do that, "the first care of the Apache medicine man is to have on the field of battle some fresh boughs of the ash, whose leaves are used in dressings. Quite as important, also, is a quantity of mescal root . . . which is roasted and carried with them as food. When it is chewed and the nutritive part extracted, there remains in the mouth a wad of woody fibers. . . . The doctor first lays on the wound a fresh ash leaf; he then places on it a plug of the chewed mescal fibres, and thrusts the whole into the wound." After the danger of hemorrhage was entirely over, "the next step is to go deeper for the first plugs were only pushed into the orifices of the wounds. They now fill the entire track of the arrow or bullet to its extremity with a [mescal] tampon which they allow to remain a short time." [14] After a prescribed period, the chewed mescal pack was removed and herbs were applied to the wound, accompanied by shamanic rituals and incantations.

No stranger to these ancient herbal healing preparations and ceremonies, Mary Peña, a contemporary Apache healer and the director of traditional programs on the Mescalero Apache Reservation, presents public lectures which include demonstrations of Apache medicines. Mrs. Peña carries exhibits with her that contain mounted and framed samples of herbs used in healing. Among them are sumac berries, yucca fruit, black walnut, piñon nuts, chokecherries, wild tea, wild onions, parched corn, and mesquite beans. Her displays list the names of the medicines in the Apache language and tell which ones treat various ailments. For example, greasewood (*Covillea tridentata, Larrea tridentata*) is used to ease the pain of arthritis, wild mint (*Mentha arvensis*) soothes a sore throat, wormwood (*Artemesia frigida*) is an earache medicine, and Spanish hat (species unknown), collected on the sacred mountain of Sierra Blanca at Mescalero, is effective in treating colds.

Not all ailments required the use of herbs. For example, pain was sometimes combatted with pain, as when a toothache was eased by "placing the tip of a hot awl into the cavity." [15] In setting broken bones, more than likely a frequent occurrence in the Southwest, splints were created from sotol slats or from any flat wood or planks handy. Warm horse manure was applied to the limb prior to immobilization, and then the set bone and board were wrapped with buckskin or rawhide strips.

Opler wrote about another Apache healing custom, bloodletting, a therapeutic remedy occasionally practiced without ceremony.[16] For rheumatism, a skilled practitioner (who was not necessarily a shaman) cut open a vein on the back of a patient's hand, and the pain was believed to flow out with the blood. When fatigue was the problem, blood was drawn from the legs with prickly pear spines. John G. Bourke, an early observer of traditional Apache medicine, reported that "the Apache scouts when tired were in the habit of sitting down and lashing their legs with bunches of nettles until the blood flowed. This, according to their belief, relieved the exhaustion." [17]

To reduce fever Apaches cooked willow and quaking aspen leaves in water and drank it as a tea. Spurge, also called *Euphorbia*, was chewed raw when it was essential to induce vomiting.[18]

Each Apache, then, could be his or her own healer once the remedies that helped cure the minor ailments were known. If healing was not forthcoming, an herbalist was consulted; if the medical situation did not improve after that, the problem required the services of a shaman. If the healer was unsuccessful in producing a cure, it might be, as Opler reported, that the shaman had angered the power, which caused it to withdraw its protection.[19] But there was something else as well. If the cure designed by the shaman failed, he or she became the target of revenge by the friends and family of the ailing Apache. This vulnerability was one factor that could prevent an individual from assuming the role of a "healer of the sick," according to Bourke, along with the "dread of punishment for failure to cure or alleviate sickness or infirmity."[20]

The penalty paid by an unsuccessful shaman varied among Native American groups from turning the individual over to the relatives of the deceased to a tribal custom of killing the healer after he lost six patients.[21] "While the killing of a medicine-man under such circumstances has never been witnessed by whites," Hrdlicka stated, "the evidence must be regarded as conclusive."[22]

The death of Cochise, one of the most famous of all Chiricahua Apaches, is an excellent example of a healer's power turned to evil and of a cultural more regarding a shaman's failure. As the old chief lay dying in 1874 from either "dyspepsia or some form of stomach cancer,"[23] his son Taza and a party of warriors left Cochise's side. Convinced that bewitchment by a healer using his power for evil purposes was the cause of Cochise's failing health, Taza believed that if the shaman/witch, whom they had previously identified, could be found and forced to remove the spell, Cochise would live. The well-armed party of warriors located the shaman and brought him, with his wife and children, to the chief's deathbed. It was too late; nothing could be done, and Cochise died shortly after that on June 8, 1874.

The fate of the witch is unclear. Al Williamson, then a clerk in the trading post at Fort Bowie, wrote, "I never saw or heard anything more of the witch and his wife and children, so I suppose they were put to death."[24] Contemporary author and historian Dan

Thrapp's version is similar to an 1886 report in the *Arizona Daily Star* by Fred G. Hughes, an employee of the Chiricahua Reservation in Arizona, who wrote that "by an extraordinary amount of talk and persuasion by agent Jeffords and others they were induced to let him [the witch] go."[25] Sweeney, Cochise's biographer, supported Hughes's version because, by being present on the reservation, Hughes "would have known the details better than Williamson."[26]

A similar account exists in a report by L. Edwin Dudley, the superintendent of Indian affairs, to E. P. Smith, commissioner of Indian affairs in Washington, D.C., dated June 30, 1874.[27] Dudley described seeing the war party of twenty-seven warriors, led by Taza, "going for the witch to compel him to cure their chief. The party were thoroughly armed, having among them eight breech-loading guns, and all were well mounted. I asked what would be the fate of the supposed witch if he failed to cure Cochise, and was told they would hang him in a tree and burn him to death. The agent believed he could save his life at the proper time, and I have no doubt he did so."

In the time of Cochise, at least one Apache shaman was reported by Andrews to have been shot during an army attack on one of the villages. Soldiers captured the man's medicine pouch and discovered five stones and a seashell inside.

The stones were carbonate of lime, and were cut out of pieces of beautiful stalagnite from some cave or spring, the stone being handsomely striped with black and fawn-colored veins. Four of the stones apparently constituted a set of tamponers. The largest was about five inches long, cylindrical and slightly tapering, and was just about the right size to enter a wound made by an army musket-ball. The others were of successive sizes, smaller and probably used in the same way on the wounds made by the very small stone arrowheads of the Apaches and other tribes of that region. The fifth stone is supposed to be a charm only. It represents in form the Texan armadillo and the stone is ingeniously cut in such a way that the bands of color show stripes across the back like the rows of scales on the armor of the armadilla [*sic*]. . . . The sixth object was a sea-shell, perforated and suspended to the neck by a string. . . . When shown to the squaws captured in the assault, the latter exhibited great emotion, and begged that they might be thrown away, otherwise they said not a single soldier would live to return to his camp.[28]

As an example of the effect time and modernization have had on Apache shamanism since the days of Cochise, in 1977 Boyer published an unusual article about Apache healing.[29] An elderly Mescalero Apache woman with advanced diabetes avoided modern scientific medical care and relied instead on the traditional healing methods practiced by shamans. A healer herself, she suspected that her illness was caused by supernatural powers, witches, or ghosts, but was disappointed again and again when cultural cures failed to help. In 1973 she became convinced that the faith healer Oral Roberts could treat her from afar (he was in Tulsa, Oklahoma, more than five hundred miles from the Mescalero Apache Reservation), reasoning that if witches could bewitch by shooting arrows into people across long distances, there was every possibility that healing could be similarly accomplished. The woman sent Roberts a donation in a letter describing her misfortune and asking his assistance. He wrote back, thanking her and sending his blessings by mail. Her ailments grew worse; an abrasion on her foot became gangrenous. Warned by local hospital physicians that she needed immediate medical intervention, she instead traveled to Tulsa alone to see Oral Roberts. Unable to meet with him, she returned to Mescalero and had her leg amputated by a Public Health Service physician.

This situation raises at least one intriguing question from the standpoint of cultural customs. Which shaman(s) failed the patient? Initially, the treatments she performed on herself were ineffective, so she likely sought the services of other, more specialized healers. When their efforts didn't help, the woman appealed to Oral Roberts, then to the Western scientific medical profession's healers, went back to Roberts again, and finally went to the Public Health Service physicians. If the old-fashioned pattern of putting to death an unsuccessful shaman were followed to the letter in this case, imagine the consequences.

Regardless of the specific purpose of the healing ceremonies, most Apache shamans incorporated *hoddentin* into the ritual. *Hoddentin* is the pollen of a variety of cattail that grows near water throughout the Southwest and is considered sacred. This pollen was applied by the shaman to the body of the patient, then to the bodies of the other participants (family members, friends, chanters), and at last to his own head and into his mouth. Pollen was used as well outside the formal healing ceremony. In days of old, a shaman would walk in front of a wounded warrior riding a horse or mule, pray for him, and scatter pollen. Sacred *hoddentin* was also a tonic to restore energy, a holy powder to be thrown to the sun for good luck before embarking on the warpath, essential to the puberty ceremony,[30] and utilized in preparing a corpse for burial. Francesca, an Apache woman, told Bourke, "When a person is very sick the Apache make a great fire, place the patient near it, and dance in a circle around him and the fire, at the same time singing and sprinkling him with *hoddentin* in the form of a cross on his head, breast, arms, and legs."[31]

Pollen wasn't exclusively reserved for healing rituals, however. Eric Stone believed *hoddentin* to have been "a prehistoric food [that] has persisted in sublimated form as a ceremonial powder, its ingestion being in historic times only practiced as a rite. . . . The theurgist . . . while repeating a prayer . . . sprinkled hoddentin in a specified manner over and around the invalid."[32] As food, *hoddentin* has absolutely no taste, which may be why it lost its appeal. Then again, the early Apaches were very creative in preparing dishes comprised of natural vegetation and might have relied on the pollen as a "filler" of sorts. Whatever the case, *hoddentin* lost its status as a foodstuff but attained a higher position as a ceremonial article.

Apache shamans incorporated other sacred objects into their healing ceremonies as well. One was identified by Stone as a "rhombus,"[33] or, more familiarly, a bull roarer. This flat wooden object was seven to eight inches long, with a round knob on one end to which a cord was attached. Wavy, parallel lines were engraved on one side, each tinted a different color, denoting the hair of an Apache god and lightning. The fetish was tied to a long horsehair or leather thong and then whirled rapidly above the head, producing a sound similar to a gust of rain-laden wind. It was believed to entice wind, rain, and crops to aid in a patient's recovery.

Apaches also wore totems made of wood that had been struck by lightning. They were very thin, carved slats of pine, cedar, or fir cut in the shape of a human body. These small amulets were frequently attached to children's cradleboards, but adults depended on their rain-bringing properties and their ability to protect Apaches in trouble.

A most sacred item, the medicine cord, was described by Bourke. "There is probably no more mysterious or interesting portion of the religious or 'medicinal' equipment of the Apache Indian . . . than the medicine cord. . . . Less, perhaps, is known concerning it than any other article upon which he relies in his distress . . . the Apache look upon these cords as so sacred that strangers are not allowed to see them, much less handle them or talk about them," he wrote.[34]

Bourke's description of a medicine cord shown to him by an old Apache friend includes the fact that it had four strands, each stained a different color—probably yellow, blue, white, and black. By the time he saw the ancient artifact, its colors had faded. A former Apache scout sent him another medicine cord, this one having three strands, decorated with beads and shells strung at intervals. "That the use of these cords was reserved for the most sacred and important occasions," he wrote, "I soon learned; they were not to be seen on occasions of no moment, but the dances for war, medicine, and summoning the spirits brought them out, and every medicine man of any consequence would appear with one hanging from his right shoulder over his left hip."[35] Only the chief healers are permitted by custom to make medicine cords, which must be sprinkled with pollen before being presented to the owner. They were once worn on the warpath and were thought to provide divine protection against injury from enemies. Medicine cords also enabled their owners to identify thieves, ensure abundant harvests, and cure illnesses.

Frank C. Lockwood wrote about Apache sacred clothing, saying that the "medicine hat" and an "elaborately constructed ghost-dance headdress" had powers to "cure sickness" and provide a shaman with "insight into the future, whereby a man could see and forestall the coming of an enemy." The medicine shirt, according to Lockwood, "was an artistically ornamented shirt of buckskin. The decorations were symbolic of the sun, the moon, the stars, hail, rain, lightning, rainbow and clouds, among elemental objects, and of the snake, the centipede, and the tarantula among animals. The medicine shirt also possessed the magical quality of providing security for the warrior against the arrows and bullets of his foe."[36]

Along with honoring sacred objects used in healing ceremonies, Apaches had and still have a great regard for legends and other

Unidentified Chiricahua Apache bride in traditional wedding costume. Note the abalone shell necklace, a symbol of water and life. (Frisco Native American Museum)

stories told about their ancestors in days long gone. These tales are part of the broad concept of Apache medicine because it is from the legends that Apaches learn values and processes to call upon for assistance when necessary. One legend in particular was a favorite of the son of a former Chiricahua warrior. He told this tale about a secret mountain to author Eve Ball.

Before the Chiricahuas were sent to Florida they used to go to a mountain south of where Deming [New Mexico] is, to hold their dances. Once they were all around the mountain. One lady and her little boy went out on the plain to get some seeds for food—far from the foot of the mountain.

They were out there and cannot see far. And before they know it soldiers circle all around them.

"Look, Mother! Soldiers!"

There was an interpreter with the Cavalry—an Indian scout. They used to have Indian scouts with the soldiers to do the fighting for them. The interpreter call to the lady, "You know how far you are going to go? You watch that sun, and you see."

She tell him, "You just shut up and do what I say. Come over here and we are going to cut your neck."

She brave woman.

The bugle blow and the soldiers come. She been going backward toward the mountain and she speak to the Secret Mountain: "Today, with you looking at me I don't want nobody to do bad things to me."

Soldiers are coming with swords all ready. She call the mountain her brother; and she turn to it and make the Apache distress signal. Nobody can refuse to respond to that sign. I can't tell you how it is made; it is just for Apaches.

When she turn 'round soldiers riding their horses right into that mountain. You can see nothing after while but their boots and the horses' feet sticking out. And lots of saddles laying around.

For many, many years you can see those things. Maybe if you go there now some of them still left.

The Chiricahuas were watching from the mountain, and they can't understand what become of soldiers until she tell them.

And that's how Secret Mountain save that lady and her boy.[37]

A Chiricahua Apache learns faith from this tale—faith in supernatural powers and their ability to protect an Apache from danger.

It is not unusual for legends, tales, and stories to contain references to mountains, for they hold great power in Apache lore. In them, the sacred *Gah'e*, the Mountain Spirits, reside. The night dance of the Mountain Spirits is performed around a huge, roaring fire and is the most spiritual custom in the Chiricahua Apache culture. It too is based in legend. In 1948, J. Wesley Huff interviewed Clarence Bullis, a drummer and leader of singers whose ancient music is an essential component of the dancers' ritual. Bullis told Huff, "The dancers are endowed with the full powers of the gods they impersonate, and are held in great respect by the people who dare not touch them. Every mark, every bell, every symbol on their costumes has its own meaning and represents something from heaven, from the earth or from beneath the ground. It is taboo for anyone to recognize the impersonators as men they know. . . . They are Spirits of the Mountain. . . . I wouldn't dare say they are men."[38]

The dance is still faithfully performed and represents one of the fundamental structures of the Chiricahua Apache culture. It is a deeply stirring sight.

However, all the rituals and ceremonies, all the beliefs, all the natural remedies the Apaches had discovered, and all the environmental hardships they had experienced and overcome could not have prepared them for one incomparable event in their lives and in the history of the world: the arrival of the Spanish and the contagious diseases they brought with them to the Southwest.

3

Newcomers

✳ ✳ ✳ ✳

Popular mythology describing the entry of the Spanish into the Southwest has produced Hollywood-like images of handsome bearded men clothed in billowing, colorful silks. Sitting tall on sweating stallions, these *conquistadores* covered their heads with silver helmets that flashed in the blazing sun and rested their hands on sharpened swords of steel that gleamed in the pure, white desert light. Behind them trudged dedicated religious men, Franciscan friars, murmuring incantations. They shuffled their sandal-covered feet through swirling brown sand clouds and folded their hands in front of them in prayer, preparing to bring the Word, on behalf of cross and crown, to all the indigenous peoples. In the rear of the miles-long caravan were carts, wagons, and hundreds of men, women, and children guiding huge herds of ambling, bawling livestock. Not as readily visible, however, were the billions upon billions of infectious germs in the Hispanic pioneers' blood, cells, bones, respiratory passages, and alimentary canals that accompanied the separate waves of newcomers to the Southwest.

Just forty-eight years earlier a sailor named Columbus had opened the ocean to the west of Europe to travel. It would be another sixty-seven years before the first permanent English settlement was established in North America at Jamestown, and eighty years would pass before the Pilgrims stepped on Plymouth Rock.

More than likely, the newly arrived Spaniards and

Mexicans had partial or total immunity to most European ailments because of prior exposure. No doubt, though, they were worried about new illnesses laying in wait for them in the unfamiliar environment. To offset that possibility they brought with them their body of medical knowledge, called *curanderismo,* which included reliable, age-old healing techniques and traditional cures known as *remedios* that were effective against minor illnesses. These included approximately sixty medicinal herbs, such as anise, coriander, chamomile, dill, garlic, mint, oregano, and rosemary. But would these natural medicines be as effective in their new home as they were in the old? No one really knew.

On these journeys, clergymen often served as the medics, but when the destination was reached, *curanderas* (female healers) and *curanderos* (male healers) assumed their community roles. There were problems right away, similar to those encountered by Native Americans who had earlier migrated into the same area. The plant medicines on which *curanderismo* was based had to be changed to accommodate the new circumstances. Herbs that were abundant in the soils of Spain and Mexico did not prosper and even died in the Southwest. On the other hand, certain new and unfamiliar plant *remedios* grew freely in the arid climate. After the Hispanic pioneers became friendly with the Native Americans, they shared medicines and eventually discovered mutual compatibilities. For instance, both groups believed in the supernatural causes of illnesses, although the specifics of the tenets differed. As friendly as the early exchanges were, however, the Native Americans were unprepared for and unprotected against the medical consequences of their contacts with these newcomers.

One example of a contagious ailment brought by the new arrivals was the common cold. In the process of zealously establishing a regional outpost for the greater glory of the Spanish Empire, at least one tired and rundown *conquistador* or Spanish-Mexican pioneer must have sneezed and loosed the first rhinovirus on the new land. One need not speculate too long about the effect that respiratory convulsion had on the indigenous populations. The sneeze could have resulted in pneumonia, pleurisy, or death among a group whose immune systems had never been exposed to this most prolific of ailments.

"Before America was discovered by Columbus, it was apparently one of the—if not the—most healthful continents," reported Hrdlicka.[1] He examined the skeletal remains of many Native Americans and found them remarkably free from diseases, fallen arches, and skin blemishes. This idyllic environment ended when the newcomers arrived, however, and would never be re-created.

By the late 1700s the Spaniards and Mexicans had settled permanently in the American Southwest. Comfortable at last in the new environs, they began recording their observations of the Native Americans on a regular basis. One writer, José Cortés, noted that the Apaches had

> a most bilious temperament which gives them a character which is astute, suspicious, bold, haughty, and zealous of its freedom and independence. . . . They are sustained . . . by the vigilance and caution with which they look after their health, which leads them to change their location frequently in order to breathe new air and so that the site which they abandon might be purified. . . . The Apaches are extremely gluttonous when they have provisions. At the same time, it is amazing how patiently they suffer hunger and thirst in times of calamity and scarcity. Their suffering reaches unbelievable extremes, yet their strength does not falter or decline.[2]

Daniel S. Matson and Albert H. Schroeder's classic article addresses an aspect of Apache life that contributed to good health: physical prowess. "Having been born and raised in the open country and strengthened by simple foods," they quoted their eyewitness source, Cordero, as saying, "the Apache is endowed with an extraordinary robustness which makes him almost insensible to the rigors of the seasons. The continuous movement in which he lives, moving his camp from one to the other location for the purpose of obtaining new game and the fruits which are indispensible [sic] for his subsistence, makes him agile and nimble in such a degree that he is not inferior in speed and endurance to horses."[3]

The Apaches could not have known that their small groups and mobility helped preserve hardiness and offered some protection from the invisible killers then gaining a foothold. It was quite a while before research revealed that contagious diseases need a certain number of individuals in order to thrive and become epidemic. Thus the Apaches, who could move their campsites at will, were

Naiche (son of Cochise), last chief of the free Chiricahua Apaches. Photo was probably taken during incarceration at Fort Sill, Oklahoma (1894–1913). (Frisco Native American Museum)

better able to avoid infection with the newcomers' diseases than were other Native Americans. For example, the Pueblo Indians, who lived in stable, sedentary populations along the Rio Grande in New Mexico, were horrendously affected by medical maladies brought from Europe, especially smallpox.

New Mexico mission documents disclose the health conditions in the pueblos during the seventeenth and eighteenth centuries, during and after exposure to contagious diseases:

1699   Father Garaycoechea buried 30 children.

1791   Nambé, 24 adults and 21 children died of smallpox.

1728   December, Jemez, 109 Indians died of sarampion (measles); spread into surrounding areas.

1729   Acoma, many died of sarampion during December 1728 and January 1729.

1733   Jemez (Fray Juan del Pino), smallpox epidemic during June and July.

1733   Santa Ana, smallpox epidemic.

1733   Santa Fe, many deaths in May and June, no cause given.

1736   Santa Fe, 38 deaths in November, no cause given.

1738   Pecos, smallpox epidemic.

1747   Zuñi, 200 Indians died of smallpox; number not accurate since many were not reported.

1748   Santa Fe, 68 deaths July to September, no cause given.

1748   Pecos, epidemic in August, disease not given.

1772   Laguna, 44 adults and 21 children died "de la peste."

1781   Bernalillo, Corrales, and Alameda, smallpox epidemic [these are not pueblos; they are villages still located near Albuquerque].

1781   1782, 1800, Santa Clara, severe smallpox epidemics.

1781   Santa Fe, deaths extremely high considering population, 142 in January and February.

1781   Santo Domingo, more than 230 Indians, young and old, died during February and March.

1785   Santa Fe, 75 deaths in April and May, no cause given.

1789   Santa Fe, 50 deaths in January and February, no cause given; 45 deaths October–December.

1797   September, Santa Fe, 21 deaths.

1799   December, Santa Fe, 57 deaths.

1799   November, and 1800, March, smallpox epidemics.

1800   February, Santa Fe, 36 deaths.

1804   May and June; 1805, April and May, Santa Cruz [a village north of Santa Fe, not a pueblo], increased number of deaths, no cause given.

1804   February, Santa Fe, 24 deaths.

1805   Cochiti, epidemic of sarampion.

1805   April and June, 122 deaths.

1805   May, Santa Clara, a plague of sarampion.

1806   April, Santa Fe, 23 deaths.

1816   Picuris, more than usual number of deaths, no explanation.

1816   San Juan, smallpox epidemic in spring.

1816   Santo Domingo, 78 deaths from an epidemic, disease not given.

1817   Santo Domingo, 22 deaths, epidemic, disease not given.

1826   Socorro [a village south of Albuquerque, not a pueblo, although Piro Indians lived there], during April 22 persons, mostly infants, died, no cause given.

1840   San Juan, in spring, an epidemic of fever in adults and smallpox in children.[4]

Smallpox raged for 150 years in Europe before it became "the greatest [epidemic] in the modern history of the southwest," and all the forces available in the late 1700s were not enough to control the disease's rampage. "Of the 9,104 inhabitants of the mission pueblos enumerated in 1760 . . . 5,025 died during this epidemic."[5] These immovable villages along the Rio Grande in New Mexico were ideal targets for contagious diseases, in marked contrast with the mobile life-style of the Apaches, who were freer and more amenable to migration. But like the Apaches, the Puebloans themselves had no immunity to the European ailments. They were situated in small and intimate communities, had constant contact with each other, and had no way to protect themselves against the invisible enemy—disease. Although most Puebloans had readily accepted the religion of the newcomers, neither the villages' traditional medical societies nor prayers to the Spaniards' God was of medical help to them when contagion struck.

Through its missionaries and friars in the New World, the Catholic church became involved with the illnesses brought by the colonizers. The clergy, of necessity, assumed the often hopeless task of treating ailing Indians with available but ineffective remedies. For example, when someone became obviously ill with the first signs of smallpox—high fever and vomiting—the Catholic missionaries and friars carefully prepared potions and teas from herbs in an attempt to palliate the symptoms. Prayers were offered as oozing pustules erupted, and Pueblo patients were bled to lower their fevers by opening a vein with anything handy, sometimes a sharp rock. The incubation period of twelve days was followed by a high fever and vomiting, and many victims, delerious from fever, plunged into the Rio Grande to cool themselves. The shock of the ice-cold water caused many more medical complications, and frequently death. If the patient survived to this stage of the epidemic, three or four days after the fever subsided the characteristic skin eruptions appeared. This was the most dangerous time of the disease. A week or ten days later the pustules dried up and formed scabs, which eventually fell off. However, the virus could remain alive inside the discarded scabs for weeks and could be transmitted from person to person or carried from place to place. (Most everyone has heard the tale about the smallpox scabs placed deliberately in the folds of blankets before the blankets were issued to Indians.) Permanently scarred and disfigured after the illness, the surviving patient was immune from smallpox but was psychologically devastated and lived in terror of the newcomers on horseback, who, he had reason to believe, had brought this and other frightful afflictions to him from another land.

Apache contacts with Pueblo peoples, while not frequent, were certainly taking place during this time. Depending on the purpose of the visit, whether to trade or to raid, the Apaches' nearness to villagers exposed them to the contagious diseases lurking in the pueblos. Too, army officials, Indian agents, and others whose business took them into Apache country carried the communicable diseases with them. Literally and figuratively, the Apaches were surrounded, and they were susceptible to the communicable diseases that infected all Native Americans. In their favor, however, was their ability to flee—to establish a campsite far from an outbreak and to either never return to the original place or to come back at some date far in the future when the danger had been reduced to a minimum.

Aiding in creating circumstances favorable to transferring ill-nesses were Apaches living elsewhere who arrived to visit friends and relatives. These well-meaning visitors added to the conditions necessary for diseases to flourish: they increased the number of people in one site, and they themselves carried illnesses from one location to another. But without a stable, substantial population and community base, such as the Pueblo peoples had, the *full force* of epidemic diseases never struck the Apaches while they were still a free people.

Many researchers have examined the impact contagious ailments had on Native Americans, but one, William Griffen, an expert on the Apache presence in the Southwest, stated that Spanish officials expected an epidemic every eighteen to twenty years.[6] Frequently, it was sooner. In 1780, 1797, 1799, and 1800, many people of all ethnic backgrounds died of smallpox in the Mexican states of Chihuahua and Sonora. Apaches in the area, whether permanent residents or visitors, fled in terror.[7]

By February 1844, when the same area was under Mexican con-trol, the Janos, Mexico, peace establishment, where Apaches were issued rations and sheltered, practically collapsed because of small-pox.[8] Most Apaches fearfully abandoned the site, even though re-cords reveal that only five people had been afflicted and three had died. The number of Apaches in the area originally is not known, al-though a few months before, some six hundred had received rations.

In addition to smallpox and more minor ailments, many Apaches suspected the Mexicans of deliberately causing them to become ill, even after the Southwest came under United States jurisdiction. This is clearly expressed in a letter written on November 21, 1857, by a New Mexico Indian agent, Dr. Michael Steck, to his supervisor, the superintendent of Indian affairs, General J.C. Collins. Steck was visited by a group of Mimbres Apaches who were "ill, exceed-ingly poor, almost naked and actually in a starving condition." To avoid problems with the U.S. Army, this group had been living near Janos and occasionally receiving rations from the government of Mexico. They had suffered much from a "disease" and many died. The Mimbres Apaches told Steck they believed they had been poi-soned, and Steck did not dispute that claim. He had heard rumors to that effect from the citizens of Janos. On closer questioning, the Mimbres Apaches described the symptoms that killed their loved ones, and Steck concluded that they resembled "those of poisoning by arsenic, probably administered as part of their rations."[9] Arsenic can taste remarkably like garlic and would have been a flavorful additive to the rations drawn by the Apaches. There is no further information in Steck's papers as to what actions Superintendent Collins took, if any.

Two months before writing that letter, Steck had corresponded with General Collins about another matter, this one concerning the Coyotero Apaches of Arizona. Writing about returning Coyotero prisoners to their tribal captains, he said that "fifteen had died from diseases contracted here and the remaining nine were ill of fever or diarrhea when turned over. It was therefore best to send them to their country and friends at once, as to have kept them here two [more] months would no doubt have proved fatal to one half of the few that were left."[10]

One problem compounding treatment of diseases was an inability to diagnose with a high degree of certainty. True, major ailments could be identified easily, but symptoms such as fever and diarrhea characterize so many ailments that just guessing what was wrong often produced an incorrect diagnosis. Then too, treatment options were extremely limited, especially in remote areas like the Southwest, regardless of which government occupied the region.

Referring to the medical catastrophes that occurred among the natives, P. M. Ashburn declared in a 1936 article, "The outstanding result of the conquest was the rapid disappearance of the Indians from Canada to the Argentine."[11] (This sentence may be misunderstood. Indians did not flee from Canada to the Argentine, but Indians all along that geographical route disappeared.) An even more striking statement came from an affected group of Mexican Indians, the Mayans, who, despite the devastation of smallpox and other diseases, kept a chronicle in the sixteenth century. "Great was the stench of the dead," wrote a diarist. "After our fathers and grandfathers succumbed, half of the people fled to the fields. The dogs and vultures devoured the bodies. The mortality was terrible. Your grandfathers died, and with them died the sons of the king and his brothers and kinsmen. So it was that we became orphans, oh, my sons! So we became when we were young. All of us were thus. We were born to die!"[12]

While smallpox was the major malady affecting southwestern Native Americans, it was only one of several epidemics that devastated the indigenous populations. Another medical condition against which most southwestern Indians had no immunity was malaria, even though the arid atmosphere was antagonistic to the disease, which was common in Europe during the sixteenth, seventeenth, and eighteenth centuries. It is hard to believe that individuals ailing with the fevers and chills of malaria would board boats in Spain (en route, mosquitoes could breed in water casks and bilge water in the sailing vessels) to travel to Mexico and then attempt an overland trip of many months. Yet the ailment was ostensibly not present in the damp, lowland regions of the southwestern countryside, including Arizona and New Mexico, until the arrival of the newcomers. Might there be some other explanation? William McNeill proposed a different hypothesis: "Suitable anopheline species . . . probably already existed in the New World, tinder for infection with the malarial plasmodium. . . . Only so is the rapid development of malaria as a major disease factor in the New World credible." [13] Eventually the drug quinine was developed and distributed to fight malaria, but a vaccine against another highly contagious disease, measles, was still more than a century away.

The measles virus stormed across the land, from south to north and east to west, infecting most of the Indians it encountered and leaving behind survivors very sick with fever, pneumonia, and middle ear infections.

Another deadly ailment, tuberculosis, was also the subject of great concern on the frontier and all across the country. Tuberculosis bacilli are among the oldest organisms on earth. They have been identified by paleopathologists in the bones of Stone Age skeletons and among Egyptian remains. The pulmonary variety of tuberculosis loves unsanitary and crowded conditions; coughing, sneezing, and spitting; and close conditions where people regularly intermingle. And it loved Native American villages as much as it loved the Spanish frontier towns.

Hrdlicka called tuberculosis

the chief . . . scourge to the North American Indian and Eskimo. . . . Eventually in some cases practically whole tribes became infected with this disease and large numbers perished. . . . the discovery of the continent by Columbus was the direst misfortune that ever happened to a race of people. That the whole race did not perish was due to their large fecundity, great distribution, relative isolation of many of the tribes in forests, or mountains, the wholesome way of life of a great many in the open, their fleeing away when an epidemic began to develop in their midst, and eventually to the gradual building up of at least partial immunities in their bodies.[14]

Nonetheless, "frontier conditions tended to compound medical problems," reported John Duffy.[15] Yes, and the medical misfortunes in the Southwest increased dramatically with the arrival of the next group of newcomers, the Anglo-American pioneers, lured out of the cities of the East by the promise of a healthy life among the canyons and mesas of the West.

4

Contagious Diseases, *Curanderismo,* Home Remedies, and Doctoring

For approximately forty years, from 1850 to 1890, four million men, women and children rode, walked, and were carried across America's prairie in an enormous and unprecedented relocation away from the dense, humid unwholesomeness east of the Mississippi. Air pollution was a problem then too, but not because of complex chemical compounds or automobile emissions. In the middle 1800s the eastern United States was filled with deadly contagious diseases. John Duffy graphically described a common situation when he wrote, "Myriads of flies engendered by human and animal wastes hovered over dining tables and kitchen counters, spreading typhoid and other disorders, while the drainage from privies carried pathogenic organisms into the wells and springs which provided drinking water."[1] No wonder healthy people left to find a better life in the vast reaches of the West that promised so much. As an act of mercy, they took with them nearly 750,000 sick loved ones who spat, coughed, limped, leaned, scratched, and bled their way along trails they prayed would lead to a long life in the rarefied, pure air and healthful climate of the Southwest.

Many easterners familiar with popular theories about causes and cures of illnesses believed in the idea of a "health frontier" amid mesas and mountains of the West and Southwest. Some pioneers must have known in advance that the region had a clinical history of its own, dating back more than one hundred years to the days when explorers and trappers first exposed the indigenous peoples to the "white man's diseases." But the stalwart easterners made the journey anyway, unable to resist the lure of new opportunities.

Along the way there were always Indians to be feared, and even the thought of ambushes or raids was enough to strike terror into many hearts. Long-winded horror stories had filtered back to the East—frightening tales about dead bodies strewn around the countryside after unprovoked Indian attacks. In certain sections of the trail west, it was reported, hungry buzzards circled, staking out the next meal still alive on the earth below. Also, it was practically a given that a wagon train could count on some draft animals becoming ill and falling along the wayside. To complicate matters, trails were frequently washed out, causing long delays during which food and water supplies could be exhausted. Although danger appeared in many guises, still the settlers came, prepared to bury their loved ones on the trail west if necessary.

A young married pioneer woman named Susan Magoffin kept a diary of her journey west in 1846–47. Describing the prairie grave site of a Mexican who died from consumption, Magoffin wrote, "The grave is dug very deep, to prevent the body from being found by the wolves. The corpse is rolled in a blanket—lowered and stones put on it. The earth is then thrown in, the sod replaced and it is well beat down. Often the corral is made over it, to make the earth still more firm, by the tromping of the stock. The Mexicans always place a cross at the grave."[2] Children died too, and that, perhaps, was the worst of it.

Other ailments such as toothaches, snakebites, earaches, poison ivy, measles, mumps, and respiratory distresses, fatal and nonfatal, routinely accompanied pioneers on their adventures. Most caravans carried home remedies such as camphor, quinine, citric acid to counteract scurvy, opium, whiskey, castor oil, and essence of peppermint—all standard fare.

Snakebite was especially dangerous for those who occasionally walked beside the procession to stretch their muscles, sore and aching from sitting or driving teams of horses or oxen for endless hours, days, and months. Carbolic acid, kerosene, and turpentine served as external antiseptic solutions, but it was whiskey, one of the few easily available pain killers, that was given internally as soon after a snakebite as possible. (We know now that was a bad idea because it hastened the spread of venom through the body.) True stories are told of men bitten in the finger or toe who cut off the entire digit, believing that amputation was the only way to save their lives. Another, less dramatic, emergency treatment involved the snake itself. If it could be killed, it was cut into pieces and sections of its meat were applied directly to the bite. In a few minutes, the white snake flesh would turn green, 'tis said, because it pulled the poison out of the victim's body. Raw beef slabs and fresh chicken flesh were used for the same purpose once the travelers had settled in their permanent locations.

Accidents along the road were especially injurious to children. Falls, broken bones, injuries caused by livestock, and, quite commonly, getting run over by wagons were routine. Added to these perils were ordinary ailments that contributed to children's discomfort, such as the miseries of blisters, mosquito bites, diarrhea, and, for the youngest, diaper rash and other "hot" or "sore" spots that are part of a baby's world. For some of these irritating medical situations, mothers prepared a concoction of sage, borax, alum, and sugar.

In the mid-nineteenth century, well before antibiotic therapy, the slightest trauma or disease in an extremity could mean gangrene and amputation. Infection occurred in nearly all wounds, and there was often no way to control the deadly consequences. On the trail west, frequently the only "surgical instrument" available to remove a limb was a dirty or rusty saw with teeth dulled from years of use. When the damaged limb was amputated, usually with whiskey as anesthesia, the wound was sealed shut with a red-hot wagon bolt.

In the middle 1800s, typhoid fever,[3] transmitted through contaminated food or drinking water, raged on the Santa Fe Trail from Missouri to Kansas and then south across the countryside to New

Mexico. Wagon trains usually camped near water, which was often at the bottom of an incline, down a hill and off the road. Human wastes left far from the ponds and streams by previous travelers seeped through the ground or were washed by rains toward the flowing water. Animals, wild or domesticated, were less careful, depositing their excrement wherever they stopped. Forced to drink and fill their wooden barrels from any available supply, thirsty pioneers often fell ill from typhoid fever well before they reached their destination.

Travelers who arrived in Santa Fe, New Mexico, in December 1847 were met by a typhoid fever epidemic among the soldiers quartered at the United States military post there. During the preceding three months there had been twenty-nine cases and ten deaths, with the high mortality rate attributed to the unsuitable climate and a wholly inadequate military diet. Standard army fare was grossly deficient in vitamins and minerals, and often the deprivation of adequate nourishment was sudden. Many soldiers had come from farm families whose diet was abundant and balanced. Then they joined the military and found themselves in remote outposts like Santa Fe, seven thousand feet above sea level, an altitude that could have temporary adverse effects on those from lower regions.

Unaccustomed as some men were to the extremes of weather in the West, they also had a good deal of trouble accommodating themselves to the unfamiliar—and uncomfortable—military environment, especially the close living conditions and other hardships of army life. Enlisted men frequently slept outdoors in tents, impossibly crowded and tucked into each other like spoons. When one man had to leave in the middle of the night to use the latrine, all shifted over to the other hip as one to let him pass. Army personnel were often so seriously weakened physically from malnutrition and unsanitary conditions that, despite state-of-the-art medications and treatments provided by the government, they became increasingly susceptible to death-dealing diseases.

Civilians managed no better than the military in southwestern towns, villages, and settlements. A poignant personal situation was expressed poetically by Indian agent Michael Steck in a letter to his parents from Santa Fe dated October 9, 1864, in which he wrote about the death of his wife: "Another of the chords that bind us to earth has been severed. Another pure angel has been added to the bright throng in heaven . . . thank God she died as she had lived, at peace with the world and with the certainty of a happier home hereafter. She often talked with me about death, saying that she was not afraid to die, and half an hour before she left us she said, 'don't leave me dear. I am worse' and directly added, 'you will have to let me go now.' " The remainder of the letter describes her last moments, even up to the end, when "without a murmur or even a sigh, she fell gently asleep in death."[4] Mentioned also in the letter were Mrs. Steck's symptoms of chills, diarrhea, difficulty in breathing, and her "lingering disease," all characteristic of a number of contagious ailments that were running wild in the Southwest and Mexico in the middle to late 1800s.

✳ ✳ Frontier Diseases

Looking back in time from today's perspective, it is apparent that three main groups of microorganisms were the invisible frontier killers: bacteria, protozoa, and viruses. Of these, bacteria, the parasitic survivors of the earliest stages of life on earth, usually exist in delicate and healthy balance within the human body. The lowest parts of the digestive tract contain hundreds of species of bacteria, the mouth's saliva washes away bacteria that adhere to mucous membranes, and bacteria can be grown in the laboratory from healthy skin. Not all bacteria coexist so benignly in or on their human hosts, however. Some are dangerous, virulent, and even deadly. The *Pneumococcus* bacterium, normally not hazardous, is a common throat inhabitant, but in a tired, rundown, hungry, or malnourished person, it can quickly flare into pneumonia. Pneumonia is an inflammation of the lung(s) in which the air sacs fill up with so much pus that air is excluded and the lung(s) becomes solid. Death may result.[5] *Meningococcus*, another bacterium present in the throat, can climb upward into the brain under the same physically vulnerable circumstances as described above and cause meningitis, a serious medical condition characterized by an intense headache, fever, vomiting, convulsions, delirium, and death.[6] *Salmonella* and *Shigella* bacteria in the bowel may also become harmful and can cause gastroenteritis, septicemia, bacillary dysentery, and other types of intestinal distress. Venereal diseases are the result of bacterial invasions that need not be limited to the sexual organs. The eye ailment trachoma results when *Chlamydia* bacteria cause the conjunctiva of the eyelid to become inflamed and to ooze a purulent discharge. If untreated, the eyelid turns inward so that the eyelashes brush up against the cornea and blindness ensues,[7] a condition that several Chiricahua Apaches suffered during the latter years of their incarceration. None of the bacterial diseases mentioned above, however, has had the impact on humanity of the infectious disease called tuberculosis.

Caused by the bacillus *Mycobacterium tuberculosis* and formerly known as consumption and phthisis, the disease begins with inhaling an airborne bacillus into the lungs. The microorganism spreads rapidly to the nearest lymph nodes, but an individual with healthy immune reactions can still deter the disease at this point. In others it may smolder for years before flaring up to produce the symptoms of coughing, sneezing, fever, weight loss, sweats, and bloody sputum. This highly contagious infectious disease caused millions of deaths worldwide before antibiotics were discovered.[8]

That tuberculosis had a devastating effect on peoples of all ethnic backgrounds is indisputable, but it was especially catastrophic within Native American groups. Federal officials called it the "scourge of the Indian race" and cited comparative studies which showed that the "prevalence of tuberculosis among Indians is greatly in excess of that among the white race."[9] In 1913 there were approximately twenty-five thousand Indians needing medical care for tuberculosis while available hospital facilities could accommodate only a few hundred. The commissioner of Indian affairs, in a report to the secretary of the interior, stated that "the situation is so grave that immediate action should be taken."[10] But nothing helped.

Alex Hrdlicka wrote extensively about the epidemic of tuberculosis among Native Americans and identified a major cause of contagion: poor sanitary conditions. In an incredible depiction, Hrdlicka described infected individuals expectorating on the floor of their own homes or homes they were visiting; common use of dirty bags, quilts, and blankets among healthy or ailing family members; unclean eating utensils, unwashed and shared by all; not isolating tubercular individuals; passing a pipe from mouth to mouth without caution; and living in very crowded, overheated rooms.[11] While they were incarcerated in Alabama the Chiricahua Apaches suffered greatly from tuberculosis. They lived in tents and spit and coughed so much that the canvas eventually served as a handkerchief, catching all the bacilli in its weave. When the tents began to deteriorate because of the wet climate, legend has it that Army seamstresses made clothing for the prisoners from the salvageable canvas, with no regard for the contamination the material contained. More likely, the tents were burned.

By no means was the lack of sanitation confined to Native American homes. Tuberculosis was so widespread that very few individuals or families of all backgrounds escaped exposure in the nineteenth century. It was such a serious threat to the public health that it generated hundreds of national debates, theories, reports, articles, books, and speeches by leading physicians of the day. Most of the recommendations for treatment included a change of climate to one that was sunny and dry. Naturally, the West and Southwest came to mind. There was room to breathe in the West. A patient could see the sky, feel the sun, and drink the pure water. And at a time when there was no cure for tuberculosis, the environmental qualities offered by the country west of the Mississippi were far better than any palliatives available elsewhere.

A U.S. Senate report published in 1913 includes a state-by-state survey that records the numbers of Native Americans suffering from tuberculosis. After stating that "available records of the past no doubt contain many errors due to the wide distribution and inaccessibility of the Indian population," the report places the death rate from tuberculosis at 12.1 per 1,000 for Anglos, 33.9 per 1,000 for blacks, and 35.4 per 1,000 for Native Americans.[12] In other words, American Indians were almost three times as likely to die from tuberculosis as Anglos. To counteract the terrible consequences, each Indian tribe devised its own culturally based treatment.

Apache remedies for tuberculosis and other diseases equally as devastating were based in tradition. Because Apaches believed tuberculosis was caused by worms, their healing ceremonies included powerful purgatives using a root they called "narrow medicine." The root was pounded into powder and heated in water by putting four hot stones into it. As the shaman prayed and chanted,

Chiricahua Apache warrior Notalq, a member of Chatto's delegation to Washington, D.C., in 1886. Notalq was imprisoned at Fort Marion, St. Augustine, Florida, but no further information exists as to his fate. Note beads of perspiration under his lower lip. (Frisco Native American Museum)

the mixture foamed and the Apache drank it. The patient was then blessed with *hoddentin* and placed outdoors in the sun until he vomited or defecated the worms.[13]

Compared with wetter regions of the nation, the Southwest and its people were minimally affected by the protozoan disease called malaria. Malaria was so common that it seemed to be the most prevalent contagious disease on the prairie. Transmitted by the *Anopheles* mosquito, which ingests the parasites along with the blood of an infected person as it feeds, the protozoa multiply in the mosquito's stomach, invade its salivary glands, and then are transferred to the next human bitten by the mosquito. In the new host, the infection results in bouts of shivering, fever, sweating, anemia, and enlargement of the spleen. The eccentricity of the ailment places a strain on the body and weakens an individual so seriously that resistance to opportunistic ailments is impaired.

Before quinine,[14] home remedies were the treatment of choice, and they varied greatly. Marc Simmons's ancestor, a doctor in Mississippi just before the Civil War, wrote a prescription for malaria in his journal: "Take a lump of cow excrement as large as a hen egg from a cow pie dropped in the month of May. Wrap it in a rag and put it into a pitcher with a little sage, horsemint, and other sweating herbs. . . . Drink plenty to cause sweating." [15]

Amebic dysentery doesn't need mosquitoes to spread its infection. Also caused by protozoa, it is disseminated through food and water contaminated with human feces. Dysentery was especially virulent when wells and latrines were close together, as was the case during the Chiricahua Apaches' incarceration in St. Augustine, Florida. The parasites hibernated for days, months, or years after the initial infection and eventually produced diarrhea, indigestion, weight loss, and anemia. Worse, ulceration of the intestine, and infrequent formation of abscesses in the liver, lungs, testes, or brain, resulted in many cases. Death was always possible.[16]

Unlike bacteria and protozoa, viruses have no metabolism of their own and are parasitic in the most fundamental sense by being wholly dependent on the host cells for reproduction. Contagious ailments, all potentially fatal, such as smallpox, mumps, measles, influenza, and the common cold were the results of viral infections among every ethnic group on the frontier. Although some of the ailments were contained through inoculation and vaccination, *access* to the life-saving medicine was crucial. From time to time the Apaches were offered medical care by the occupiers, including treatment in the form of vaccination against the dreaded smallpox, but often the effort was short-lived due to shortages of the vaccine. William Griffen reported that "while Spaniards began inoculation against smallpox around the turn of the nineteenth century, apparently they never finished this service to the Apaches despite their recognizing that epidemics . . . were the root of considerable upset among the Apaches."[17] True, the Apaches and other Native Americans feared contagion, but it was the Mexican pioneers who had settled in villages in northern New Mexico who were reluctant to be vaccinated against smallpox. A massive public education effort had to be undertaken before volunteers came forward to receive the protection. Nearly everyone without prior exposure, except those who were vaccinated, became infected.[18]

Jason Betzinez, a Warm Springs Apache, wrote about being camped near Silver City, New Mexico, while he and his group were being moved to the San Carlos, Arizona, Apache Reservation under army supervision. While the soldiers were resting, some of the Warm Springs women traded in the Silver City stores and unknowingly brought smallpox back with them in cloth and other goods. Shortly after the group arrived at San Carlos, an outbreak fatal to many occurred. The Warm Springs Apaches who did not become ill moved into the reservation's northern mountains, once again running from disease and hoping to avoid the illness. Those who were sick, according to Betzinez, did the best they could at the lower altitude.[19]

The smallpox virus incubates for ten to twelve days, and then symptoms of fever, headaches, nausea and vomiting, and muscular aches appear, followed in a few days by a rash. Then lesions arise, grow into vesicles, and finally become oozing pustules. In the last stage, scabs form which fall off after one or two weeks.[20]

Although immunization has now virtually eradicated the disease, standard medical treatment was limited at best before smallpox vaccine became available. Simmons reported that "most help came from Franciscan friars who often did double duty as doctors. They possessed a small stock of medicine brought up from Mexico and also made use of local herbal remedies. In addition, they practiced phlebotomy, or the bleeding of patients. This practice entailed opening a vein with an unsterile instrument called a fleam and collecting the blood in a basin. The idea was that a surplus of blood contributed to the fever associated with the disease."[21]

During early 1805, Santa Fe's only doctor, Don Cristoval Larrañaga, returned from Mexico with 4 children who carried live cowpox in their arms. From these, 257 children in the area were vaccinated against smallpox in an arm-to-arm campaign. In 1806, the effort ended when viable fluid was lost. But Dr. Larrañaga never stopped trying. In 1808, cowpox fluid crusts were sent from Chihuahua, Mexico, with the following directions: "Some ten or twelve crusts are taken and being ground in a very clean mortar, the powder is put in a paper and with a drop of water, wait until it remains in a very flexible dough and with the point of the lancet or needle, it is taken and introduced to the children the same as if it were fluid vaccine, with respect to which it gives the same results, and is even more sure in arresting smallpox than when the inoculation is performed with the fluid from the crusts."[22]

The Delgado family, Hispanic pioneers who were among the early settlers of Santa Fe, had one *remedio* for three diseases: smallpox, scarlet fever, and diptheria. Their recipe read: "Pulv. Digitalis 1 Gr., Zinc Sulphate 1 Gr., Water 4 oz., Sugar ½ teaspoonful, three times a day as a preventative. For disease, a teaspoonful every 2 hours. A teaspoonful for an adult, ½ for a child."[23]

The Chiricahua Apaches' remedy for smallpox and other diseases was demonstrated in healing ceremonies and other spiritual rituals. In the Apache view, offenses against the Mountain Spirits, representatives of the Apache deities, caused epidemics; natural catastrophes such as earthquakes and eclipses were warnings of the epidemics to come. When the Chiricahuas received an omen, the Mountain Spirit dancers performed for four nights, and, as one old Apache reflected on days long gone, "we never got the smallpox."[24] He was sadly mistaken. In addition to widely available information regarding all aspects of the disease which disproves his statement, the Amerind Foundation's museum in the Apache country near Dragoon, Arizona, has a rare acquisition—a bow and several arrows made by Geronimo. At a private showing for Chiricahua Apaches in March 1991, the curator pointed out a design carefully carved by Geronimo on the inner aspect of the bow. Clouds and mountains are represented in the scene, as are four tents spotted with dots still red after a century. When asked, the curator agreed that they might depict smallpox or measles.

That the Apaches were terrified by smallpox was confirmed in an unusual way by Teresa Pijoan, a cryptographer and mythologist. In deciphering petroglyphs in the Comanche Gap area of north-central New Mexico, Pijoan noted the presence of smallpox or chicken pox as dots on figures scratched into the rocks. She identified one group as Kiowa warriors and another as Apaches, who are fleeing from the spotted Kiowa stick figures. "Apaches would see the spots and run," she declared, also stating that "one of the things the Kiowa learned from the United States Cavalry was how to glue spots on. They would take tree sap and rub it over the pox spots so they wouldn't fall off." [25] If true (is it really possible?), the army was much more innovative and clever in its military strategy against the Indians than many people imagined. For example, charging soldiers (or Kiowas friendly to the army) wearing pasted-on red spots might drive the Apaches backward into a military ambush.

The Kiowa, keepers of pictorial calendars, drew representations of epidemics on hides. One that I have seen shows a figure of an individual with smallpox in the winter of 1839–40; a second shows a measles patient in the summer of 1877; and a third shows a cholera victim in the summer of 1849. Of the three, the first two look somewhat alike because the figures are covered with dots, but the cholera victim has his fists clenched and his legs drawn up in pain.[26]

Cholera, an acute bacterial infection of the small intestine, causes severe vomiting, diarrhea, and eventual death. After exposure to feces-contaminated food or drinking water, it takes one to five days for the symptoms to begin. Very suddenly and with great force, the patient becomes so seriously ill that the resulting dehydration and electrolytic imbalance in the body fluids causes death within twenty-four hours. Outbreaks are rare when good sanitary conditions exist.

Burning human waste was often prescribed to fight cholera, along with a home remedy consisting of a hot herbal enema of granulated bayberry bark, white oak bark, sumac, or wild cherry, taken early in the attack. When vomiting occurred, peppermint or spearmint tea soothed the stomach. Two hours after the first cup, the patient was given another, this one made from goldenseal, gentian, or bayberry. Goldenseal (*Hydrastis canadensis*) was and is a popular multipurpose herb preferred by almost everyone.[27] In cholera patients, the remedy produced healing of the mucous lining of the rectum, which alleviated some of the distress.[28] In all situations, however, disinfecting the area was necessary. As noted earlier, if the Chiricahua Apaches needed to cleanse a location, they called upon their longtime favorite plant, sagebrush, to serve as a fumigator; a more dramatic action consisted of burning the area to sterilize it.

＊　＊　＊　Herbal Remedies

Sagebrush, called *chamiso hediondo* (*Artemisia tridentata*) by southwestern Hispanics, was not considered a fumigator by Spanish and Mexican pioneers, although it was widely used in *curanderismo*.[29] As a tea, a powder, or heated in lard, the herb cleansed the skin and inhibited bacterial growth. It was also burned as incense and was sipped in a tea that would stimulate sweating, for example, to break fevers. The preparation was bitter and might have caused a gag reflex in sensitive patients, so the sufferer was advised to drink it slowly and in small quantities. As cold tea, it was said to stimulate digestion and help avoid maladies related to diarrhea and constipation.

For gastrointestinal distress caused by diarrhea, dysentery, or stomach ulcers, Native Americans and Hispanics both liked mesquite (*Prosopis juliflora*) in the form of a tea made from the pods, leaves, and bark. Mesquite gum was also used after it had been soaked in water until dissolved. This preparation was believed to settle the intestines after stomach flu, food poisoning, and surgery, and was a soothing remedy for sore eyes and sore throats. For constipation, a rounded teaspoon of a familiar remedy, *cascara sagrada* (*Rhamnus purshiana, R. californica*), was called upon to produce results by morning.[30]

Symptoms of colds, flu, and croup in babies were treated with a variety of herbs and herbal preparations, among which was *ajo* (*Allium sativum*), the well-known and humble garlic, which was crushed and steeped for a day or so in honey. The Hispanic patient then ate one or two teaspoons of the mixture to quell fevers or swallowed a whole clove with water every three to four hours to dislodge mucus from the lungs. Ground garlic as a poultice was applied to carbuncles by the Cheyenne Indians. When the lesion opened, garlic was used in water to rinse out the infection.

Chamomile (*Anthemis* spp.) could be used as drops to relieve earaches related to a cold as well as drunk in tea. For coughs, *osha* (*Ligusticum porteri*), the most widely used herb in the Southwest among Hispanics, was helpful. *Osha* loosened phlegm in lung infections and was soothing to sore throats and queasy stomachs. Grated *osha* was mixed with salt and taken as an emetic, or steeped in whiskey to treat malaria. It was also used as a soak for superficial infections and boils.[31]

A patient with an ailment characterized by fevers, such as malaria, could try *canela*, a tasty herb known for its ability to reduce temperatures. *Canela* sticks (*Cinnamon* sp.), occasionally accompanied by *ajenjibre* (*Zingiber officinale*), or ginger root, were crushed and sipped three times daily in tea.[32] The *curanderismo* pharmacy had a *remedio* for nearly every ailment. In instances of serious illnesses, though, everyone on the frontier was totally at the mercy of the diseases before preventions or cures were discovered.

For example, before Louis Pasteur led the way in 1885 toward a successful inoculation against rabies,[33] 15 percent of those infected with the virus succumbed, reported J. Frank Dobie, one of the most respected writers of the American West. The one hope of surviving a bite from a rabid animal was to find a "madstone," a stone that looked like it had been processed through the intestines of an animal. The stone was moistened with warm milk and applied to the wound. If it didn't stick to the skin, the patient was presumed not to have been infected. If the stone adhered, it was believed to be drawing poison out of the wound. Then it would be put into a vessel of warm, or hot milk, and the liquid would turn green from the poison.[34]

Marc Simmons disagreed with Dobie's mortality statistics. In an article about rabies in the Southwest, Simmons put the death rate at 100 percent and never referred to the "madstone." Instead, he mentioned the Hispanic *remedio* that placed *trementina*, the gum from a piñon tree, over the bite. The gum also drew out the poison and prevented infection. Mint mixed in a tea with salt was supposed to keep the patient free from the disease. Simmons added, "Home remedies, of course, were a waste of time. Once the malady had infected a human, death was the inevitable outcome. But before that happened, the victim suffered high fever, delirium, convulsions, paralysis, foaming at the mouth and, finally, coma." To prevent dogs from becoming rabid, Simmons wrote, Spaniards living in the Southwest fed their pet dogs garlic, believing that the strong odor would keep the virus away.[35]

While symptoms of rabies pointed clearly to a diagnosis, it was often difficult for ethnic healers and physicians in the Old West to accurately define some ailments. When the main symptom was fever, the cause could be one of several diseases, and the healer's task became one of correctly determining the problems without much assistance. Actually, if the patient was misdiagnosed, it often was of minimum consequence because available treatments were so limited. Even when the ailment was more or less certain, medications were primitive compared with today's sophisticated technology. In 1858, military hospitals carried the best and latest available drugs. Fort Burgwin, near Taos, New Mexico, was considered well stocked, relatively speaking, even though it was a modest army outpost. Fortunately, the records kept by its physician, Dr. William Wallace Anderson, are very complete and offer insight into the medical practices of the time. The following items are noted on the supply list:

Glycerine, 2 oz.	Finet-ferric Chloride, ¼ lb.
Spirits of ether nitric, ¼ lb.	Aromatic Sulphuric Acid, ¼ lb.
Pith. of Sasafras, ½ oz.	Washing sponge, 8 to 10 oz.
Citric Acid, ¼ lb.	Brandy, best quality, 2 gal.
Madeira, 1 doz. bottles	Arsenic, 3 lb.
Sodae. bicarb., 2 lbs.	Potass. Nitrat., ½ lb.
Alcohol, 2 gal.	Lycopodium, 1 lb.
Brandy, cooking, 1 gal.	Wine, cooking, 1 gal.
Wine, sherry, 1 doz. bottles	Port, 1 doz. bottles
Whiskey, Scotch or Irish, 1 gal.	

Dr. Anderson charged a range of prices to civilians seeking medical treatment. Kit Carson paid twelve dollars for a single visit (diagnosis not recorded), and a local rancher was charged ten dollars. Amputating the forefinger of a "halfbreed" cost twenty-five dollars, but six visits to a desperately ill "Mexican with typhoid" cost the patient one hog and three dollars worth of corn. A woman treated over a period of time for rheumatism paid one chicken and ten eggs.[36]

A review of Dr. Anderson's extensive patient notes reveals that the most common mid-nineteenth-century complaints in the Taos area were wounds—from gunshots, knives, and arrows. Next, and in no special order, were broken limbs, dysentery or chronic diarrhea, respiratory illnesses, exposure, typhoid, bad teeth, abscesses as a result of secondary infection, rheumatism, scurvy, gonorrhea or syphilis, and infant illnesses including colic, whooping cough, measles, and scarletina.

Dr. Anderson's medical kit, separate from the medical supplies at the hospital, carried a small selection of drugs to be administered during house calls. Opium was prescribed for many conditions, as a tincture (laudanum) in pills or as morphine, which often was sprinkled directly into wounds. Quarter or half grains of opium, plus leeches, were prescribed for wounds to control pain and prevent shock. Dover's Powder, a preparation of one part *ipecac* (a shrub containing an alkaloid which acts as an expectorant and emetic when taken internally; too much is toxic) and eight parts "sugar of milk," was given to patients with dysentery.

Medical services during childbirth on the frontier cost a dollar for each mile the doctor traveled, but more at night or in bad weather. And when the vagaries of nature arrived, they often did it with great style. Dust storms, blizzards, earthquakes, fires, droughts, and floods, combined with attacks by Indians, outlaws, and Mexican renegades, made travel very hazardous. Too, the esteemed physician might not be a well-educated doctor; the years of formal medical training were few a century ago, and occasionally just a little medical knowledge and a few dollars to open an office enabled an individual to establish a medical practice.

Midwives were more numerous than country doctors, often more accessible, and more willing to accept meat, produce, fruit, or gingham as payment for their services. But midwives were subject to the same conditions of weather and physical danger as were physicians, so the laboring mother often had to be her own obstetrician.

Hispanic mothers-to-be depended on female relatives for information about herbs such as cinnamon and spearmint that were used as cathartics, tonics, and prenatal aids and could be taken as soothing teas. Garlic, raw and fried onions, and chamomile could be rubbed on the expectant mother's body to hasten delivery. When a woman's strength ebbed during long and difficult labor, the smoke of burning coriander seeds was wafted toward her in the belief that breathing it in would revitalize her.

Pregnant Native American women followed the customs of their tribes. For example, when the Apaches were on the move to avoid hostile encounters, pregnant women were expected to fall behind when contractions began and not jeopardize the others' safety. Hidden in the shelter of a boulder or behind a bush, suffering intense labor pains, the Apache woman birthed alone and in silence, lest she betray her presence. Afterward, she would gather up her newborn and sneak off, usually at night, hoping to rejoin her tribe in a few hours or days.

On the Great Plains, a Cheyenne mother-to-be knelt on a hay-covered robe in a special tipi and pushed her baby out while she firmly grasped an upright pole planted in the ground in front of her. A Hopi mother, high on a mesa in Arizona, walked around a special room while she and her husband awaited the birth. From time to time he pressed his knees on the small of her back and shook her to hurry the birth.[37]

Clearly, customs related to health and healing differed from tribe to tribe and across the cultures of the Southwest, but terrible medical afflictions respected no ethnic boundaries. However, history shows that the vast majority of emigrants and pioneers lived fairly healthful lives with only rare episodes of sickness. Various Indian peoples in the West were prone to horrifying casualties from occasional epidemics and plagues, but aside from those, their life spans might be long, relatively speaking, unless cut short by wounds or by the rigors of life in the open.

One significant contribution to the ease with which epidemics gained a foothold was the vitamin-poor diet most individuals of every background ate. For instance, frontier army posts served a standard fare of salt meat, cornmeal, bread, soda biscuits, syrup, lard, black coffee, and beans, beans, beans.[38]

A balanced diet providing even the minimum amount of appropriate nourishment to military personnel was a rarity, and the same was true for the rations issued to Native Americans by the Spanish, Mexican, and American armies. Distributed at "subsistence stores" on military posts, rations were bribes and were a favorite way of keeping the peace. Griffen noted that in 1791, the Spanish presidios were protecting some Apaches and providing them with weekly supplies of "corn or wheat, meat, brown sugar, salt, and cigarettes." By 1831, the political circumstances had changed and the weekly rations were discontinued by the Mexican government. Many Apaches left the presidios and returned to raiding, one of the traditional ways they obtained food. About fifteen years later, according to Griffen, Apaches were again receiving rations from the military in Janos and Corralitos, Mexico, indicating that the subsistence system was again functioning.[39] In the 1870s, on Arizona's San Carlos Reservation, Apaches received weekly or twice weekly handouts of "flour, sugar, coffee, beef, and unwanted soap. Each native who answered roll call was given something like five and one-half pounds of freshly slaughtered beef, four pounds of flour, and supplementary rations."[40] Vegetables may have been included among the "supplementary rations." If so, it was not recorded, nor is it certain from historical documents exactly what health conditions the lack of fresh fruits and vegetables in a reservation diet caused among the Apaches. It is known, however, that the Chiricahua Apaches greatly enjoyed fruit, directly from the trees when possible, while they were away from the Spanish and Mexican presidios and off the American reservations.

The outdoor life of the Apache people created superior physical conditioning, which in turn contributed to generally excellent health. An early document compliments the Apache people for their strength, ability to endure, intelligence, quickness, and leadership.[41] Given these outstanding qualities, all of which have their foundation in good health, one wonders what the Apaches would have thought of some of the "old standbys" preferred by pioneer doctors to treat less vigorous southwesterners:

Jalap: Tuberous root of a Mexican plant, used as a cathartic or purge
Tartar Emetic: Crystals of antimony and potassium tartrate, employed usually as a sedative or an emetic
Calomel: Mercurous chloride, used as a laxative purge
Blue Mass: Laxative made by rubbing up metallic mercury with licorice and other excipients

Paregoric: Tincture of opium and camphor, to check diarrhea

Nux Vomica: Beans of an East Indian tree which contain
strychnine, used as a stimulant

Belladonna: Leaves and root of the deadly nightshade
containing atrophine, used as a stimulant and to decrease all
secretions of the body except the urine

Arnica: Dried flower heads of a plant native to the Old West,
used as a tincture to relieve sprains and bruises

Digitalis: Dried leaves of the Foxglove plant, used as a heart
stimulant

Seidlitz Powder: A pioneer effervescent anti-acid containing
bitartrate of sodium and potassium, bicarbonate of sodium
and tartaric acid

Ergot: Derived from spawn of a fungus which grows in the
flower of common rye, used to stimulate uterine contractions
and in the treatment of certain hemorrhages

Blaud's Pills: Carbonate of iron, given in cases of anemia

Asafetida: A gum resin, used as a stimulant and carminative in
the alimentary canal[42]

"Granny medicine" was used side by side with the more formal
medical remedies in many different "cures" for ailments. Karolevitz claimed these home remedies were "a strange conglomeration
of superstition, religious fervor and simple ignorance—but it was
practiced with great faith and not for financial gain." He listed quite
a few trusted "granny medicines," among them the following:

Oil of geese, wolves, bears or polecats for rheumatism; common
salt with scrapings from pewter spoons for worms; scorpion oil as
a diuretic in venereal disease; tonic made by soaking half a bucket
of rusty nails in vinegar as a blood purifier; brandy and red pepper
for cholera; to remove warts, rub them with green walnuts, bacon
rind or chicken feet; scratch gum with iron nail till it bleeds, then
drive nail into wooden beam to relieve toothache; wrap legs in
brown paper soaked in vinegar to relieve aching muscles; onions
boiled in sulphur molasses for laxative; and warm brains of freshly
killed rabbit applied to child's gums to relieve teething pains.[43]

While grannies and their remedies were everywhere, old-time
physicians were more often located on or near military posts or had

a formal or informal affiliation with army physicians. One of the concerns of both military and civilian health authorities on the frontier was the role sanitation, or the lack of it, played in spreading contagious diseases. At Fort Davis, Texas, during the years 1868–72, a physician named Daniel Wiesel was post surgeon. Only thirty years old, the doctor assumed all the medical responsibilities as he saw them, including preparing a cookbook that stressed the use of recipes containing watercress growing in a nearby creek [44] to combat widespread scurvy among the troops. While Dr. Wiesel established post and hospital truck gardens to provide fresh vegetables, he was unsuccessful in improving other conditions. He lamented the lack of personal cleanliness among the garrison; the men bathed infrequently in a creek that was fouled with drainage from the stables. Garbage was strewn everywhere, sinks and other open holes were filled with rotting refuse, and the guardhouse and barracks were so overcrowded that they were perfect breeding grounds for disease.[45]

Unfortunately, Fort Davis was not an exception. Sanitary measures were not understood or were ignored during the 1800s and early 1900s. Flies infested outdoor toilets; spitting was an acceptable social practice, and saloon keepers washed their spittoons in the same ditch water used by townspeople for cooking and drinking; dead animals lay where they fell and wild dogs fed on their decomposing corpses; and animal dung was everywhere. It's a wonder that so many people survived.

In areas where men congregated and prostitutes worked, such as boomtowns, mining villages, and railroad construction camps, another malady appeared quickly: venereal disease. Hrdlicka believed syphilis in its current form did not exist in pre-Columbian America,[46] a conclusion derived from his careful examinations of skeletal remains. He found no signs of syphilis in the skulls and other bones, where it would characteristically have appeared, of American Indians in the Southwest and in northern Mexico.[47] There is considerable dispute about this issue, however. Benjamin Gordon stated that syphilis had been identified in three skulls (possibly Indian) found in Pecos, New Mexico, and in South American natives.[48] The issue has not been resolved, and the debate continues.

Chiricahua Apaches relied on high moral standards and cultural patterns to control the promiscuity that could lead to sexual disease. If a woman committed adultery, for example, her husband was expected to cut off the tip of her nose, a practice with roots in antiquity.[49] Naturally, this action did not cure any disease she might acquire, but it surely was a deterrent to extramarital liaisons. Chiricahua men who committed adultery suffered no such humiliation.

Venereal diseases alarmed the Chiricahuas, and they developed specific ceremonies which were conducted by healers who knew the cures. Remedies varied, but several were preferred. Mud (found later to contain sodium sulfate and sodium magnesium chloride) from a special creek in Arizona was used, and compresses were made from quaking aspen bark. The affected anatomical areas in men were plastered with poultices, and women's vaginas were packed with the preparations.[50] That women alone were at fault in transmitting venereal disease was made clear by an Apache whose father was a shaman. Talking with Morris Opler, the man remembered, "My father couldn't do much for him (the patient) because he was sick with the disease from a woman."[51] According to Opler, the Apaches believed that a ceremony or treatment for venereal disease could not be effective unless the patient revealed the identity of the person from whom he had received the disease. In this particular case, the patient was so ill and his wife so loving and forgiving that she urged him to speak out. He refused and died shortly thereafter.

Opler also reported two stories told to him by other Apaches about venereal disease. During the ceremony to cure the ailment, medicine from pounded and boiled roots of a locust tree was given to the patient by the shaman. One individual told Opler that administering the preparation must be done in conjunction with the patient bringing the woman who had given him the disease before the shaman. If the man refused, nothing could be done for him. Another man said, "When there is a hard boil down there, they recognize that it is very serious and hard to cure. When it breaks, they have a medicine to put on it. They use a ceremony and drink medicine."[52]

Whether or not the locust tree medicine was effective has not been revealed, but it shouldn't be surprising if it cured the lesion. Then, as now, belief in the healing properties of cultural remedies had an enormously positive effect on patients. It was when strange new diseases were introduced into an area, and became lethal, that previously reliable ethnic healing patterns collapsed beside dying individuals and families. There is another factor to the predictable failure of cultural healing techniques: when a people are denied access to the natural medicines and curing ceremonies that form their culture's healing traditions, the tradition breaks down.

In particular, the Apaches' imprisonment ensured that familiar medicinal herbs could not be collected and prepared for use before being coupled with the spiritual ceremonies that were so integral to traditional healing. Even if the rituals had been conducted, however, the assault upon the Apache people by powerful contagious diseases could never have been successfully treated with plant remedies. At the time, deadly diseases such as tuberculosis had no known cure in patients of any ethnic background.

The Chiricahua Apaches, however, were destined to suffer an unrestricted attack by communicable illnesses while they were confined in Florida, Alabama, and Oklahoma. Their recovery as a people, at least in terms of population, is still not complete more than one hundred years after the final surrender. Also incomplete are answers to many questions about what actually happened during that incarceration. These uncertainties haunt many of today's descendants of the survivors.

5

Incarceration

in Florida:

Fort Marion

For the United States government, the long-awaited opportunity to crush the free-roving and troublesome Chiricahua Apaches began in the spring of 1886. Outwitted, angry, and desperately tired of chasing these Indians, the army had been repeatedly frustrated by its inability to capture the agile and superbly conditioned Apaches in their homelands. The strong and hardy men, women, and children escaped from the soldiers time and time again in Arizona and New Mexico by calling upon their superb physical resources, excellent health, and unsurpassed knowledge of the terrain and environment. But the pressure created by an all-out military strategy eventually had its effect.

The end of the Apaches' traditional way of life began when the Chiricahuas left the San Carlos Reservation on May 17, 1885. Fleeing east into New Mexico, the two separate groups, led by Naiche and Chihuahua, eventually parted. A little more than a month later, on June 23, 1885, in the Bavispe Mountains of Sonora, Mexico, Chihuahua's band heard shots. The warriors diverted army troops long enough for the women and children to hide in a cave. But it didn't matter. A sergeant and his men

Chiricahua Apache women and children from Chihuahua's band as prisoners of war newly arrived at Fort Bowie, Arizona, in spring 1886. Note the armed soldiers guarding the group. (Arizona Historical Society)

---

found them, shot at them, and dragged them out. Some were killed and were left where they fell. All the survivors, regardless of the severity of their wounds, were marched hundreds of miles overland to Fort Bowie. Said Eugene, son of Chihuahua, "Not one of the women, not even the wounded, was permitted to ride. . . . I don't know how long it took us to reach the fort, but when we did we were locked in a building. Some food was thrown on the ground for us as though we were dogs . . . women were put to digging ditches [latrines] . . . even the wounded ones."[1]

Later, Chihuahua and his warriors reunited with Naiche's band at a previously designated spot. The men shared their worries about inevitable capture or surrender, and most agreed they couldn't hold out much longer. They were concerned about the fate of the women and children who had been with Chihuahua, a torment made worse by the warriors' belief that the soldiers would take sexual advantage of the Apache women. Subsequently, after a long and tedious negotiation, Apache leaders from these groups met with Brigadier General George Crook and his military party at Cañon de los Embudos in Mexico on March 25 and 27, 1886, to talk about surrender. At the first session, the notorious shaman and warrior Geronimo monopolized the discussion with complaints about his reputation being ruined by rumors and innuendo. He tried to convince the general that he was the innocent victim of gossip, and not responsible for the highly publicized murderous actions attributed to him. The weary general held his ground and insisted that both groups surrender and that Geronimo stop his tirade or the talks would be canceled. Two days later, when they all met again, Geronimo was quiet and Chihuahua took the lead. He surrendered, shaking hands with the military men and assuring them of his good intentions. Naiche and Geronimo did the same, but of the three Chiricahua Apache leaders, only Chihuahua and his warriors later arrived at Fort Bowie in the company of army officials and scouts. Naiche and Geronimo had second thoughts and rode off, taking some of their followers. An unscrupulous man by the name of Tribolet had sold them some bootleg whiskey, which precipitated their flight.

When Chihuahua and his warriors rejoined their women and children at Fort Bowie, a reporter was waiting to record the notable event. In a special dispatch to his newspaper, the *Los Angeles Times*, Charles Fletcher Lummis wrote on April 6: "The Chiricahua Apaches who surrendered to General Crook March 29 [actually March 27], and arrived here April 3, in charge of Lieut. Maus, will be sent to Fort Marion, St. Augustine, Florida, as prisoners of war. The squaws and children go too. . . . The prisoners are giving a grand dance to-night at their camp. . . . The prisoners know that they are going away, but don't know where. They take it very philosophically. Chihuahua . . . hoped he would not suffer imprisonment too long, because he would lose a wagon he had at the reservation."

Lummis's description portrays an excited and vigorous band of Chiricahuas getting ready to depart the next day.

All this morning the bronco camp was a scene of confusion. The bucks were greasing up their hair, and gathering their cartridges. The squaws were . . . catching and saddling the mules and horses, and packing cleverly upon them the blankets, muslin "tents," pots and cups, canteens, baskets, and hunks of jerked meat. . . . A queer procession it was that wound down Apache Pass and out upon the dusty plain. Here was a gaily painted scout wearing the army blouse, and with his rifle or carbine across his saddle. . . . Next you might have seen a burro so hidden by big bundles that

Monochrome of Chiricahua Apaches preparing to board train at Holbrook, Arizona, for incarceration at Fort Marion, September 1886. This illustration depicts some of the more than 400 Apaches whose peaceful way of life on the White Mountain / San Carlos Reservation came to an abrupt halt. (National Park Service)

only his slender legs and comical head were visible, while on top and bestride of the whole aggregation would be a squaw, with the peculiar Apache cradle under one arm and across her lap, while the other hand was occupied with whip and bridle . . . the strange passengers were loaded into the emigrant sleepers, and now are trundling eastward.[2]

Lummis didn't mention that the military band played "Auld Lang Syne" as Chihuahua's group left the fort.

Among those to be the first Chiricahua Apaches incarcerated in Florida were Today, Tanzea, Nausen, Cosner, Shunarday, Chechet, Stallock, Donshedan, Soz, Goody-goody, Gocsi—Chatto's kin, Jozhya, Parlo, Sozone, Couporal, Siele, Sizzen, Kaleson, Harry, Katar, Kerozona, Spudy, Bender, No Slim, Stone, Conaenato, Bahaley, Backlom, Jim, Nigharzen, Notar, Whenoshe, Bezanas,

Monochrome depicting recently arrived Chiricahua Apaches marching at night through the streets of St. Augustine toward confinement at Fort Marion, September 20, 1886. Note curious townspeople. (National Park Service)

Fatty, Natchez, Bushozen, Bisha, Josanan, Coyonke, Kashonar, Shiltinoo, and Elskeney.[3]

Unknown to any of them at the time, they had started on an odyssey that would result in nearly three decades of incarceration for them, their relatives, and their friends. Worse, imprisonment became a death sentence for many of the prisoners. It started with a seven-month stay at Fort Marion in St. Augustine, Florida. There, some newly arrived Apaches quickly felt the first symptoms of tuberculosis and within days or weeks became seriously ill. If any consideration had been given by authorities to the medical consequences the Apaches might suffer during incarceration, there is no record. On the other hand, it is difficult to believe the issue of health, or the lack of it, was overlooked, given the widespread contagious illnesses of the day. The obvious conclusion is that the Apaches' well-being while in captivity was not among the government's priorities.

Monochrome portraying crowded conditions of incarceration on the ter-replein at Fort Marion. Tourists and sightseers mingle with the Apaches. Actually, the tipis were much closer together, housing more than 500 pris-oners of war. Armed guards were stationed in the bastions on all four corners atop the fort. (National Park Service)

At a private meeting with the secretaries of war and interior and a famous Indian foe, Lieutenant General Philip Sheridan, President Grover Cleveland apparently verbally approved the decision to incarcerate the Chiricahuas in the small facility on the Florida seacoast that had once confined hostile Plains Indians. Fort Marion was on the president's mind because the facility had been the subject of a two-year debate in the Senate, where an appropriation of $10,000 for repairs was mired down in the Committee on Military Affairs.[4] It is not unreasonable to conclude that the president's selection of Fort Marion was political, made with an eye toward forcing the legislation out of committee and onto the Senate floor for a vote. Fort Pickens, a much larger facility off the coast of Pensacola, three hundred miles to the west of St. Augustine, was empty and could easily have held all the prisoners without crowding. And the president knew that, having been made aware by his advisers and members of Congress. Yet the much smaller Fort Marion remained the president's choice.

Leaving Bowie Station on April 7, 1886, by train, Chihuahua's group arrived at St. Augustine on April 13. The seventy-seven prisoners of war had been guarded during the entire two-thousand-mile journey by thirty soldiers under the command of First Lieutenant J. R. Richards, from Company E, Eighth Infantry. The Apaches carried baggage consisting of "square packages tied with ropes; black tin cans and buckets and pots; packages of splendidly tanned and highly ornamented skins; bundles of dried meat, sacks of meal, blankets, coats, odd-looking blankets and a variety of other plunder," which "spilled promiscuously into trucks (wagons), amid jeers of the colored porters who were hauling the stuff."[5] Having no way of knowing what they would need, the Apaches had brought whatever they had.

The prisoners' arrival in St. Augustine was chronicled by a reporter from the *Florida Times-Union* on April 14, 1886. He described a pathetic scene, mentioning that when the doors of the train were opened, "dirty, ragged, half-clad, and with long unkempt locks of coarse black hair flying loose about their heads," the Apaches emerged. "In their eyes, they were typical savages," wrote the reporter. "First came the men, each with shoulders and head wrapped in a blanket and all marching with expressionless faces and stately gait; then came the young bucks with less dignity and fewer blankets, as well as fewer clothes of any kind; then straggling along one by one, came the young women, girls, and children . . . lastly came the old women, each hugging a baby or bundle, and a wounded squaw in a truck, her head shrouded in a blanket, brought up the rear."[6]

The Apaches were herded like livestock from the train to the fort. Crossing the drawbridge over the dry moat that surrounded Fort Marion was a new and terrifying experience, especially if the prisoners looked over their shoulders and saw the wooden bridge rise behind them. Chihuahua's followers had never before been within the walls of a fort capable of being surrounded with water—not in the Southwest. The families were broken up immediately, even though this punitive action had neither been agreed upon nor discussed in the negotiations. On the contrary, one of the reasons for surrender was to join families together, and the government representatives gave their word that this would be done.

The first clash of cultures in captivity, that of ancient taboos versus military realities, began right after the families were separated. The men and older boys were taken by boat to Anastasia Island, just across a waterway, and left with food, fishing tackle, and oil to light the lamps in the lighthouse. Occasionally a boat arrived and brought more food, but the Apaches were expected to catch and cook fish for themselves. It is possible that the warriors and boys actually went eighteen days without solid food before being brought back to the mainland. Although eating fish was a violation of a powerful cultural taboo, it was a prohibition that government officials refused to recognize, not only in Florida but throughout many of the long years of confinement.

Although beef was issued in small quantities at the fort, one of the mainstays of the government rations was fish. Another source of protein, pork, was part of the military diet, but pork was also forbidden to the Apaches by their cultural customs because hogs ate snakes and taboo marine life. The staples—beans, rice, hominy, turnips, potatoes, onions, bread, sugar, and coffee—that were part of the Apaches' basic rations in captivity were nourishing but couldn't make up the lack of protein. With the deficient food supply, the good health the Chiricahua Apaches enjoyed while a free people began to deteriorate. In Arizona and New Mexico, meat had been obtained by hunting and raiding, but these traditional activities had obviously ceased. Now the fearsome Apaches were totally dependent on their captors for food—a situation that shifted power dramatically. But still the cultural mores prevailed: the Apache prisoners of war would eat no fish or pork, and hunger moved in to increase the downhill slide of the people's health. To fill their bellies they invented meals comprised mainly of the sparse amounts of beef each prisoner-of-war family received. Woodward Skinner said that "the most common dish was a soupy beef stew made with a mixture of flour and fat. . . . The women often made a pastry from wheat flour and water. The dough was worked thin by tossing it from one hand to the other, being unleavened like hardtack, . . . it would be kept for a period of time without becoming rancid. . . . They liked coffee, but they would never drink cow's milk or feed it

Rear view of Fort Marion, with tipis on the terreplein, ca. early 1887. The North River and Anastasia Island (facing the fort) were graveyards for the 18 to 24 Chiricahua Apaches who perished here during seven months of incarceration. (National Park Service)

to nursing babies, a fault that may have contributed to babies dying in a weakened condition. However, women sometimes nursed their babies for years."[7]

Ruey Darrow, daughter of prisoners Sam Haozous and Blossom Wratten Haozous, confirmed Skinner's statement in a 1989 interview, saying of her father (who was just a boy in the days before the final surrender), "He nursed at her [his mother's] breast until he was five years old because that was during the times when they didn't have anything to eat."[8] The same situation was occurring under the supervision and control of the military officials at Fort Marion.

The army reported that the Chiricahua Apaches were doing quite well at Fort Marion. In an August 20, 1886, report from Lieutenant Colonel Loomis L. Langdon, Second Regiment, U.S. Artillery,

Commanding Post, St. Francis Barracks, St. Augustine, Florida, to the assistant adjutant general, Headquarters, Division of the Atlantic, at Governor's Island, New York, Langdon seemed particularly pleased with the situation. He wrote that Chihuahua's people "have the run of the place" and were "allowed full liberty within the walls. . . . The general health of these prisoners is good. There have been, however, two deaths among them," despite having what he decided was "the best of medical attention. . . . They were supplied with all the medicines needed."[9] The two deaths in four months were children, and there is no indication in this correspondence that Langdon thought anything was amiss.

However, in another report to the same superior officer dated just three days later, Langdon stated, "These Indians were brought here on the 13th of April last. Since then four of them have died, three children and one adult male. There now remains of the original number, a total of seventy-three."[10] Langdon was suddenly clearly worried.

In that same month, Acting Secretary of War R. C. Drum was instructed to determine how many more Indians could be incarcerated at the fort. He sent a telegram to Langdon asking, "What number of Indians—men, women, and children—can, in addition to the number now at St. Augustine, be accommodated there? Should it be determined to increase the number by some four or five hundred, what preparation would be necessary and what probable expenditure required?" Langdon replied, "Can accommodate seventy-five men, women, and children in addition to those now here. Fort Marion is a small place. . . . Would recommend no more Indians be sent here."[11] Lieutenant General Philip Sheridan, the officer credited with saying "The only good Indians I ever saw were dead," disregarded Langdon's response and ordered hundreds more Chiricahua Apaches to be sent from the San Carlos Reservation at Fort Apache, Arizona, where they were learning to be farmers, to Florida. Before the diaspora ended, 502 prisoners and a supervisory army staff would be jammed into less than an acre of ground—inhumane conditions that aided and abetted the spread of virulent contagious diseases.

The procedures to incarcerate the next group of Chiricahua Apaches began three months after Chihuahua's band left Arizona. Keeping certain Chiricahuas on the Arizona reservation with the San Carlos Apaches had created a volatile situation, so the government considered the alternative of relocating these nearly four hundred industrious Indian farmers. Chatto, a United States Indian scout and formerly one of the most brutal Chiricahua Apaches, with a delegation of a dozen of his peers, most of whom had served in the United States military as scouts, were summoned to the nation's capital. There they listened to Secretary of War William C. Endicott extol the virtues of living in Indian Territory (now part of Oklahoma). Officials believed that Chatto would agree with them about a reservation to call home, preferably located east of the Mississippi River, possibly in Indian Territory, and would influence his relatives and friends at Fort Apache/San Carlos to concur. The government underestimated him. Chatto told the secretary of the interior, L. Q. C. Lamar, that he did not want to leave Arizona where he and his tribe were very happy and productive as farmers. Disappointed but in what appeared to Chatto to be a spirit of friendship, Lamar then offered to provide the Apache delegation with more farming implements back home. Chatto was pleased, and the Apache group left Washington believing they had made their point. But the government, hypocritical once again, had lied, and less honorable plans were in the making, even though Chatto had been presented with, and carried, a "certificate of good character" signed by Lamar and a beautiful silver medal, another present from the secretary of the interior.

On the return trip to Arizona, the thirteen Chiricahuas and their military escort traveled by rail to Carlisle Barracks in Pennsylvania, where at least four Chiricahua Apache children were in school, and then continued their journey to the Southwest. They could not have been aware of the flurry of telegrams among military and civilian officials across the country about the status of the Chiricahuas still at Fort Apache and of Chatto and the other delegates then on their way home. The group was within two days of reaching Fort Apache/San Carlos when the train unexpectedly, under orders, turned around and headed eastward. At Fort Leavenworth, Kansas, Chatto and the Apaches were detained as prisoners for nearly two confusing and worrisome months, and finally were told they would not be able to return to their homes.

A confidential telegram ordering the incarceration of Chatto and his group was sent on August 26, 1886, by Lamar to Drum. The message read: "I think it is the wish of the President that the Indians

Chatto as an old man on the Mescalero Apache Reservation in New Mexico, still wearing the peace medal he was awarded in Washington, D.C., immediately before being shipped to prison at Fort Marion. Chatto died in an automobile accident in 1936 at Mescalero. (Frisco Native American Museum)

who came to Washington should, none of them, return to Arizona within reach of communication with those at Fort Apache until transfer to Fort Marion has been consummated." [12]

It is important to call attention to the words "I think" in the communiqué. Lamar's beliefs were taken as direct orders by Drum and became the basis for Chatto's group's incarceration. As rationale for the action, the authorities convinced themselves that Chatto would use his influence to dissuade other Apaches from agreeing to leave Arizona and might even cause a breakout from the reservation if he was permitted to return.

On September 12, 1886, Chatto and the others left Fort Leavenworth under guard and were taken by train to Fort Marion. There the Apache scouts were imprisoned right beside the people they had betrayed during the years the Chiricahuas were free.

At least one military officer, Captain John G. Bourke of the Third Cavalry, long familiar with the Chiricahua Apaches, was worried and angry about the government's treatment of Chatto and the other scouts. Writing to Herbert Welsh, an Indian advocate and officer of the Indian Rights Association in Philadelphia, Bourke aired his concerns. Calling the actions against the Chiricahua scouts "a very disreputable thing," Bourke listed all of Chatto's contributions to keeping the peace among the Apaches, his assistance in the capture of Geronimo, and his general services to the army. His treatment by the government was, to a furious Bourke, "a most contemptible outrage, one of which I can tell you much more than I dare write, as I don't know whether this will reach you or not. If our government is to build up an Indian policy, based on treachery, lying, and double dealing, it can't blame the Indians for being good imitations of bad models." [13]

Chatto's own words and thoughts about the government's actions against him, spoken several years later to General George Crook, were still full of hurt.

> When I left Washington, I expected to go back to Camp [Fort] Apache. A letter came from General Miles stating that it was a bad place for Indians at Camp [Fort] Apache. All the white people were down on us and the other Indians also. He told us one part of the country belonged to Washington, the other part on the other side was Arizona, so he would put us on the Washington

side where there were good people. . . . From Fort Leavenworth we were taken to a place where Chihuahua was. . . . The letter said also that we could raise lots of horses, cattle . . . that there would be plenty of room on it for all [our] stock.

It was another lie, for obviously there was no room to raise livestock on the terreplein at Fort Marion. During the conversation with Crook, Chatto took from his breast the medal that had been presented to him and asked Crook, "Why did they give me that, to wear in the guard-house? I thought something good would have come to me when they gave me that, but I have been in confinement ever since I have had it."[14] The general's answer, if any, was not recorded.

On the third day after Chatto's people arrived at Fort Marion, the largest Apache group to be incarcerated as a unit joined them. Three hundred and eighty-three Chiricahua and Warm Springs Apaches had left Fort Apache by train under guard on September 7, 1886. Ruey Darrow recalled, "Papa [Sam Haozous] was a boy when they left for Florida and he told me that he remembered roll call that day. The soldiers called everyone to a central point and then split them up."[15] Chiricahua Apache Jason Betzinez, a young farmer at Fort Apache at that time, wrote in his autobiography, "All the men, women, and children were lined up and surrounded by soldiers. The commander ordered the men and boys into a building where he informed us that we were now prisoners of war. We were separated from our women and children, who were assembled in other camps, while we were placed under guard in tents . . . they loaded us all into wagons and started us off under armed guard for Holbrook, Arizona . . . out in the country, we were loaded on a train and shipped east."[16]

Two former army scouts, Chiricahua Apache Kuni and Warm Springs Apache Rogers Toklanni (he had married a Chiricahua woman, Siki, and remained with her throughout the period of incarceration), also recalled the day. "One day near noon," Kuni said, "they [the soldiers] told me they wanted to count the Chiricahuas. They surrounded us with scouts and soldiers. Five scouts were mounted. . . . They told us that where we were going it was the same as it was there. We were scouts in one place and would be in the other. When they had surrounded us, the White Mountain Indians

[Fort Apache] drove off our horses and cattle; they went to our farms and took what they wanted while we were surrounded. . . . They told us that we were going to be taken off, but not very far away, about a day's travel by railway." Toklanni added,

> The White Mountain [Fort Apache] Indians said that the Chiricahuas were bad. Their chiefs had been talking against us. . . . The officers told us we would be sent to a good country and we would have more houses and farms than we had at Camp Apache. "You have plenty here," they said, "but you will have more there and better stock. Do not be afraid, you will not be hurt. You are going to a good country." We did just as they told us. The day they rounded us up at the post all the men, women, widows and poor of the tribe that had stock had it driven off by the White Mountain Indians, who stole it.[17]

As with Chatto and the other scouts already confined, previous service and loyalty to the American military was not taken into account by the government officials involved in this plan. Kuni and Toklanni were herded onto the train and sent to Florida with the others.

Skinner was quite graphic in his descriptions of what happened to the members of this large group during their long journey from Arizona to Florida.

> Most of the captives had never ridden a train and were hesitant to get aboard. They were rudely assisted by the soldiers. *All windows had been closed and nailed shut* [italics mine]. The Atchison, Topeka, and Santa Fe special was composed of 12 cars, 10 coaches for the 383 Indians [there was no place to lie down and sleep] and two cars for the 84 soldiers and nine officers. . . . The route to Florida was slow and routed to permit crowds of people to see the feared Apaches during frequent stops. Never in American history had an Indian tribe been subjected to such conditions and receive ridicule [*sic*]. . . . For example, the Apaches were given buckets and cans which were supposed to serve as chamber pots. . . . The many babies had their built in disposals [cradleboards] which simply permitted the urine and excretion to be eliminated to the floor . . . the windows could not be raised to permit fresh air to enter. . . . The stench in every car was simply fearful.[18]

Angie Debo believed that "the tubercular infection that was to decimate them during their captivity began on this journey. If there was any source of contamination on the train, all were exposed." [19] Mildred Cleghorn recalled what her father, a child prisoner of war named Richard Imach by his captors, said about the food. "The people received a can of food with the lid open and were given a utensil. They didn't know what it [the food] was and so they wouldn't eat it." [20] Warm Springs Apache Sam Kenoi said, "The soldiers came with hardtack barrels and fed us," an action that took place the only time the prisoners were allowed off the train. During the rest of the journey, said Kenoi, "The soldiers kept making motions as if they were going to cut our throats every time they went through the train to give coffee. . . . On that train we slept the best we could sitting up. Little children were put in the rack where you put the packages." [21]

John Anthony Turcheneske, Jr., believed that sealing the windows shut "set the stage for ensuing illness and its ultimate consequences." His research and interviews revealed that aboard the train, "buckets which served as latrines were rarely, if ever, emptied . . . sanitary facilities for washing were nonexistent. Rations once opened were set aside only to be eaten again. Severe and sometimes fatal cases of food poisoning developed, for no one thought to tell the Apaches that food once taken from containers had to be consumed immediately or otherwise discarded. In what can be described only as the effluent of humanity," concluded Turcheneske, "women gave birth to babies, and children and old ones beyond redemption passed away." [22] And the train continued on.

Eugene Chihuahua greeted the large number of his relatives and friends when they arrived almost two weeks after leaving Fort Apache/San Carlos to travel to the train station at Holbrook, Arizona. "They were almost dead," he said, "they were almost naked, they were hungry, and they were pitifully dirty." [23] No wonder. It had always been the Chiricahua Apaches' practice to leave a campsite before the situation regarding disposal of human wastes became acute. Living as they did in temporary shelters known as wickiups, built of branches of brush, it was a simple matter to move on when sanitary conditions required migration.

Their loyal advocate and friend George Wratten was not with this group; he would appear at Fort Pickens as an interpreter with the

Naiche/Geronimo band later in their captivity, so this large number of prisoners of war had no one on whom they could rely for accurate information.

Compounding the terrible conditions of the journey was the fact that many of the uprooted Apaches had not had a chance to bathe or change their clothes before leaving the reservation. Skinner mentioned the presence of "vermin in untold quantities," as well as the "filthy" train cars. To make matters worse, a near-carnival atmosphere prevailed among onlookers in depots where the train stopped in its cross-country trip. Little did the prisoners know that strangers gawking at them would become commonplace in the future when, with the concurrence of the military, they would be exploited as tourist attractions in Florida and Alabama. In Jacksonville, Florida, for example, hundreds of residents gathered to gape at the Apaches as they detrained and walked to a ferry waiting to take them to St. Augustine. "A more dirty, disgusting, strong scented mass of humanity never alighted from a train in Jacksonville," wrote a reporter from the *Florida Times-Union*. "And the stench that came from the cars was worse than ever came from a nest of ten year polecats." [24] No mention was made of one of the root causes of the odor—windows that the government had ordered nailed shut.

Based on interviews with Raymond Loco, descendant of the famous Chiricahua Apache chief Loco, John Shapard wrote of a scene in Holbrook, Arizona, that reflects the chaos and confusion present when this biggest group of Chiricahuas left for Fort Marion. Left behind as the train slowly rolled along were "the tribe's livestock, dogs, and several piles of belongings that could not be fitted into the two baggage cars. The personal belongings were quickly picked over by souvenir hunters. The horses were rounded up by the soldiers and later sold at auction at Fort Union, New Mexico. The camp dogs, which had faithfully followed the tribe from Fort Apache, were distraught at being separated from their masters and ran pitifully, howling and yapping, beside the train. Some kept up for almost 20 miles."

Raymond Loco told Shapard on December 27, 1963, that when the train was just out of Holbrook, "the inside of the sealed passenger cars became blackened with smoke from the engines" which had filtered into the coaches and made breathing a choking effort. Motion sickness and nausea, caused by the smoke, the train's swaying motion, and the hot September sun streaming in the windows, brought on vomit which had to be spewed onto the floor. "The odor made still more prisoners sick," reported Loco, "and they added vomitus to the urine and feces" resulting from the sudden sickness. "Within a matter of hours," Shapard stated, "the floors of the cars carrying the Indians were covered with the smelly slime and were so slick that an adult could not stand without clutching the seats for support." Complaining was useless, as was taking matters into their own hands, for, reported Shapard, "apparently the Apaches had been told they would be shot if they opened the windows."

Lieutenant William Strover, one of the officers accompanying the train, corroborated these incredible circumstances in an interview dated July 24, 1924, with the *National Tribune* (Washington, D.C.). "Something had to be done to clean up the cars, but ordinary methods would have been inadequate, so when the train stopped for the morning feed, the superintendent had each car washed out with a hose and a powerful stream of water. Of course, it was not a pleasure to go into one of these cars after this cleaning, but it was the only way to make it possible for any human being, other than an Indian, to enter them at all." [25]

These Chiricahua Apaches arrived at Fort Marion on September 20, 1886, and seventy-six cases of sickness, sixty of which were the intermittent fevers of malaria, were treated in the next ten days; one woman died. Worse, within the coming three months, eighteen men, women, and children [26] would die, including some from the Chiricahua Apaches with Naiche's band, who arrived on October 25, and those with Mangus, who arrived on November 7.

As shocking as the eighteen fatalities in such a short time are, the · number may be too low. DeWitt Webb, the acting assistant surgeon and medical officer for the Chiricahua Apaches at Fort Marion, gave a speech before the Duchess County, New York, Medical Society in September 1887, one year after most of the Apaches arrived at St. Augustine. Looking back, Dr. Webb reported twenty-four deaths overall—one man, seven women, and sixteen children.

While he was in charge of the medical care of the prisoners Dr. Webb became overwhelmed by the dramatically increasing number of ailing and dying Apaches. Desperately needing help, Dr. Webb asked for a hospital steward to assist him, and his request was met. Each morning the entire camp was carefully looked over by both men. As Webb stated in his New York speech, "only by the most careful attention could we avoid the occurrence of a serious outbreak of disease." While close medical monitoring of the prisoners may have prevented contagion, one fact of life at Fort Marion certainly contributed to the proliferation of illnesses: local residents and tourists were encouraged to visit the Apache prisoners of war. There was a great deal of interest in St. Augustine about the prisoners, and before long they had become a popular attraction, adding even more people to the crowded conditions at the fort. But while most of the visitors had at least a partial immunity to infectious diseases the vulnerable Apaches had none. As tourist attractions, the Chiricahuas were quite popular; as fertile territory for furious infections, they were incomparable. Although it normally would be unusual for a government to permit outsiders to mingle freely with prisoners of war, this policy, as it pertained to the Chiricahuas, continued far into the future.

As another example of peculiar governmental actions, the prisoners were also permitted to leave the fort on guard-supervised excursions into town. Free to roam the city in groups of fifteen to twenty, these former terrors of the Southwest, removed from their traditional way of life by just a few months, became quasi celebrities. During these visits to the streets and shops of St. Augustine they were exposed even more to infectious diseases, and many brought the deadly germs back to the fort with them. Certainly the military was aware of the deaths and illnesses that were occurring among the prison population, but still they allowed the Apaches to intermingle with the city's citizens.

The first outbreak of malarial fever occurred at the fort two days after the arrival of the large group in September 1886. Dr. Webb thought the long train trip and dramatic change to a seacoast climate was responsible for bringing the illness "to the surface." His conclusions may have been correct, depending on the presence or absence of a conspiracy of circumstances. If the average period of malarial incubation varies from twelve days to ten months, and if the Apaches were on the move for thirteen days, they may have been infected while being transported from Arizona to Florida. Although the windows in each train car were nailed shut, it is certainly possible that mosquitoes entered the cars when the food was being distributed or when the prisoners were allowed out of the train to eat. The location of that stop was said to be near the high and dry town of Albuquerque, New Mexico, which normally has very little standing water favorable to breeding mosquitoes. Should a heavy rain fall, however, the hard caliche New Mexico soil has difficulty in absorbing all the water at once, and ponds, pools, and puddles can sit for days, becoming fertile territory for mosquitos.

In all, Dr. Webb treated twenty-eight cases of malarial fevers during the first flare-up at Fort Marion. Most of these were of the intermittent type, in which the patient's body temperature periodically rises and falls and often returns to normal at night. The capricious fevers were controlled by quinine in solution, three ten-grain doses per day, so that in less than a week the first outbreak had disappeared. However, malaria routinely recurs without warning, and 152 of the 473 Apaches in confinement at that time were treated for this ailment before the end of September 1886.[27]

During that month, Dr. Webb also treated sixteen cases of remittent fever, characterized by temperature fluctuations that do not return to normal. No deaths occurred from these recurrent fevers, nor were there any deaths that month from another ailment that disabled fifty-nine Apaches: acute diarrhea. However, there were seven cases of and four deaths from dysentery—three of them children. Although the doctor's suspicions about the cause of this illness were not reported, a contaminated water supply was probably to blame.[28] A well had been bored in the courtyard which produced an abundant supply of water, but the casemate utilized as a toilet was close by.

One adult male died in those early days of captivity from a "fatal swoon," according to Dr. Webb. He may have suffered some type of heat exhaustion, which would be a predictable reaction of desert dwellers to the steamy Florida weather; the available records do not add any details.

Alicia Delgadillo, former administrator of the Fort Sill Chiricahua/Warm Springs Apache Museum in Arizona's Cochise Stronghold, recalled a conversation she had years ago with an elder. "The old ones said that a long time ago their relatives told them that when they were so sick [in Florida], they were given some liquid medicine but told not to swallow it. They washed their mouths out with it, spit it out, and their mouths became filled with blisters after that."[29] No written record remains of this incident, and there is no way to determine what medicinal preparations were given to the Apaches in an effort to combat these and other ailments or to prevent other illnesses from gaining a hold.

During the autumn months of October and November 1886, a number of children still being nursed at their mothers' breasts became ill with bronchitis; six died. Dr. Webb believed the outbreak of the respiratory ailments was largely due to the poor condition of the mothers, who had "not yet become accustomed to the change in locality, and . . . for that reason, their milk was of poor quality."

The children who remained healthy behaved like any other children would, despite the unfamiliar circumstances. Dr. Webb spoke of the son of Chihuahua, perhaps Eugene, although the leader had other children with him as well during the first months of internment. While playing with the other children the Chihuahua boy was pushed off the top of the fort and fell to the bottom of the dry moat, striking his head on the stairs that led down into the broad ditch. Although he lay unattended in convulsions for nearly half an hour, he spontaneously recovered and had no symptoms thereafter.

Referring to the noncontagious diseases experienced by the Chiricahuas at Fort Marion, Dr. Webb reported two deaths due to "old age" among the women, adding, "Except Nana, there are no very old men in the tribe. The fortunes of war has [sic] prevented the men from attaining great age. The women, however, grow old and live on until they look like centenarians." Before incarceration, that is.

The physician listed twelve cases of neuralgia, possibly a result of the dampness, treated at the time by hypodermic injection of morphine and "the internal administration of quinine." A child of the scout Dutchy died from epilepsy, and the wife of Hosea (José?) was diagnosed as having "Hystero Epilepsy" after the death of her baby from bronchitis. Four cases of rheumatism were treated by Dr. Webb in the early months, as were the residual effects of old gunshot wounds received while the Chiricahuas were still free. Dr. Webb was impressed with the Apaches' healing ability: "Many of the Indians show remarkable recovery from gunshot wounds, even where the joints have been implicated." He referred to one injury in particular, saying the bullet had entered "above the patella, [passed] beneath it," and came out "below the head of the tibia, and yet the man has as good use of the joint as ever."

Two deaths occurred among newborns from a specific illness

Dr. Webb diagnosed as "Tetanus Neonatorum," explaining that it was a "disease unknown to them in Arizona, but as we all know, common enough here."[30]

Of all the ailments teeming unchecked among the Apache prisoners of war, tuberculosis was the most common . . . and the deadliest. Strangely, in his Duchess County speech Dr. Webb did not state the actual number of prisoners who died from this disease. He did say, "Of the deaths from tuberculosis, all but the child, a little girl, showed symptoms soon after their arrival and ran down very slowly. The case of the little girl was of very rapid development and of a short course until the end. The treatment of these cases was more difficult than that of almost any other, as finding little relief from medicine, they were averse to taking any, and the appetite failing, they could scarcely be induced to take food, and they ran down, making no sign for weeks, until they died."

Writing in the first decade of the twentieth century about tuberculosis among Indian people in general, doctor, scholar, and observer Alex Hrdlicka identified several of the external conditions that must be present in the environment if contagion is to occur.

> The healthy and the unhealthy spit freely . . . the sputum being usually covered with a pinch of sand or earth and thus remaining. Its removal is at best rare or incomplete. . . . Various articles, as bags, quilts, blankets, etc. used by different members of the family, and occasionally given away, are never washed or otherwise cleaned. . . . The tuberculous . . . eat with the same utensils. . . . They sleep with others until the symptoms of their disease become too annoying. Their soiled clothing is in no case washed separately. . . . They visit their neighbors freely. . . . All exposure to heat and cold which is liable to bring on abnormal conditions of the respiratory apparatus, actual disease of the air passages or the lungs, and frequent neglect of such conditions, strongly promote in the Indian the development of pulmonary tuberculosis.

Hrdlicka urged education to combat continuing infection. "The Indian must be taught how to live, how to prepare his food, how to take care of the young, of the old, and of the sick, and what precautions to use against the spread of consumption . . . introduction of a simple and practicable method for the disposal of the infected sputum . . . cheap and easily destructible articles as toilet paper . . . the exclusion of flies . . . the isolation of all cases . . . general cleanliness of houses and their contents, of clothing, and of the person . . . an improvement in nutrition." In confinement, the Apaches were not able to adequately protect themselves by following these basic guidelines, which had been known for quite some time by their captors. No one assisted the prisoners in understanding how to avoid contagion, and they did not have the liberty to learn for themselves. "Want and consequent debilitation," added Hrdlicka, are "certainly responsible for a percentage of the cases of pulmonary tuberculosis."[31]

Army officials, cognizant of the medical dangers inherent in the close, damp, and crowded environment of the fort and aware that Fort Pickens would provide a healthier environment, did nothing to change the circumstances, not even after more and more tubercular children became critically ill with secondary ailments such as marasmus,[32] a seriously debilitating illness experienced by at least six youthful patients, three of whom died. Said Dr. Webb, "One of them, still living, is remarkable for the length of time the little fellow has lived, a mere shadow. Certainly for four months past, his death might have been looked for any day, yet the little fellow has lived on, cared for most tenderly by both father and mother, who have devoted themselves to his care for many months."[33]

More than one hundred years later, a visitor may still cross the drawbridge over the now water-filled moat and enter and then emerge from a dark, cool, stone passage into the brilliant, sunny courtyard of Fort Marion. To a person standing in the center, directly ahead is the door of a chapel with casemates on either side—empty, dark, and damp rooms that were used for latrines, a jail, storage facilities, classrooms, and kitchens. These vaults also temporarily quartered Chihuahua's group until the Sibley tents arrived from army stores and were erected, enabling the first group of Chiricahua Apache prisoners of war to be moved from wet casemates to the unprotected and exposed area called the terreplein atop the fort overlooking the water. The only staircase inside the courtyard leads to this area. Here, there was no shelter from the elements, sheets of rain furiously pounded the brick and mortar floor, and the cold winds of winter blew unobstructed off the sea. And here, still today, the summer temperature and humidity cause a visitor from Apache country to dehydrate even quicker, it seems, as so much water comes into view over the parapet.

At Fort Marion there was room for no more than 150 *persons*, according to the military correspondence. It was here, however, that 130 Chiricahua *families* of 3 or more individuals, totaling 502 persons, were ordered to live in extremely crowded conditions in packed tents, to cook over open fires in spare corners of the ramparts regardless of the weather, and to sleep on the always moist brick and mortar floors. Here the children looked out over four-foot-wide parapets to see the water below them, thought at first by one young adult Apache male to be a "limitless field of waving grass. . . . Never before had we seen such a great body of water."[34]

Surely the unfamiliar and restraining physical conditions at the fort contributed greatly to the overall deteriorating health of the Apache prisoners, but one must not overlook the devastating psychological effect that incarceration had on a once proud and free people. That the Chiricahuas were superb specimens of healthy human beings had been commented on by Spanish, Mexican, and American observers over a period of centuries. But at Fort Marion, the Chiricahuas had no choice but to submit to governmental regulations designed to manage enemies of the state. All the Chiricahuas' strength, all their might, all their power and resistance were so assaulted and insulted by the concept[35] and processes of incarceration that their health, physically and psychologically, was literally stripped of defenses that had been generations in the making. Vulnerable on every level of their being and assailed by an unhealthy climate, it is no wonder that the Chiricahuas fell victim quickly to diseases. Military weapons were no longer needed. Through the diseases acquired during incarceration, the people were decimated in a way that armed conflict could never achieve. Many humane and caring American citizens were worried.

Aroused by public opinion favoring the Chiricahuas that grew out of continuing newspaper reports about the ongoing medical catastrophe at Fort Marion, the Indian Rights Association of Philadelphia sent its corresponding secretary, Herbert Welsh, to Fort Marion in March 1887, six months after the prisoners arrived. Welsh's first examination of the facility led him to conclude, "Fort Marion is entirely inadequate to contain with safety and convenience the 447 prisoners now within its walls. The ramparts are closely crowded with tents, so that but a narrow space is left for passage way. Most of the tents are crowded with occupants. . . . I noticed scraps of bread or meat lying about. . . . The rations [are] less than they obtained on the reservation, where they were able to procure a considerable supply from hunting, and vegetable and fruit food from the mescal, various roots and seeds, and the prickly pear. . . . The rations are insufficient." [36]

We do not know if Welsh was aware of the cultural food taboos and that, because of those prohibitions, the Apaches were not eating their full portions. The list of rations upon which Welsh based his statement includes no mention of fish or pork, nor are there any official comments recorded about the Chiricahua Apaches' cultural customs. According to one author, there was no doubt, though, about the intent of the American government vis-à-vis the Chiricahua Apache prisoners of war, even while Welsh was visiting. "They starved them," Skinner said tersely, "and didn't give them any clothes to wear." [37]

Winter in St. Augustine was nearly at an end during Welsh's inspection, and he noted that "the clothing of the Indians during the Winter has been totally insufficient and unsuitable. Most of them wore only the rags which they brought with them from Arizona. During cold days when . . . great coats were necessary, the Indian children were obliged to keep within the tents for protection. Many of them had nothing to cover them but a calico slip." [38] Six months after incarceration, the government still had not provided any clothing. The prisoners had to sleep on freezing bricks, and adequate clothing would have buffered their bones. And could they stay warm when it became necessary to leave their tents several times daily to use the latrine in the casemate below?

Welsh had strong comments in his report about the fort's sanitary conditions. He had made a careful inquiry while he was in St. Augustine, and the sergeant on duty showed him one of the caverns where, reported Welsh,

a copious stream of water was introduced by which drainage was secured directly to the sea. But even this precaution, and the free and constant use of carbolic acid as a disinfectant, is not sufficient to prevent an unhealthful condition of affairs if the present

Courtyard of Fort Marion today. Stairs at rear left lead to terreplein. Capped well, the only source of the prisoners' water, is in center background. Directly behind the well is the casemate used as a toilet; the proximity of the well and the casemate caused health problems among the prison population. (H. Henrietta Stockel)

large number of prisoners be continued in the fort during the approaching summer . . . filth cannot be prevented from being absorbed by the sandy soil and highly porous coquina stone of which the fort is composed. The danger of contagious disease attacking these Indians . . . is, in my judgment, a matter worthy of prompt and serious consideration.[39]

He did not mention the proximity of the latrine to the well that was the only source of drinking water at Fort Marion.

Welsh was also disturbed about the inactivity of the people, especially the men.

No effort is being made to give these male adult prisoners any training in handicrafts, farming or other industries. They are employed occasionally in the light and insufficient labor of keeping the fort clean, and in a few odd jobs from time to time. Beyond this, so far as physical work is concerned, their time is passed in idleness. . . . The result of this condition of things, if permitted to continue much longer, must be disastrous, whether considered from a physical or a moral standpoint. At present there is no hopeful outlook for these men; no means by which their abundant physical vitality is being trained and developed in the ways of civilization.

Welsh's report concluded with his own outrage about the Chiricahua scouts being imprisoned alongside those they had helped to capture or convinced to surrender. He considered the government's actions in this regard a violation of "a fundamental principle of just and wise policy in the treatment of Indians . . . for not only have the innocent been condemned unheard, but the meritorious have received the punishment of the guilty." In a footnote, Welsh reported that on March 28, thirteen days after he submitted his findings, an agent of his organization "saw the President. . . . He merely said in regard to the Apache Prisoners that there was not time to separate the guilty from the innocent ones before taking them down there. There was an urgency about it that did not admit of delay. He did not think there was such a crowded condition as to endanger health." [40]

Debo said Welsh's report "created a sensation." [41] A public outcry ensued and the government was forced to consider making changes. But as the wheels of bureaucracy slowly rolled, the Chiricahua Apaches continued to die, despite the traditional healing ceremonies conducted at Fort Marion for those who became ill. Something significant was missing from these rituals—the familiar healing herbs that were an essential component of a healing ceremony. The medicinal plants needed were nowhere to be found in Florida. But at least one ritual was held without the natural medicines after so many sickened and perished. Led by Ramon, the oldest shaman, the participants improvised and designed their own musical instruments, using what was available. Ramon's drum had been left behind in Arizona, and so he fashioned one from an iron kettle holding a little water, with a soaped rag drawn tightly over its mouth. No mention is made of the material used for the drumstick, which is usually a willow stick with a loop on one end, but it is clear that the *Gah'e*, the Chiricahua Apache Mountain Spirit dancers, had brought their sacred paint with them.

As Ramon thumped his drum, the dancers prepared their bodies with sacred colors. Each man was painted a basic green-brown, with yellow on each arm and an insignia in yellow on his back and breast. Each held two wands ornamented with representations of blue lightning. An ailing child was inside a tent in the northwestern sector of the terreplein, and so the dancers performed their age-old steps in that area of the terreplein first. They charged around, stabbed at the air with their wands, and stomped their feet on the bricks, all in an effort to drive the evil spirits away.

A woman appeared out of a tent, knelt before the dancers, and held her sick baby up toward them. The *Gah'e* swooshed their holy batons around, over, under, and upon the cradleboard that held the baby as the mother turned her child toward the four directions. Each of the dancers in turn took the child in his hands, pressed the baby to his breast, lifted the cradleboard to the sky, lowered it to the earth, and turned to the four directions, all the time "prancing, whistling, and snorting."[42] The child's mother and her friends simultaneously pierced the night with their shrieks, trills, and ululations.

There is no record of whether that child recovered, but if not, the baby probably would have been buried at North Beach.[43] However, Ruey Darrow said that her father, Sam Haozous, told her the dead were taken across the water in boats by the military and buried on Anastasia Island. "Now," said Darrow, "they've built condominiums on top of the burial ground."[44] Skinner reported yet another version. Speaking of the military processes that were implemented on the death of a prisoner, he said frankly, "They dumped them overboard in the river and later their bones washed up on shore."[45] Shapard's interviews revealed that "the Apaches who died . . . were buried in the sand dunes across the bay on the ocean side from the fort with no markers."[46]

More than likely, relatives and friends witnessed the burials from the terreplein, unless the corpses were transported in the darkness of night. While it is presumptuous to imagine exactly what the Apaches' reactions were to the military's burial methods, it is fair to conclude that—given their ancient cultural customs regarding water—shock, astonishment, and horror were among the responses.

When I questioned him about these and other circumstances of the Chiricahua Apache incarceration at Fort Marion, Luis Arana, the historian at the fort for the last thirty-five years, had a surprisingly concise answer. "The United States government is not the only government that has sinned," he said matter-of-factly,[47] and would add nothing else, not even a positive statement, to his succinct comment. But another aspect of the incarceration at Fort Marion demands attention. For despite all the hardships, sicknesses, and deaths, and despite a wailing, mournful song—a lament of sorrow and loneliness—sung each night to the stars and the seabirds by an Indian voice streaming out of one of the fort's watchtowers, a dozen Chiricahua Apache babies were born and survived incarceration at Fort Marion.

6

Incarceration
in Florida:
Fort Pickens

✳   ✳   ✳   ✳

A small band of about thirty-five Chiricahua Apaches congregated on the parade ground at Fort Bowie, Arizona, in early September 1886. Led by Chief Naiche, son of Cochise, and by the notorious shaman and warrior Geronimo, these bedraggled friends and relatives of the St. Augustine prisoners had just surrendered.

Having eluded capture for more than fifteen months, they had become a source of continuing frustration to a powerful United States government who couldn't control, contain, or arrest the fifteen warriors and their wives and children. To the ranchers, settlers, and pioneers in the southwestern regions where the Naiche band roamed, the Chiricahuas were hated, despised, and ruthless murderers, thieves, and wild savages. Their actions and reputation gave rise to many myths; some are based in truth, some in half-truths, and some clearly are outright fabrications. For instance, one frontier story concerns General George Crook. It is said that he thought the Chiricahuas were such skilled strategists and formidable enemies that he devised a unique method of evaluating their status. "It was said that often after a fight with a hostile band he [Crook] would have a surgeon who was along with the outfit perform an autopsy on some of the dead bucks to find out what they had been eating. If cooked food was found in their stomachs, he knew that the Indians had not been pressed hard. If acorns, berries, and such stuff as they could get hastily was found, he knew he had them coming his way."[1] But no matter what the government or military did, the Naiche band remained free.

It was the public's outrage that caused the festering circumstances to erupt. Fed up and furious at the authorities for their ineptitude in subduing the Chiricahuas, citizens in Arizona and New Mexico got together and demanded that something, anything, be done to rid their countryside of the hostiles. The political pressure thus created was felt all the way to the halls of Congress and into the White House. In time, the lumbering bureaucracy finally responded, but in a surprising manner.

Believing it was unable to seize the Chiricahua Apaches with military force, the army negotiated. The moment was propitious—one of those rare occurrences that changes the direction of history. At exactly that time the Chiricahuas were weary of running, hiding, and fighting. Also, the warriors were aware that some of their wives, children, and kinfolk were already incarcerated and they were eager to see them. As a motivating force among Chiricahuas, families have always been among the strongest determinants of actions. To those at the negotiations with General Nelson A. Miles, Chief Naiche in particular seemed concerned about his wife and daughter (to be named Dorothy by her captors), who had left San Carlos/Fort Apache for Florida with the large group six months earlier.

During the surrender conferences, Miles promised the men that if they capitulated they would be reunited with their loved ones in the East. The general also made the alternative quite clear: if the Chiricahuas continued to resist, they would be hunted down and exterminated to the last individual, no matter how long it took. "Surrender and you will be sent with your families to Florida, there to await the decision of the President as to your final disposition. Accept these terms or fight it out to the bitter end," is said to have been the general's message, delivered to the Chiricahuas in the field by Lieutenant Charles Gatewood, a man they knew and respected.[2]

"Miles promised Geronimo that the people would be returned to their homelands in two years," said Mildred Cleghorn, born in captivity and currently chairperson of the Fort Sill Chiricahua/Warm Springs Apache Tribe. "Geronimo knew that if they didn't go along with the military this time, the name Chiricahua Apache and all it meant would not survive into the future. Not all of the headmen agreed with the idea of giving up, but Geronimo was able to convince most of them that surrender was the right thing to do. Of course, the army's promise to allow the people to return in two years was never kept by the government, and the warriors were not permitted to be with their families until almost a year after they arrived in Florida."[3] But during the discussions, the conditions offered by Miles became acceptable, and, in Skeleton Canyon, southeast of Fort Bowie, the Naiche band of Chiricahua Apaches lay down their arms for the last time. It was September 5, 1886, but the Apache wars were still not over. One more group of ten Apaches, headed by Mangus, son of famous Mimbres Apache chief Mangas Coloradas, was still free.

At the time of the historical surrender of the Naiche group, Mexican authorities were in hot pursuit and were especially eager to get their hands on Geronimo. To avoid meeting up with those hunters and with civil authorities from Tucson, who were also catching up with the wanted Apaches, General Miles, Naiche, Geronimo, and military and civilian personnel hurriedly fled Skeleton Canyon and reached Fort Bowie the same night. Three days later the rest of the small band arrived at the fort under military guard. On September 8, a few hours after the last of the arrivals reported in, this group of Chiricahua Apache prisoners of war left Fort Bowie in wagons. In the background an army band once again played "Auld Lang Syne." To those present, the scene was reminiscent of the time nearly six months earlier when Chihuahua's people departed under the same circumstances. The Naiche band's first destination was the same as Chihuahua's—approximately ten miles away in the nearby town of Bowie Station, where they were loaded on a train headed for Florida.[4] No time was lost.

The wide, well-traveled route among cacti and other desert shrubs the wagons carrying the prisoners took from Fort Bowie toward Bowie Station has now narrowed to a winding path approximately a mile and a half long. From the parking lot toward Fort Bowie along the foot trail, a hiker walks in a direction opposite that taken by the wagons. Nonetheless, there are several landmarks remaining that were in existence when the Apaches passed by: the foundation of a Butterfield Overland Trail stage station; Siphon Canyon; the ruins of a Chiricahua Indian Agency administration building; a cemetery full of white grave markers designating those who had died mainly as a result of conflicts with the Apaches; the site of the Battle of Apache Pass; Apache Spring, once an ample source of water in the desert but now only a trickle; and the hillside ruins of the first Fort Bowie. Along the course, one can open the gate to the fort's old graveyard and step inside the enclosure, but no remains rest beneath the earth. All the bones have been moved, and there is only one wooden marker left. Inscribed "Little Robe," it is reputed to mark the final resting place of one of Geronimo's sons, a boy who died long ago from forgotten causes. A cholla cactus grows directly in front of the memorial, a gift from nature.

Whether Geronimo acknowledged his child's grave as the caravan rushed past the post cemetery is not known, but he and the others probably had the subject of death on their minds. With the final surrender now a reality and the uncertainty of what lay ahead, this band of Chiricahua Apaches, perhaps the most infamous in history, had no way of accurately predicting their fate at the hands of their enemy. All they had to count on were the promises made by the military during surrender negotiations—that they would be imprisoned with their women and children. Unknown to the prisoners, those assurances were shaky. Expecting nothing less than unconditional surrender, President Grover Cleveland became angry when he learned the details of the actual negotiation. He accused Miles of insubordination in making any commitments to the Chiricahuas and called his advisers together to develop an official plan that would supersede all previous actions.

Just three weeks before, in a series of telegrams anticipating the capitulation, the president, Acting Secretary of War R. C. Drum, and General Miles had debated the destiny of the Naiche group. President Cleveland stated he hoped "nothing will be done with Geronimo which will prevent our treating him as a prisoner of war, if we cannot hang him, which I would much prefer."[5] A decision was eventually reached in the highest councils of the government, and the chosen activities began to be implemented.

On September 6, 1886, orders were issued by Captain William A. Thompson, Fourth Cavalry, from the headquarters of the Department of Arizona in Willcox, instructing members of the Fourth Cavalry and Apache interpreter George Medhurst Wratten to "take charge of the surrendered Chiricahua Indian prisoners of war and proceed with them to Fort Marion, Fla."[6] This direction was supposedly the result of an earlier telegram to headquarters from Drum, dated September 4, 1886. However, there is "no record . . . of a telegram of September 4, 1886 or any other date from the Acting Secretary of War to General Miles, directing him to send Geronimo and band to Fort Marion, Fla. *No such order has been given*"[7] (italics mine), states a telegram dated September 18, 1886, from J. C. Kelton, acting adjutant general, to O. O. Howard, the commanding general of the Division of the Pacific. Regardless of any improprieties or illegalities, however, the actions necessary to incarcerate the Naiche group proceeded without interruption.

"When they put us on that train at Bowie," said Jasper Kanseah, who at the time was an orphaned thirteen-year-old horseholder for his uncle Geronimo, "nobody thought that we'd get far before they'd stop and kill us."[8] When the train halted for the first time, two days later, they were in San Antonio, Texas. This train, like those before it that carried Apache prisoners of war, became filthy with human waste. Raymond Loco recalled, "The old people say that the train . . . had no sanitary facilities and that the aisles of the train were slick with human waste and vomit. . . . In the picture of Geronimo and the train in San Antonio, the streaks on the side of the train were vomit."[9]

Brigadier General D. S. Stanley, commanding the Department of Texas at San Antonio, had been instructed by Drum to take charge of the prisoners and hold them until further orders were issued. Stanley reported on September 10 that the band was quartered at the fort in the quartermaster's depot under guard. While the Chiricahua Apaches waited in San Antonio, Miles's "suggestion to locate the Indians at a military post west of the Mississippi was rejected outright, and a vindictive attempt to place them in Fort Jefferson, a yellow fever hole in the Dry Tortugas of the Florida coast was rejected immediately. A better place was Fort Pickens, on Santa Rosa Island, in Pensacola Bay."[10]

They remained in San Antonio, not knowing their fate, until October 20, when Lieutenant General Philip Sheridan ordered the fifteen warriors and their interpreter, George Wratten, to be sent to Fort Pickens, near Pensacola, Florida. The eleven women, six children (including a baby several weeks old), and two enlisted scouts were to be separated from the warriors and sent to Fort Marion in St. Augustine.

The selection of Fort Pickens to confine the Apache men was made, according to some reports,[11] as a result of political lobbying by a group of influential citizens of Pensacola. In a letter to their congressman, P. H. M. Davidson, they listed the advantages of incarcerating the Apache prisoners of war at Fort Pickens: the Santa Rosa Island fort was a superior location from a sanitary point of view because it was on a remote island; it was twice as large as the St. Augustine facility; the Fort Barrancas troops would be able to guard the prisoners; and since the Pensacola forts were subordinate to the commander at Fort Marion, Colonel Loomis Langdon, the prisoners would be as much under his jurisdiction as if they were at Fort Marion in St. Augustine. The congressman agreed and contacted the War Department. Soon afterward, the move was under way.

On Friday, October 22, 1886, at four o'clock in the afternoon, a special train left San Antonio and was expected to arrive at Pensacola early Sunday morning. The railroad cars separated there, with the one containing the women and children scheduled to continue on to St. Augustine. Upon reaching Pensacola, the coach containing the fifteen warriors and thirty soldiers from the Sixteenth Infantry was switched off onto a side track. The Apache men left the train and were marched single file between double rows of soldiers toward a steamer that was to ferry them across Pensacola Bay to Fort Pickens. Along the short passageway a crowd of approximately two thousand sightseers had gathered, hoping to see an Apache from the notorious band they had read so much about. In the harbor, dozens of small boats waited to catch sight of the prisoners. People were intrigued, fascinated, clamoring to have a look at the nation's most famous Indians. It had been that way on every stop the train made: gawkers and sightseers filled railway stations and lined the tracks, hoping to catch a glimpse of Geronimo and his colleagues. What they saw at the last stop in Pensacola was a parade of husbands and fathers who had just experienced the first of many broken promises. Contrary to the assurances made, and to the expectations of the

Chiricahua Apaches near San Antonio(?), en route to Fort Marion, St. Augustine, Florida, September 1886. Geronimo is in the first row, third from right; Naiche is fourth from right, and Ha-o-zinne, his wife, is in the top row, fourth from right. Warrior woman Lozen is in the top row,

third from right. Jasper Kanseah, as a youth of 13, is in second row, far left. Note new boots worn by Geronimo and Naiche, probably from the sutler's store at Fort Bowie. (National Park Service)

Chiricahua warriors, they would not see their wives and children for another year, nor would they be incarcerated beside them. As time would also reveal, neither would they be released in two years.

There is no written record of the warriors' response to being taken under guard from the train while their women and children were diverted, but it is known that Naiche and Geronimo regarded "the separation of themselves from their families as a violation of the terms of their treaty of surrender."[12] So wrote Brigadier General Stanley from San Antonio on October 25 to Major General J. M. Schofield, commanding officer at Headquarters, Division of the Atlantic, in New York City. Although white interpreter George Wratten confirmed the warriors' version of the events and the promises made about their families by military officials in Skeleton Canyon, no action was taken to change the situation. Naiche, Geronimo, Perico, Fun, Ahnandia, Napi, Yahnoza, Tissnolthos, Beshe, Geronimo's son Chappo, La-zi-yah, Motsos, Kilthdigai, Zhonne, and Hunlona, along with their military guards and Wratten, arrived at their destination on October 25, 1886. Skinner said that Geronimo was chained into the boat at his own request because he was terrified of so much water.[13]

Five days earlier, on October 20, 1886, the final Apache holdouts had surrendered. Mangus, two warriors named Fit-a-Hat and Goso, three women (including Mangus's wife, Dilth-cley-ih, who was the daughter of famed Mimbres Apache chief Victorio), and five children were captured in Arizona along with twenty-nine mules and five ponies. On October 30 they left Holbrook, Arizona, on a train bound for Florida. The same fate awaited them: the three men were ordered sent to Fort Pickens, and the eight women and children continued on to Fort Marion. But Fit-a-Hat, who was elderly, died en route and his body was left at Fort Union, New Mexico. Mangus tried to escape by slipping out of his handcuffs and jumping through an open window as the train was passing at thirty-five miles an hour through Colorado. After he was caught, he said he had fled because he overheard the guards planning to attack the women. Feeling unable to protect them and the children, he preferred death and believed his effort to escape would be so punished. He was wrong. Mangus was bruised as a result of his fall from the window but not seriously injured, and the journey to Florida continued, with Mangus being very closely guarded after that. This last band of Chiricahua Apaches to be imprisoned arrived at Fort Pickens on November 6 and, following the same procedures as Naiche's group, crossed Pensacola Bay by boat.

Access to Fort Pickens today is overland. One way to reach the fort, which is located at the tip of a barrier island named Santa Rosa, is to cross a toll bridge that extends from the small town of Gulf Breeze to Pensacola Beach. The right fork in the road leads toward the fort, nine and a half miles away. High-rise motels line both sides of the two-lane road that separates Pensacola Bay on the right from the Gulf of Mexico. Preservation of sand dunes on the gulf side necessitates tall chain-link fences surrounding some of the mounds but doesn't preclude small pathways on the bright white sand to the blue-green water among other, less restricted dunes.

As one enters the Fort Pickens area, which comprises more than a dozen acres of land, tall sea oats wave from both sides of the road. Yellow pines become more numerous toward the western end of the island. Birds nest safely in their specially designated area, which is off-limits to human visitors. Although the sand dunes seem higher here, they vanish eventually, just before the fort looms into view.

The first sign of the buildings that constitute Fort Pickens, now part of Gulf Islands National Seashore, is an American flag waving in the breeze. The second sight is a huge gap in the wall enclosing the area. An accident on June 20, 1899, more than a decade after the Apaches left, blasted the hole when a fire ignited a magazine containing black powder. National Park Service rangers say that bricks from the explosion landed one and one-half miles away across the bay. With the exception of the missing area, known as Bastion D, the fort appears well preserved. It is constructed of massed earth and masonry (21.5 million bricks were laid by slave labor during the years 1829–34) and was intended to guard the island and the entrance to Pensacola Bay. Its size allowed large numbers of infantry, up to two thousand, to be quartered there. The army's job was to prevent an invading land force from occupying the island.[14] Like Fort Marion at St. Augustine, the sallyport-covered entrance opens into a courtyard lined with casemates. There is no terreplein here, however, upon which tents could be pitched, and so the Chiricahua warriors were initially housed in the caverns off the south courtyard. When they arrived, in late October, they were each issued one blanket, two pairs of trousers, two knit undershirts, two pairs of cotton socks, and one pair of field shoes. The clothing was not enough to protect the Chiricahuas against winter weather.

"You've got high humidity year round here except occasionally in October," David Ogden, interpretive specialist at Fort Pickens, told me. "In winter the weather is nasty, bitter cold. In January and February our temperatures range between forty and fifty degrees during the day and between the high twenties and low forties at night. Usually the humidity is between 70 and 80 percent, and there's a fairly steady twenty-mile-an-hour wind blowing across this island. There's not much protection. The casemates the Apaches stayed in didn't have windows or doors, and the wind just howled through that place. It was bone-chilling cold."

And in summer Fort Pickens is incredibly, breathtakingly hot. The sun blazes and the sand burns while whole armies of insects bite and snipe. The island was filled with rattlesnakes when Naiche, Geronimo, Mangus, and their followers were incarcerated there, but none are visible today. However, literature distributed at the fort urges respect for the small mammals and reptiles that inhabit the structure and advises visitors to seek shelter and avoid high places during thunderstorms.

While the weather and animal life were factors to be considered when the fort was actively occupied, the fort itself posed the major danger to health. "One thing the army always complained about was that the quarters were basically unhealthy since the casemates tend to stay damp," Ogden told me. "And if you sleep on the brick floor in the damp casemates, it's not terribly healthy." Ogden didn't have detailed knowledge about the physical conditions present at Fort Pickens when the warriors arrived in 1886, but "the quarters had not had any repair work since 1861 or so; there were no windows or doors to speak of, and there were rotten boards in [the rooms] that had wooden floors. For the first six months the warriors just lived in the casemates along the wall with open arches and the brick and sand floors. It's likely that they were sleeping on straw."

When asked about sanitation at Fort Pickens during the time the warriors were incarcerated, Ogden replied, "Basically, there were no sanitary facilities at the fort. Since these old brick structures were designed not to be occupied under most circumstances, many of them didn't even have quarters in them. When the fort was occupied during the Civil War, troops just camped out in the parade ground. There is no record of how they disposed of their waste. I suggest that there were chamber pots probably in some of the officers' quarters. This island is deserted enough that it's very likely that the men would have continued with whatever their habits had been prior to that."

Ogden was unaware that Chiricahua Apache customs called for leaving a campsite when it became unsanitary. Obviously, at Fort Pickens that couldn't have been done. "The disposal of human waste would not be the sort of thing that would normally find itself in military reports," he commented. "Up until the 1890s, in the Spanish-American War period, the sanitation practices of the army were somewhat lacking, at best. There were a lot of diseases caused in encampments from having dug latrines next to wells, for instance."

If someone became ill, "there would have been a medical officer attached to the army post. The main quarters were at Fort Barrancas, across the water," said Ogden.[15] The post surgeon visited Fort Pickens at least twice a week to monitor the health of the seventeen warriors (fifteen from the Naiche/Geronimo band, plus Mangus and Goso), which remained good with the exception of a few accidental injuries such as contusions or cuts and routine ailments such as temporary bowel disorders or reactions to the smallpox vaccinations the men had received. Langdon had four large tents in storage at Fort Barrancas. Plans were to quarantine any warriors who became ill by isolating them in the tents, thus removing them from the prisoner population. It never became necessary to ferry the tents across the bay to Fort Pickens, nor to transport ailing Apaches to Fort Barrancas. Many Apache relatives and friends at Fort Marion had become quite ill and were dying; what was it about the incarceration at Fort Pickens that kept sickness away?

"They fed them," declared Skinner[16] in a direct reference to the insufficient rations provided the prisoners at Fort Marion. Yes, but it took a complaint by Geronimo about the meager rations at Fort Pickens to increase the amount they could cook on their three mess pans and four frying pans, and drink in their eighteen tin cups. On orders from the high command, the new allowance of food was based on one hundred rations and comprised 75 pounds of pork, 125 pounds of fresh beef, 112.5 pounds of flour, 15 pounds of beans or 10 pounds of hominy, 10 pounds of coffee, 15 pounds of sugar,

Geronimo, Naiche, and Mangus at Fort Pickens, Florida, 1887. Note the stripe across the faces of Geronimo and Naiche. The casemates behind the prisoners are similar to those occupied by the Chiricahua Apache men. These open, cavernous rooms offered almost no protection from the weather and would have been more suitable as storage facilities than as living quarters. (Arizona Historical Society)

4 pounds of soap, 4 pounds of salt, and 0.5 pound of tobacco. It is not known whether they ate the pork.

The warriors had much more room at Fort Pickens than did their relatives and friends incarcerated in St. Augustine. They lived in two casemates that had fireplaces, but most of the cooking was done outdoors over wood that had been provided by the army. Supplementing this supply was wood collected along the beach by the prisoners. It is strange to think of the fearsome warrior Geronimo, under military guard, walking barefoot on the hot, white sand with his trouser legs rolled up, carrying driftwood in his arms. Throughout the years of incarceration, Geronimo did many things that would have been totally out of character had he and the Chiricahuas still been free in Arizona and New Mexico. For example, contrary to Apache customs, which rigidly defined the roles of men and women, the warriors had to perform physical labor at Fort Pickens. Under natural conditions it was the women who did most of the hard work while

The open casemate at Fort Pickens, where seventeen Chiricahua Apache warriors were incarcerated. The right wall contains a fireplace that should have been used for cooking, but the men preferred to prepare their meals outdoors over fires of driftwood. Sleeping accommodations were straw pallets on the brick floor. (H. Henrietta Stockel)

the men provided the food and protected their homes. But in captivity at Fort Pickens, circumstances were much different.

The years of abandonment had given free rein to varmints and vegetation at the fort, and the formerly mighty and brave Chiricahua Apache men were in the right place at the right time to rid the fort of its unwelcome brush, animals, and snakes. According to Langdon, who wrote about the prisoners of war on June 28, 1887, to the assistant adjutant general, Headquarters, Division of the Atlantic, "they scrape, paint and pile shot and shell; they clean the grounds of weeds and dirt that has accumulated in a quarter of a century; they root out from the chinks of the walls the plants and young trees that are constantly getting a foothold there, and they are also engaged in setting out Bermuda grass in the parade ground." While performing these duties, they also removed a large amount of debris—broken bricks, rotten planks, and stones—that had accumulated in the ditches and on the grounds around the fort. A prolonged drought had lowered water in the cisterns to a critical point, so when time permitted, the Apache men dug wells among the dunes near the fort to obtain water for cooking and washing.

Langdon also reported, "Their light and continually varied employments keep them in good health, not only by the exercise they thus secure, but by preventing their brooding over fancied wrongs or chafing under a confinement, which, even under mildest rule, must be radically different in its surroundings from the free life to which they have been accustomed from childhood." In the same letter he commented on the conduct of the prisoners, saying, "There has been no occasion to reprimand, much less to punish a single one of these Indians since their arrival here. Of course, no credit is due them for behaving well when it is clearly understood that an offender will be promptly put in irons. But they deserve commendation for their cheerfulness of demeanor, for their prompt alacrity in obeying orders and for the zeal and interest they show in the duties assigned to them." [17]

In response to the curiosity of Pensacolans, and as was being done at St. Augustine, Langdon began allowing tourists to visit the fort and mingle with the prisoners of war in early February 1887. Every applicant for a pass had to be cleared by the commander himself at Fort Barrancas before purchasing a fifty-cent adult's ticket or a twenty-five-cent child's ticket from a boat captain for the ride across the bay and back. Charitable visitors, mainly women, brought gifts of clothing and food to the warriors and left them small amounts of money. Word spread quickly about this newest tourist attraction in the Pensacola area, especially since 1887 was a time when excursions were fashionable and the railroads offered a wide variety of tours. Trips to Fort Pickens were so well advertised that 150 tourists arrived from New Orleans on Sunday, November 28, 1886. One day there were 459 visitors at the fort; there were never less than 20. On these occasions Geronimo became a star attraction while Naiche, the son of the great leader Cochise, preferred to observe the tourists from afar, providing they weren't ranking officers or high-placed politicians; for those honored guests he came out of the casemate.

Forever sly and crafty, Geronimo realized his own popularity and devoted his considerable natural talents to promoting himself. He sold souvenirs to the tourists—trinkets he had carved from driftwood, buttons from his clothing, even his mark on a piece of paper. Perhaps Geronimo's long-standing fear of being murdered in captivity abated when he assessed the Chiricahua Apaches' latest function as tourist attractions.[18] It didn't take any of the prisoners long to adjust to the role of quasi celebrities and gracious hosts to large parties of curious sightseers. The Chiricahuas knew how to survive amid even the most adverse conditions.

It is extraordinary that despite their exposure to thousands of excursionists, the damp and humid climate, the extremes of winter and summer weather on the island, and the severe disruption in their natural life-style, none of the seventeen warriors at Fort Pickens became ill with a life-threatening ailment. As more and more visitors to Fort Pickens came away impressed with the Chiricahuas' attitude and adaptation to incarceration, public opinion began to build in favor of the warriors. "Everybody in Pensacola was sympathetic with the prisoners," said Skinner in a conversation at the National Park Service Headquarters Visitors' Center in Gulf Breeze, Florida. Apparently the empathy extended even farther geographically, for, according to Skinner, "the *New York World* ran a story that said the group had been sentenced to a 'lingering death.' That brought everybody to Fort Pickens."[19] Public pressure reached a crescendo as more and more people became "very strongly divided in their opinions" about the Apaches at Fort Pickens. "I had heard that some people agreed that a possible solution to the . . . problem was to ship them off to the east, confine them in forts, and maybe they would all die off. It certainly could have been the sentiment from someone in Arizona, it could well have been the sentiment of the president at the time, and any number of folks," said Ogden.[20]

Once again the government was embarrassed by its policies toward the Chiricahua Apaches. Something had to be done, so a decision was made to permit the wives and children of the warriors to join the men at Fort Pickens. The rest of the prisoners of war at Fort Marion were to be "released" as well, but the plan was to send them on to incarceration at Mount Vernon, Alabama. News of the physical conditions and high number of deaths during confinement in St. Augustine had also reached the public, and demands for relief were being heard around the country and in Washington, D.C. By evacuating Fort Marion of its prisoners of war and secluding them in the mosquito-infested woods of Alabama, the military hoped to divert public attention from the ailing and dying Indians.

After the required bureaucratic procedures were followed, on April 27, 1887, twenty women and eleven children left St. Augustine in one railroad car that would take them to Fort Pickens. Eight other coaches held guards and the remaining prisoners of war, who were on the way to a new place of confinement at Mount Vernon, a town thirty miles north of Mobile, Alabama. Twenty-four of their children, relatives, and friends had died in less than one year of incarceration at Fort Marion.

The women whose husbands were confined at Fort Pickens were given the choice of either joining them or being transferred to Alabama. The wives of Motsos, Tissnolthos, and Chappo Geronimo did not go to Fort Pickens; one of Ahnandia's wives joined him but another stayed on the train. In a letter to Herbert Welsh of the Indian Rights Association dated June 23, 1887, Colonel Langdon, writing from his office at Fort Barrancas, asked Welsh's help in understanding why these women refused to join their husbands. He wrote about Motsos, whose wife took their three children to Alabama, "His case is particularly hard because he is remarkably attached to his family. There may have been some intriguing to effect this separation on the part of the chiefs, who only had to keep silence to prevent her coming here." Next, Langdon addressed Tissnolthos's situation: "The other squaws believe that at the time of the transfer to this place [Fort Pickens], this woman, being rather young, was sent away to the Indian School at Carlisle, Pa." Of Chappo he declared, "He is the most intelligent Indian in the lot. His wife did not come. She too is supposed to have gone to Carlisle." Ahnandia's wife

> is here. But the man has a boy four years old who was not sent here. As I understand the case, the boy's own mother when living on the Reservation in the West used to get drunk and when in that condition beat the child. The grandmother of the child has been taking care of it and at the time the separation of the prisoners at Fort Marion was made and preparations were in progress for

transferring the squaws and the children that belonged at Fort Pickens to that fort, this old grandmother, when questioned about the child, said it belonged to "no one." She and the child have gone to Mount Vernon Barracks.

Langdon urged Welsh to use his influence to bring the wives and children mentioned to Fort Pickens and concluded his remarks by stating, "You will be glad to know that not one Indian, squaw, or child has died since these people have been under my charge at Fort Pickens."[21] It is not certain what results his request achieved.

Naiche and Geronimo each had three wives come to Fort Pickens, and Mangus and Perico each had two wives join them. Geronimo's wife Ga-aa, also known as She-gha, arrived at Fort Pickens suffering from Bright's disease.[22] On June 28, 1887, Langdon's routine report described a woman, possibly Ga-aa, who was sick with a cold in the chest. She was not considered seriously ill. Records do not reveal whether Ga-aa deteriorated during the hot, wet months of the summer, but she died on September 28, 1887, the only Chiricahua Apache to do so at Fort Pickens. Ga-aa was buried in the Fort Barrancas military cemetery after being transported across the bay, accompanied by Geronimo and the soldier guards.

The families occupied casemates that were formerly officers' quarters at Fort Pickens, while the men who lived alone remained where they had been assigned initially. Visitors were now limited, and without the presence of sightseers the entire situation became more normal insofar as family life was concerned. Women assumed their wifely and motherly duties while the men continued their chores under supervision of the military. Because of the heat during most months of the year, the hours of labor expected of the warriors each day were abbreviated. They worked from eight in the morning until eleven, and then on some days from one to three in the afternoon or from four to six, depending on the sea breezes.

In his August 9, 1887, report, compiled before the death of Ga-aa, Langdon addressed the health of the forty-eight prisoners at Fort Pickens, confirming that several cases of sickness had occurred.

Among these cases was that of one woman who was ill a long time from very large eruptions following vaccination, and there was another woman who was dangerously ill from erysipelas.[23] It

Rare profile photo of Geronimo, taken at the St. Louis World's Fair in 1904. Still a prisoner of war, he was by this time a national celebrity and sold his photograph, autograph, and handmade bows and arrows from a very popular private booth at the Louisiana Purchase Exposition. When business slowed, he entertained customers by singing and dancing. (Frisco Native American Museum)

seems remarkable that there has not been a single death among these Indians since the first of them landed at Fort Pickens over eight months ago. Some mortality was to be expected, considering the changed conditions of food, climate, personal liberty, and the prospects of the future under which they are now living. In particular, the climate is one of the things entirely different from that to which they are accustomed. The nights are warm and exhausting. . . . Yet these Indians seem, somehow, to thrive. What a second year will do for them remains to be seen, but at present they are remarkably healthy.[24]

Langdon's reference to a second year at Fort Pickens for the warriors and their families was prescient. They remained at the fort until May 13, 1888, when they were moved to Mount Vernon. Before they left, at least one birth occurred—a child was born to Perico and one of his wives. Skinner believed this was the only child born at Fort Pickens, but Eve Ball's sources state that one of Naiche's wives birthed a male child shortly before everyone was moved to Mount Vernon. The baby was weak and couldn't make the trip, according to the post surgeon, and so was placed in the care of a nurse named Wells. She called the baby George, after George Wratten, and became so attached to the child that she fled with him from Florida to Pennsylvania, where she reared and educated the boy with loving care. When he was grown, Nurse Wells confided in him and he learned his identity. He took his wife's last name, and they called their first child Mark de Marinella. When Mark grew up, he too was told the family background, and he began a search for his relatives. He found the descendants of Chief Naiche living on the Mescalero Reservation in New Mexico and drove to the Southwest to meet them. Ball wrote, "After some further doubt and delay, he was accepted by the Naiches as the grandson of their father."[25]

Five of the warriors' older children remained at Fort Pickens after all the other Apaches had gone. The boys, who had by then received first names, were Ira Goso, Calvin Zhonne, Chappo Geronimo, Eli Hunlona, and his brother, Bruce Patterson. They were waiting to be taken to the Carlisle School in Pennsylvania to join other Chiricahua Apache children who had been forcibly removed from their families in Fort Marion and sent away to receive an education. On

June 22, 1887, the boys left Fort Pickens to journey to Mount Vernon for one last goodbye before they continued on to Pennsylvania. Of the five, only Calvin Zhonne survived the dreaded tuberculosis that killed about half of the one hundred or more Chiricahua Apache children far from home at the Carlisle School.

7

The

Children

✳   ✳   ✳

More than 160 Apache children of all ages were prisoners
of war at Fort Marion, and Fort Pickens held 5. What
was to be done with these youngsters? They were, after
all, the innocents in the deadly drama that had occurred
between their parents and the military. To its credit, the
government's conscience was tweaked about these youngsters, and the pinch appeared in correspondence dated
May 12, 1886, when Chihuahua's followers were still settling in at Fort Marion. The secretary of the Board of
Indian Commissioners, E. Whittlesey, wrote to Secretary
of the Interior L. Q. C. Lamar concerning educating the
seventeen boys and eight girls under the age of fourteen,
and two somewhat older children, who could also be considered potential students. There was no national policy
regarding education at the time; specific criteria for determining who was eligible to partake in learning varied
according to the educator or government administrator
consulted. Whittlesey suggested that twelve to fifteen of
the Chiricahua youths be sent to the Principal Hampton Normal School in Hampton, Virginia, an educational
institution for "Negro" students. One prominent instructor, Captain R. H. Pratt, the superintendent of the United
States Indian Industrial School in Carlisle, Pennsylva-

nia, heard or read about the Apache children and on May 29, 1886, contacted Adjutant General R. C. Drum. Carlisle was already populated with Indian students from many tribes, and Pratt claimed the varied Native American census in his school had given him much experience in managing the education of Indian children. He was proud of his abilities, and prouder still of his dealings with governmental entities. Time passed, and no answer to his letter came from Drum. He wrote again, this time to Commissioner of Indian Affairs J. D. C. Atkins. Stating he believed that it would be difficult to convince the Apache parents to release their children to him, Pratt suggested that he be allowed to take one of his Chiricahua students to St. Augustine. Four Apache boys had been at Carlisle for about three years, having been sent to the school from the Arizona reservation. Pratt reasoned that perhaps the parents of the potential Apache students would be easily swayed to surrender their children to him for instruction if a Chiricahua student convinced them of the benefits of education at Carlisle. In his letter to Atkins, Pratt also softened an earlier approach by recommending that the parents not be forced to surrender their children. In the letter to Drum, he wasn't so sensitive and must have believed that a harsh point of view was the cause for his being ignored.

A. B. Upshaw, the acting commissioner of the Office of Indian Affairs, followed through by writing to military authorities in St. Augustine on July 22, 1886, asking for certain pertinent information about the children: how many were between the ages of five and twenty-one, how many were between six and eighteen years old, the condition of the fort, the cost of repairs, what the salary for a teacher in St. Augustine would cost, and the officials' views as to the best means of providing for the education of the Apache children.

By the time the inquiry arrived, a school was already operating at Fort Marion. Religious sisters from the Congregation of the Sisters of St. Joseph spent one and one-half hours each morning with the children, taking them off the parapet down into the courtyard and casemates where simple lessons could be taught without distractions. Still, on October 13, Lamar wrote to Pratt asking how many children the Carlisle School could accommodate and properly train. The same correspondence was sent to General S. C. Armstrong, the superintendent of the Normal and Agricultural Institute in Hampton, Virginia; to Mr. P. H. Bridenbaugh of the Juniata Collegiate Institute and Indian Training School in Martinsburg, Pennsylvania; and to John Bellangee Cox, the solicitor of the Lincoln Institute's Indian Department in Philadelphia, Pennsylvania.

By that time most of the women and children had arrived at Fort Marion from Arizona. In just a short time, Naiche's dependents would join them, and in two weeks or so after that, the few women and children who surrendered with Mangus would appear.

When all the correspondence sent by the administrators was in, Lamar notified Secretary of War W. C. Endicott that in order to relieve the crowded condition of the fort, it had been ascertained that Pratt could accommodate about 125 more pupils at Carlisle than were attending at that time. Lamar, however, misquoted Pratt, who had stated that the system of training and education at Carlisle was not suitable for pupils under twelve years of age and recommended that only children between the ages of twelve and twenty-two be sent there. No mention was made in the correspondence about a serious situation—the growing number of Chiricahua children who were becoming ill at Fort Marion. The only number mentioned in the exchange of letters was of seventy-five children who could be swiftly removed from their parents and sent to Carlisle.

All during October 1886, telegrams and letters were exchanged among the many parties involved in making arrangements to educate the children. In the third week of the month, Endicott reported to Lamar that there were twenty-four boys and fifteen girls between the ages of twelve and twenty-two in good physical condition and forty boys and sixteen girls below the age of twelve years physically and mentally suited for instruction at Carlisle.

On October 23, 1886, ninety-five children were identified to be removed from their families at Fort Marion, and the five boys from Fort Pickens brought the total to one hundred. Not all the youngsters were taken at once. Four were unable to travel for unknown reasons. Additionally, one child was kept in hiding by his mother. "My father [Sam Haozous] told us his mother put him in a rain barrel so he wouldn't have to leave," said Ruey Darrow.[1] Nonetheless, after the boy was discovered, he was quickly separated from his mother.

Not all of the children left the fort. Some of the youngest remained with their parents and continued to be taught by the sisters of the Convent of St. Joseph, but it became necessary for the government to enter into a contract for these services. R. B. Ayres, a brevet major general, commanded the nearby St. Francis Barracks where the army men who supervised the Apaches were quartered. On November 17, 1886, he reported to the adjutant general of the army at Headquarters, Division of the Atlantic, that now that most of the children were in Pennsylvania, "the convent has plenty of room in which to teach the Indian children, and it is conveniently near Fort Marion so that the children could go daily to and fro. It has been ascertained that the convent cannot take the Indian children to board."

When all the civilian and military permissions had been obtained, contract negotiations with the sisters began. The mother superior requested payments of $20 to $40 per month per child, depending on the grade, to teach the twenty-six girls and forty-two boys. Commissioner of Indian Affairs Atkins offered $7.50, and the exercise of give and take was under way. C. B. Agnew, of the newly formed St. Augustine Indian Aid Society, jumped into the negotiations and offered a counterproposal that would cost less, approximately "$1,000 to erect a building and $1,000 to maintain it." He suggested that teachers could volunteer their services, thus saving considerable cost. Agnew concluded his proposal by stating, "I hope that no contract may be made with the sisters when an organization so well prepared and numbering already a large membership of all denominations is prepared to cooperate with you." After more meetings and talks, on January 21, 1887, Agnew's offer was rejected by Lamar in a letter to Endicott, citing a contract that had already been entered into between the Indian Bureau and the Bureau of Catholic Missions. The sisters would receive $7.50 per pupil, but the total sum for one year of teaching all the Apache children remaining at Fort Marion would not exceed $900.[2]

Until the nuns could ready a facility for the students, "the old folks said one of the casemates was used as a classroom," Mildred Cleghorn told me.[3] Initially the children began learning in the dark and dank cavity under the direction of a young French nun, Mother Alypius, and Sister Jane Francis. Instructions in reading, writing, drawing, and singing were conducted daily from nine o'clock in the morning until noon. Somehow, the sisters had procured hats, shoes, books, tablets, and pencils for the pupils to use. The proceedings were watched over by the Apache men, who became so interested in the lessons that they too were soon drawing with crayons and singing religious and patriotic songs. "The Apache men and women grew quite fond of Mother Alypius," said Sister Mary Albert, community archivist at the Congregation of the Sisters of St. Joseph. "When another nun temporarily took her place, the adults were very reserved toward the new educator."

In conversation, Sister Mary Albert became quite enthusiastic regarding the circumstances of the children's education. "Although the government expected the children to learn only numbers and letters from the nuns and paid them only to teach children," she said, "there was much more. The adult Apaches also became part of the lessons taught at the fort, were very eager to learn, and were quite impressed with Mother Alypius. Because of the tribal concept of respect for authority figures, the Chiricahua Apaches accepted the teachers," she said. "They knew the nuns were instructing their children at the request of the United States government. Contacts between the nuns and the Apaches were wholesome. There was good humor and a good climate of relations," added Sister.

When they were allowed to walk to the convent under the supervision of the younger nuns, the children skipped and fussed and behaved like any other group of boys and girls. At the convent, they used a bathhouse on the premises to change their clothes and then played in the ocean, carefully watched over by the nuns. Later, when the youngsters were taken into the church for their lessons, said Sister Mary Albert, "like electricity, they jumped from bench to bench, so educating these children was not just a matter of teaching the ABCs. Their mental health was also important." The nuns also instructed the children in how to behave in the larger society. They believed they were making progress. "The mingling of these children with people from another culture broke down resistance. Because they were cooped up at the fort, walking to the convent also gave them some sense of freedom, as did the interaction between the younger nuns and the Apache children."[4]

Before he was sent to Carlisle with the other children, James Kaywaykla was one of these youngsters. In later years, referring to the sisters, he said, "I will never forget the kindness of those good women, nor the respect in which we held them. For the first time in my life I saw the interior of a church and . . . realized more fully that not all White Eyes were cruel and ruthless, but that there were some among them who were gentle and kind." Reminiscing about a friend who attended the school in those early days of incarceration, Kaywaykla added, "The girl passed away, people said, from heartbreak and loneliness. . . . I had not known it could happen to the young. Men took her body away in a box—a terrible thing to us. Whether she was buried, we had no way of knowing. That to us was much worse than death caused by violence."[5] Sadly, many of the young children's older brothers and sisters attending the Carlisle School in Pennsylvania would see dozens of deaths among their relatives and friends.

The school was located approximately nineteen miles southwest of Harrisburg, the state's capital. In the early history of the thirteen colonies, the site was a frontier military post. During the Revolutionary War a number of Hessian prisoners were brought to Carlisle and incarcerated there under military surveillance. In July 1863, when the Confederate Army invaded northern territory, Carlisle was shelled in the Battle of Gettysburg, and its buildings burned. They were rebuilt in 1865, but the post was abandoned in the early 1870s. In 1879 it was donated to the Interior Department for the purpose of beginning an educational establishment for Indians, and the first group, eighty-two Sioux, arrived on October 6, 1879. Forty-seven Kiowas, Cheyennes, and Pawnees appeared the following month, but it wasn't until 1886 that Pratt became interested in the Chiricahua Apache children.

Captain Pratt's appeal to the authorities on behalf of his school as *the* facility to be selected to educate the Chiricahua children was hard to deny. The school consisted of nearly fifty separate buildings on 26 acres, with 311 acres of adjacent farmland. The main facilities were academic classrooms, an auditorium, a library, a gymnasium, separate boys' and girls' trade shops, dormitories, an athletic field, an art studio, a hospital, a printing plant, cottages for faculty, and various support buildings such as the powerhouse.

In addition to academic courses such as language, geography, general lessons, arithmetic, morals and manners, reading, writing, and spelling, Carlisle's agricultural component for boys consisted of dairying, farming, hog raising, horticulture, greenhouse work, and poultry culture. The boys could also study baking, blacksmithing, bricklaying and plastering, carpentry and cabinetmaking, carriage trimming and upholstering, harnessmaking, mechanical drawing, painting, photography, plumbing and steamfitting, printing, shoemaking, stationary engineering, tailoring, tinsmithing, and wheelwrighting. Girls could study "household arts," described as cooking, housekeeping, laundering, nursing, and sewing. Music, native Indian arts such as weaving, beadwork, copper and silversmithing, along with physical culture and telegraphy were also essential segments of a pupil's education. But most important, the Carlisle School offered an especially significant and innovative opportunity to its Native American students through what was called an "outing system."

Designed for both boys and girls, the outing system enabled the students to spend at least one year in a country home, supervised by its owners, many of whom were Pennsylvania Dutch families. During this time the pupils also remained under the jurisdiction of the school and were paid periodic visits by the outing agent, who wrote a report concerning the students' health, condition, and progress. The farm homes became a vocational training ground for the children, who were often "considered as members of the family and are as carefully trained as are the sons and daughters of a family," declared the Carlisle Indian School Catalog with apparent pride.[6] Female students worked as domestics in the homes while the boys labored as farmhands in the fields. Each participant was paid one dollar to fifteen dollars per month in proportion to the kind of work they did and the ability and skill shown in doing it. Earnings were deposited in individual bank accounts, which were accessible to the students for necessities. As an added benefit, many families became quite fond of the students and kept in touch with them long after they returned to their natural parents. To show their respect and gratitude, a few Apache children took the first or last names of the local families as their own.

The outing system at Carlisle was Pratt's own plan "to promote the assimilationist goals of the federal government by placing Indian children in intimate contact with 'civilized' American society."[7] But, claimed Robert A. Trennert, "academic learning clearly played a subordinate role," especially with regard to the girls, who "spent no more than half a day in the classroom and devoted the rest of their time to domestic work." At Carlisle, wrote Trennert about the girls, "the first arrivals were instructed in the manufacture and

Chiricahua Apache children upon arrival at the Carlisle Indian School at Carlisle, Pennsylvania, from Fort Marion, November 4, 1886. Front row from left: Clement Seanilzay, Beatrice Kiahtel, Janette Pahgostatum, Margaret Y. Nadasthilah, Frederick Eskelsejah. Back row from left: Humphrey Escharzay, Samson Noran, Hugh Chee, Basil Ekarden, Bishop Eahtennah, Ernest Hogee. (Smithsonian Institution, National Anthropological Archives)

mending of garments, the use of the sewing machine, laundry work, cooking, and the routine of household duties pertaining to their sex." Consequently, when their education was completed, the young women "could find work, but only in the artificial environment of Indian agencies and schools . . . protected by a paternalistic government. Here they continued to perform tasks of domestic nature without promise of advancement. Nor were they assimilated into the dominant society as had been the original intent of their education . . . women were trained for an imaginary situation that administrators of Indian education believed must exist under the American system. . . . Few rewarding jobs were available in white society, and status was an impossibility."[8]

*Chiricahua Apache children after four months at the Carlisle Indian
School. Seated, from left: Ernest Hogee, Humphrey Escharzay, Beatrice
Kiahtel, Janette Pahgostatum, Bishop Eahtennah, Basil Ekarden. Standing, from left: Samson Noran, Margaret Y. Nadasthilah, Frederick Eskelsejah, Clement Seanilzay, Hugh Chee. (Smithsonian Institution, National Anthropological Archives)*

Although Pratt developed and implemented the educational outing concept, the practice of placing Indian children dates back to
colonial America, when ministers in New England and Virginia
took Indian children into their homes to educate them. No one,
however, formalized the educational aspect of the practice until
Pratt conducted the first outings in 1878 at the all-black Hampton
Institute in Virginia where he was teaching. A year later he had
convinced the secretary of the interior, Carl Schurz, that opening an
Indian school at Carlisle Barracks in Pennsylvania was appropriate.
"The school at Carlisle," he has been quoted as saying, would instill
"treason to the tribe and loyalty to the nation at large."[9]

Pratt's techniques were so successful and received so much congressional support that between 1880 and 1886 schools patterned

after this concept were opened at sites from Oregon to Indian Territory. Not all the outing programs survived, however, possibly due to politics, local customs, external influences, and unavoidable abuses. In the West, for example, where the cheap labor that Indian students could provide was more important than offering students the benefits of education, acculturation, and exposure to the dominant society's ways, the concept failed.

Back in the autumn of 1886, however, the future looked bright, and Pratt was eager to get his Apache program under way. Kaywaykla recalled that "officers and their wives went through the camp [Fort Marion] and selected over a hundred children to go to Pennsylvania to school. Part of them went by train, part by sea. I was with the latter and I was the youngest child to go . . . except for the terror of another separation from our people, and the uncertainty of what was to be done with us, we were well treated. Being out of sight of land frightened us, but not more than the bewildering experience of crossing New York City." [10]

Along with outing and educational experiences, other adventures lay just ahead for the Chiricahua Apache children. After they had their hair cut, they were forced to wear trousers and dresses and were lined up and given names, arbitrarily selected and alphabetically determined. Legends say the children were placed in rows of twenty-six, according to height. The tallest then received a name that started with A, the shortest with Z. Pratt separated boys and girls and alternated large and small students in chairs at tables for eight. The first lessons in English actually began at mealtimes with the youngsters learning how to pronounce the names of utensils and foods. That wasn't too bad, according to Asa Daklugie, but he thoroughly disliked having to do "women's work" such as making his bed and hanging up his clothes. Also, while taking their meals, the older and larger children were expected to assist the smaller ones beside them. As luck would have it, tiny James Kaywaykla, the youngest Apache at Carlisle, sat next to Daklugie. That the small boy was scared and lonely is best told through an anecdote recorded by Eve Ball. Daklugie told her that one Sunday morning at breakfast he was passing hotcakes from left to right. Kaywaykla, who was sitting on his right, was the last served, but there was plenty for him. However, when the maple syrup reached him, the jar was empty. James turned the pitcher upside down and only a few drops ran out.

Then the boy began to cry, a most unusual reaction in an Apache of any age. "It was the first time that I'd seen one of the Apache children [cry]," Daklugie said. "I felt sorry for him. . . . It was against the rule, but I got more of that maple syrup." But then something else happened. Said Daklugie, "The boy who brought it asked if I knew that Kanseah was in the hospital . . . that was terrible news, for nearly every Apache taken there had died." [11]

Jasper Kanseah, Geronimo's orphaned nephew, had arrived at Carlisle a few months after Daklugie. It is not clear exactly when Jasper became ill, or what the disease was, but based on Daklugie's description it probably was tuberculosis. "I am not going to die," Kanseah told Daklugie. "I don't take that medicine. I pretend to swallow it but I don't. I hide it and I will live." [12] Kanseah kept his word. After recovering from the episode and spending some time learning the ABCs, he was sent to live with a farm family as his outing experience. They introduced him to milking. Young Jasper was horrified, especially when everyone drank the cow's milk that he and other Chiricahua Apaches believed was taboo.

Pratt had also picked some "older" Chiricahua "children" to attend his school: twelve married men and one bachelor, Jason Betzinez, were among his choices. Betzinez, twenty-seven, had never been to school. In April 1887 his group of sixty-two future students traveled by train from Fort Marion to the seaport town of Fernandia, and from there to Charleston, South Carolina. They sailed to New York and then traveled by horse-drawn cabs to the tip of Manhattan, where a ferry took them across the Hudson River to Jersey City. The last segment of the trip was by train from New Jersey through Philadelphia to Carlisle, Pennsylvania. Jason was determined to be a good student in every way, and he succeeded. He studied in the mornings and worked in the school's blacksmith shop in the afternoons. Not too long after Betzinez arrived, he was sent to a farm owned by Edward Cooper in Bucks County, Pennsylvania, to begin his outing service. His exposure to farming lasted only about three months. He had to return to Carlisle because of an accident that caused his right thumb and a portion of his index finger to be removed. Jason returned to the farm in 1889 and once again combined outing activities with classwork. He remained at Carlisle nearly nine years, but in his middle thirties and in the eighth grade, he gave up his formal education [13] and entered the workaday world. Throughout his schooling at Carlisle Jason avoided becoming seriously ill, but he contracted tuberculosis one year after he left while working in a Pennsylvania steel mill. The ailment was not fatal. Jason lived to be one hundred years old and died from injuries received in an automobile accident.

Good health was not to be the destiny of very many Chiricahua students at Carlisle, however. The tuberculosis bacilli were everywhere. Unlike many students from other tribes, Apache youngsters had never acquired total or even partial immunity through prior exposure. Coupled with their physical susceptibility was the emotional trauma and confusion the children suffered, a combination of conditions that caused them to be especially vulnerable to the contagious and deadly diseases dwelling at Carlisle.

Alex Hrdlicka noted the general situation in a report about tuberculosis and Indian pupils at boarding schools: "In the nonreservation schools, a factor of importance is the depressing effect on the newly arrived child, of a radically different environment." He also described the impact of a strange language, the unfamiliar situations, homesickness, the lack of sufficiently diversified exercise, and unusual food. All of these negative aspects of change were first experienced by the Chiricahua Apache children at Fort Marion. But the risk factors increased dramatically when the children were forcibly removed from their parents and families, put on boats, then transported overland to Pennsylvania, and put into yet another terrifying situation.

In his report, Hrdlicka called for "special precaution in the large schools," which, in his opinion, should consist of (1) applying the tuberculin test to all incoming students and rejecting those whose tests were positive; (2) gradually introducing the newcomers to the changed physical conditions required in getting an education; (3) providing ample opportunity for outdoor sports, including swimming in nonpolluted pools and hiking in the countryside; (4) eating nourishing food and routinely disinfecting utensils; (5) exterminating flies; (6) limiting contact with consumptives; and (7) isolating seriously ill students.

Hrdlicka also suggested educating Native Americans on how to live healthfully, how to prepare food in a sanitary way, what simple precautions to take against tuberculosis, dispelling all the myths about the illness, and how to adequately dispose of infected sputum. He urged destruction of infected blankets and other goods by fire and the careful exclusion of flies, particularly around food.[14]

The officials at the Carlisle School were no doubt very aware of these and other necessary safeguards against contamination, as well as the possibility of a high death rate among the students, especially the susceptible new arrivals. Yet, Pratt continued to recruit prospective students from among the Chiricahua prisoners, disregarding the medical danger. Because none of the families at Fort Marion volunteered to surrender their children during Pratt's second attempt at enrollment, according to Skinner, "Pratt called them out for inspection, lined them up, and went about selecting."[15] Mildred Cleghorn's father, Richard Imach, was tall and so was selected without much ado. Another fellow, standing right beside Richard in the lineup, worked his toes and feet back and forth into the soft sand so that he was two inches shorter than his usual height. This youngster was excused.

When the first group of children arrived at Carlisle on November 4, 1886, tuberculosis was already present, and infection was immediate. Within one year more than fifteen died, and within another year the total rose to at least twenty-seven. Pratt was so alarmed that he wrote to the commissioner of Indian affairs on May 24, 1889:

Of the 106 prisoner Apaches brought to this school from Mt. Vernon Barracks in the winter and spring of 1886–87, twenty-seven have died and two others will die within two or three days. Others are drooping and will take their places soon. The school ought not to bear this affliction any longer. Quite a considerable proportion of those who remain are drifting downward. We should either be relieved at once of the care of the whole party or they should be thoroughly sifted, and those in precarious health sent to their people.

The cause of death, so far, has been, without exception, inherited consumption from venereal taint. While climate may to some extent have an influence in aggravating and bringing a speedier termination, I think the deplorable and almost hopeless conditions surrounding them have a greater influence. They have no home, no country, no future, and life has become hardly worth living. I hope that at the earliest practicable date something may be arranged covering the disposition of the whole party. If thoroughly sifted and the unhealthy disposed of, there is no possible objection to the others.

It is important that we make immediately a change for seven of the girls. Two, or it may be three, will take [to] their beds next week and we may be compelled to bury them here.

I have left of the Indian School Transportation Fund to my credit in New York, $117.89. I respectfully request your authority to send seven of these Apaches at once to Mt. Vernon Barracks under the care of one of my teachers, using this $117.89 toward paying the expenses and the balance I will pay from my Charity Fund. This action will ease the situation until a conclusion in regard to the whole number is reached.[16]

Pratt's request was granted, although the letter contained some inaccuracies, including the number of children and their location and the cause of the ailment. The number he cited, 106 children, is at variance with another letter of his that stated 112 Chiricahua Apache children were at Carlisle. Also incorrect was his statement that the children were from Mount Vernon, Alabama, although it is easy to understand his mistake. Three days after he and the last large group of students left Fort Marion on April 27, 1887, the prisoners of war were released from St. Augustine. Some wives and children joined their warrior husbands and fathers at Fort Pickens, and the remainder, approximately 360, were transported to Mount Vernon Barracks, north of Mobile, to be incarcerated there indefinitely. When Pratt was writing, the parents were in Alabama.

It is less easy to understand his conclusion regarding tuberculosis among the children. For an enlightened scholar and administrator to believe that consumption was inherited and due to "venereal taint" is quite extraordinary and clearly not true.

Pratt corresponded again with the commissioner of Indian affairs on June 18, 1889, expressing his thoughts about the effects of the children's separation from their parents. This topic had been raised publicly by at least two Indian advocacy organizations in response to growing national concerns about the children's health. Based on his previous expressions, it is fair to state that Pratt was not among the Apache sympathizers. He wrote:

I did not anticipate that it would be practicable to dispose of the whole party, now at the school, until after another session of Congress. I therefore scattered the seventy-six children remaining here; placing them on farms and in families. Only fourteen are now at the school. They were either too young to be sent out, or their health was not sufficiently firm to warrant our sending them . . . there is a general improvement in their health conditions. It would seem to be wise to continue them as at present located, at least until Fall, and I have no doubt that we are pretty well through with the mortality for the present.

Referring to the remark of Gen. Howard that these children are liable to "disease principally caused by their separation from their parents," I have respectfully to inform you that Gen. Howard is quite mistaken in that. The disease rests where I placed it in my former letter. They came here under its influence. It was chronic and, in our judgment, heritary [sic]. But there is another reason why Gen. Howard is mistaken in his statement that the disease is caused by separation from parents and in suggesting as a remedy the returning all the children to Mt. Vernon Barracks, and that is, of the one hundred and twelve who came to us from the Chiricahua prisoner Apaches fifty-nine had no parents living, and a good proportion of the others had only one parent living, of the 76 still under our care, 45 have no parents living, so that if absence from their parents causes their disease and death, they are doomed under any circumstances.

My suggestion now would be to let them remain as they are at present, at least through the Summer, and if any serious illness arises, that we send such cases to Mt. Vernon. There will be no objection to, and good might come from a thorough examination of the whole party here by a competent army physician, who has had some Indian experience. The students are, in my judgment, entirely free from homesickness, or the desire to go to Mt. Vernon Barracks. This point could also be tested by the army physician should one be sent as above suggested.[17]

The educator's letter stirred interest, and Captain John J. Cochran, assistant surgeon at Fort Adams, Rhode Island, was asked to look into the situation. He spent three days at Carlisle—June 22 through June 24, 1889—and submitted a report on July 1, 1889. Dr. Cochran listed 112 Chiricahua Apache children and described their status as follows:

> 61 are at present engaged with farmers in country, greater number in Bucks Co., Pa. and in neighborhood of Trenton, N.J.
> 27 have died since arrival at school, the first death took place on June 3, 1887 from phthisis
> 9 were sent to Mt. Vernon Barracks, Ala., May 30, 1889
> 15 present at school on dates of visit—June 22, 23, 24, 1889.

Next, the doctor listed the medical conditions of the fifteen Chiricahua Apache students at the school during his visit:

> 1 Ira Goso has scrofulous enlargement of glands on left side of neck
> 1 Harold Dodesteny has a scrofulous enlargement of glands on right side of neck, also scrofulous inflammation (chronic synovitis) of right knee
> 13 are in good physical condition, apparently.

The doctor added a caveat to his report, cautioning that because of language barriers, he had formed his medical opinions based on "appearance and manner while under observation," and not on questioning. Regarding the twenty-seven students who died in less than two years, Dr. Cochran wrote:

> 16 are reported to have died from consumption
> 4 are reported to have died from phthisis
> 3 are reported to have died from scrofula
> 1 is reported to have died from malaria with cerebral complications
> 1 is reported to have died from pneumonia
> 1 is reported to have died from tubercular diarrhea
> 1 is reported to have died from lungs diseased.

The consultant physician's conclusions and recommendations were succinct:

> From the foregoing data, appearance of the children at the school, of the school itself, its management, and surroundings,

I am of the opinion that the causes of death have been mainly due to (1) removal of Indians from the dry climate and elevated lands of Arizona to damper climate, and lower lands of Florida, Alabama, and Pennsylvania; (2) to captivity; (3) to more intimate contact with civilization; and (4) to lessened power of the savage races to resist just such diseases as the Apaches have suffered and died from. I consider the children that I saw and examined at Carlisle, Pa. and from reports that I examined, of the balance who are on farms, to be in as good a condition of health as it is possible for them to be in any part of this country away from New Mexico and Arizona, and their mode of living so radically changed as it must necessarily be, if they are to be educated and taught self dependence.[18]

No action was taken pursuant to the doctor's findings and recommendations. Many children became ill and died during their years at Carlisle, but lessons and outings continued.

As the healthy, sick, and dying pupils became more proficient in the language of their captors, some wrote letters to their parents at Mount Vernon. George Wratten and another interpreter, Sam Bowman, translated these letters into the Apache language and passed on the information. When visitors to the Alabama encampment arrived, the two interpreters helped the newcomers to understand Apache ways. In turn, visitors communicated what they were learning about the Apaches to interested parties back home. "They kept letters and reports from Carlisle which were months old wrapped up in pieces of cloth they had embroidered," wrote one schoolteacher visitor to another about the prisoners.

Finding how dear these letters were, we offered to write to their children for them in return, and we might easily have filled all our time and many days more in this service. I send you a copy of some of these letters.

To Betzinez from his mother Natklekla [sic].

My dear child:

I am thinking about you. I have no friends. I sent my one child to Carlisle. I loved you long ago. It is long since I have seen you. You are my son. You must write to me often. I want you to learn. I have no father or no mother. There are just we two. Perhaps you work. I don't know. I work too. You do not write to me. You must write to me. You must work for I am working too. We are living well here. None of your friends are sick. Do write to me. Good bye.

your Mother

One letter is from a chief named Becathlay.

My dear child:

I am going to talk to you. You must learn. Your friends are all well. We all try hard to do right and you must do so too. When you went away I talked to you. You must try to do everything right as the teachers tell you. You must be good. We are trying too. We work every day. We have nice clothes. We work and get nice things, coats and dresses and every thing we want. Your friends are all well. Nobody is sick. You must write to us again.

your friend,
Bakathlay.

Communication between the Chiricahua Apache prisoners of war and those who guarded, guided, and aided them was an almost insurmountable problem. The Apache language is especially difficult for an outsider to understand. Even the men and women who mingled and lived with the prisoners and developed a fair idea of Chiricahua Apache cultural customs were not adept at spelling or pronouncing their names. In the foregoing letters, for example, the spelling of Betzinez's mother's name should be Nah-thle-tla, and the spelling of the chief's name as written by the teacher, prior to his greeting to this child, and in the closing phrase differ. Then again, on some occasions a name could have been written correctly, even though the spelling varied; often Apache individuals responded to similar-sounding yet different names, accommodating their captors' inability to understand or comprehend. For example, according to a schoolteacher named Isabel B. Eustis, "a medicine woman named Chiskio" wrote,

My dear children.

Are you happy? You must be happy my two boys. I see well yet and I talk kind. When you went away from me I cried every day. I feel better now. We live very well here. I think we shall see each other again. You must not think about me. I don't think about myself.

your mother
Chenlozite[19]

These letters reveal a simple truth too often forgotten or disregarded by the military: Chiricahua Apache prisoner parents were no exception to the ancient instinct that directs all mothers and fathers to protect their children from emotional pain. In these communiqués, the sons and daughters are assured that all is well, that the parents are working, have fine clothes, and that no one is ill. The reality of life in Alabama was much different from that, but the children would have to return from school to see for themselves. Many never lived to do that. Additionally, the prisoners feared for their lives should they offend their captors in any way, and sending these "glowing" reports about conditions at Mount Vernon to their children was one way of gaining favor. The Apaches were nothing if not pragmatic and had obviously assessed the circumstances they faced as prisoners.

An excerpt from a report about the sick and dying children was sent by George M. Sternburg, the surgeon general of the U.S. Army, to the adjutant general. Captain J. D. Glennan, assistant surgeon of the U.S. Army, had written the original report on November 1, 1895, and Dr. Sternburg thought it important enough to bring to the adjutant's attention shortly thereafter. Wrote Sternburg, quoting Glennan,

> The practice which prevails at the Carlisle School, of retaining students there until in an advanced stage of pulmonary disease, and then sending them back to their people is a bad one. If these cases could be returned to the open air life and dry atmosphere of the western country, in the first stage of this disease, many of them would recover. As it is, they return them when there is no hope of recovery, only to become sources of infection to their people. Some of them are kept so long that they may not reach the reservation alive. I have seen a boy from Carlisle, dying from phthisis, compelled to travel in a day car until unconscious, and then twenty-eight miles in a stage, in an effort to get on his reservation before death, which was accomplished by a few hours. This

is bad in every way. If this school cannot be removed to a climate suitable and natural to the Indian, the students who become infected there should, at least, be given a chance for life by a prompt return to the western country.[20]

Sternburg's letter was written in December 1895; by then at least 37 of the 112 Chiricahua Apache children attending the Carlisle School had died. A partial list of the deceased, relevant dates, their ages, and causes of death is shown in Table 1.[21] The spellings on their gravestones at Carlisle are in parentheses.

Information about other Apache children who died as a result of diseases acquired at Carlisle is less documented, and some of the data concern youngsters from other Apache bands, such as the San Carlos. Since no description of specific band affiliation was provided, all the names and dates of death are listed below in order to avoid excluding any Apache child who became ill and perished.

Nenaco Antonio	November 26, 1879
Henery Ouka	March 27, 1882
Isabel Kelcusay	December 25, 1884
Eva Dezay	February 22, 1885
James Foxcatcher	June 2, 1885
Guy Basket	August 3, 1885
Corrinne Simohtie	January 11, 1886
Pedro Saahez	May 1886
Anthony Nuske	April 7, 1887
Roderick ?	June 15, 1887
Albert Cassadore	April 11, 1888
Ada Foxcatcher	July 19, 1888
Aaron Yatosek	August 20, 1888
Myra Kieca	April 13, 1889
Ezra Anicoon	May 3, 1889
Hanna Dechizien	May 14, 1889
Katie Dinta	May 27, 1889
Susie Reed	July 29, 1890
John Bytzolay	unknown[22]

Not all the children who died are represented in this list and Table 1. Those who were sent home are not recorded among these

TABLE 1. *Deaths of Apache Children Related to Attendance at Carlisle Indian School, 1886–1895 (based on data in Gillett Griswold, "The Fort Sill Apaches: Their Vital Statistics, Tribal Origins, Antecedents," U.S. Army and Missile Center Museum Archives, Fort Sill, Oklahoma).*

Date of Death	Name	Date Enrolled	Age	Diagnosis
June 3, 1887	Skahsejah, Frederick (Skahsoja)	November 4, 1886	18	Tuberculosis
July 5, 1887	Graham, Edna (Betahkatoth)	November 4, 1886	14	Tuberculosis
July 8, 1887	Cintanito, Seth (Cantanita)	April 30, 1887	18	Tuberculosis
August 28, 1887	Zaen, Penelope (Zanca)	November 4, 1886	17	Tuberculosis
October 3, 1887	Gatay, Eric (Yucy)	November 4, 1886	18	Tuberculosis
October 7, 1887	Neskez, Anthony	November 4, 1886	15	Tuberculosis
February 11, 1888	Marko, Sybil	April 30, 1887	19	Tuberculosis
March 8, 1888	Kankah, Judith	April 30, 1887	16	Tuberculosis
March 20, 1888	Earden, Basil	November 4, 1886	17	Tuberculosis
April 13, 1888	Yotsoza, Helen	April 30, 1887	18	Tuberculosis
April 17, 1888	Booth, Alida (Oleda Tapenaisiheinan)	November 4, 1886	17	Tuberculosis
May 4, 1888	Dechizin, Hannah	April 30, 1887	17	Tuberculosis
May 25, 1888	Chatto, Horace	April 30, 1887	9	Tuberculosis
May 26, 1888	Yaitsah, Lucia	April 30, 1887	20	Tuberculosis
June 5, 1888	Suison, Neal	April 30, 1887	?	Tuberculosis
June 22, 1888	Dakosin, Simon (Dakosu)	November 4, 1886	15	Tuberculosis
July 31, 1888	Anosaien, Eva (Inosaien)	December 8, 1886	17	Tuberculosis
August 2, 1888	Yalosla, Aaron	April 30, 1887	12	Tuberculosis
August 12, 1888	Istone, Beulah	April 30, 1887	16	Tuberculosis
September 8, 1888	Dudzarda, Rogers	November 4, 1886	18	Tuberculosis
November 12, 1888	Iancho, Nora (Izancho)	April 30, 1887	11	Tuberculosis
March 1, 1889	Esenday, Rudolph	November 4, 1886	19	Tuberculosis
March 9, 1889	Noran, Samson	November 4, 1886	19	Tuberculosis
March 31, 1889	Kiecha, Mira	April 30, 1887	21	Tuberculosis
April 13, 1889	Kechjolay, Caleb	November 4, 1886	17	Tuberculosis
May 14, 1889	Nachekea, Susie	April 30, 1887	14	Tuberculosis
July 5, 1889	Iskee, Geoffrey (Iskie)	November 4, 1886	17	Tuberculosis

TABLE 1. *Continued*

Date of Death	Name	Date Enrolled	Age	Diagnosis
October 14, 1889	Iahanetha, Maggie (Lavethla)	April 30, 1887	14	Tuberculosis
April 30, 1890	Goso, Ira	July 8, 1888	22	Tuberculosis
June 9, 1890	Dechizin, Wilbur (Deehism)	April 30, 1887	25	Tuberculosis
July 31, 1890	Balatchu, Godfrey (Blatcha)	November 4, 1886	17	Tuberculosis
August 1892	Guruz, Ambrose	April 30, 1887	13	?
September 18, 1894	Geronimo, Chappo	July 8, 1888	30	Tuberculosis
December 9, 1894	Yates, Margaret	November 4, 1886	21	Tuberculosis
January 20, 1895	Pel-coy, Thomas	April 30, 1887	20	?
March 9, 1895	Hunlona, Eli (Huhlona)	July 8, 1888	30	Tuberculosis
1895	Patterson, Bruce	July 8, 1888	?	?

names, and there is no way of knowing how many of those there were.

On December 13, 1895, Pratt corresponded with Major George W. Davis of the Office of the Secretary of War in response to a request dated December 6. The secretary had asked for a report on the deaths of the Apache children at the school. Pratt wrote, "The death rate . . . is excessive. We took practically all the children of proper age without reference to their health, which will in some degree account for this death rate." Referring to overall mortality, which included students from various tribes, Pratt continued, "During the sixteen years of the School we have handled in all 2,969 students, of these 144 have died here. Thus you will see that while these Apaches formed only one-twenty-sixth of the whole, they have contributed nearly one-fourth of the whole number of deaths."[23]

Chappo Geronimo, son of the famous warrior and shaman, was one of the students kept at Carlisle until he was desperately ill, but he was not the pupil referred to in Glennan's report. In the final days of his life, Chappo was sent while in extremis by train to Mount Vernon, where he lived only a few weeks after arriving and died of tuberculosis in his father's arms. Earlier, the disease had also claimed the lives of Chappo's wife and baby. As a tribute

Chappo Geronimo, son of the warrior, on right with unidentified friend at the Carlisle Indian School. Chappo was 22 years old at the time of surrender and had a wife (Noh-clon) and a child, who was born during the negotiations. Both died at Fort Marion or at Mount Vernon Barracks, Alabama. While a student at Carlisle, which he entered on July 8, 1888, Chappo became ill with tuberculosis; he was sent home to the prison camp at Mount Vernon Barracks on August 7, 1894. On or about September 18, 1894, while preparations were being made for the transfer of the prisoners of war to Fort Sill, Chappo was listed as "very sick"; he died before the prisoners were moved and is buried in Mobile, Alabama. (Frisco Native American Museum)

to Geronimo, the army permitted Chappo to be buried among soldiers in a grave marked by a granite stone in a military cemetery in
Mobile, Alabama. Geronimo and Chappo's mother were at the site
accompanied by troops when the young man was interred. Myste-
riously, fresh flowers are today placed regularly on Chappo's grave,
indicating that this young man, who died in his early thirties, has
not been forgotten more than one hundred years after his demise.

8

Incarceration
in Alabama:
Mount Vernon

✳ ✳ ✳

Eugene Chihuahua, son of the Chiricahua Apache headman, was excused from attending the Carlisle School
through a rare sentimental lapse in government policy.
When he realized that his children would be taken away,
Chief Chihuahua specifically requested that at least one
boy or girl be permitted to remain at Fort Marion with
him. As a courtesy to the warrior the authorities agreed,
and Eugene stayed with his father through the years of
incarceration in Florida, Alabama, and Oklahoma. When
he was quite elderly, Eugene spoke in detail about his
experiences to author Eve Ball. "We had thought that
anything would be better than Fort Marion with its rain,
mosquitos, and malaria, but we were to find out that it was
good in comparison with Mt. Vernon Barracks. We didn't
know what misery was until they dumped us in those
swamps. . . . It rained nearly all the time . . . the mosquitos
almost ate us alive. . . . Babies died from their bites . . .
our people got the shaking sickness. . . . We burned one
minute and froze the next . . . no pile of blankets would
keep us warm. . . . We chilled and shook." [1]

   "Swamps" is not a totally accurate description of the
Alabama countryside thirty miles north of Mobile, but to

Chiricahua and Warm Springs Apache leaders incarcerated at Mount Vernon Barracks. From left: Chihuahua, Naiche, Loco, Nana, and Geronimo. Although the gate at Chihuahua's right no longer exists, the wall still stands and the site of this photograph can be located today. (State of Alabama, Department of Archives and History)

the Apache prisoners of war, the climate was even more oppressive than the Florida seacoast. For one, there was very little circulation of air in the hollow where they lived during the early period of their eight-year stay in Alabama. Eugene complained that no one could see the sky from the first of three camps at two sites outside a mile-long brick wall that completely encircled the military complex.[2]

Today, the wall still exists, practically intact, and encloses the same two thousand acres. Its durable construction is testimony to the excellent building techniques used; very little repair work has been necessary in the last century. Inside the brick fence currently are the buildings and grounds that make up Searcy Hospital, a state of Alabama mental institution created by an act of the 1900 legislature. The name is a tribute to Dr. J. T. Searcy, under whom the facility was organized in the early 1900s, but the countryside's history predates the turn of the century. In the early 1700s, when the territory was Spanish, there was a fort nearby on the Mobile River that served as a port of entry and separated the Spanish from the American landholdings in that area of North America. The fort was subsequently abandoned because of drinking water problems and the medical peril from omnipresent mosquitoes, but the land continued to be utilized by the military. In 1811, the grounds at Mount Vernon contained a former military cantonment, arsenal, and barracks and was home to soldiers fighting wars with local Indians.[3] In 1824, Congress authorized the construction of arsenal buildings, and when these were completed, U.S. soldiers were stationed there until 1861, when Confederate Alabama troops took possession. After the Civil War, the property reverted to the United States and was occupied as a barracks until 1900. The post was considered one of the most beautiful in the army. Eleven original buildings of Mount Vernon arsenal, erected in the 1830s, still stand and have been under almost continuous maintenance for more than 160 years.

This location in southern Alabama was selected for a prison camp in part upon recommendations from many credible sources, including especially Captain John G. Bourke, an army officer involved in various ways with the Apaches since the time of Cochise. In the spring of 1887 the War Department was becoming more and more concerned by the deaths of the prisoners at Fort Marion, and Bourke was directed to make an inspection of the Alabama facility as a possible healthier alternative to incarceration at St. Augustine. Bourke left Washington, D.C., on Sunday, April 10, 1887, and returned about a week later, praising Mount Vernon as a very attractive area situated on a sand ridge 224 feet above sea level and surrounded by a dense pine forest. Bourke claimed the sanitary conditions were good; yellow fever had never been in the area, but people in the lowlands did suffer from malaria. Other ailments such as dysentery, diarrhea, and summer cholera did not prevail, and the air was pure and sweet. He noted that the railroad linked Mount Vernon with larger cities in Alabama, particularly Mobile just to the south. His description was convincing, and the government was desperate. Shortly after reading Bourke's report, President Grover Cleveland and his cabinet met and approved the transfer.

At one o'clock in the morning on April 27, 1887, the hungry, fearful, terrified Chiricahua Apache prisoners of war at Fort Marion were put on trains, under guard, at St. Augustine, Florida. Their captivity had not become any easier with the passing time. Three days earlier, a second group of their children had been taken from them by Carlisle's Captain Pratt, and many relatives and friends were ill and dying. Eighteen to twenty-four had already died, their bodies unceremoniously dumped in the river or carted away in boxes carried in the bottom of boats. That evening, in Pensacola, the train stopped and the wives and children of the warriors detained at Fort Pickens detrained, eager to be reunited with their men. But, given recent experiences, those who stayed aboard were not certain they would see *these* relatives again. They wailed and moaned and cried as the train to Mount Vernon slowly pulled away. It was the next morning, April 28, 1887, at 8:30 A.M., when the wheels slowly grated and ground to a halt.

No railroad station house served as a depot in the small town. A building combining Swiss architecture and wooden ornaments like those popular in New Orleans would be erected about a year later to accommodate tourists, but on that spring day, approximately 360 hot, perspiring, and frightened Chiricahua Apache prisoners of war simply detrained at the bottom of an incline. Prodded by the accompanying soldiers, the healthy, ailing, and dying men, women, and children shuffled up the hill, lugging their meager possessions.

Today the train stop once again appears as it did in 1887. The attractive dark blue depot building has been moved to a spot closer to the river and is enjoying historic preservation. From the railroad tracks that cross a paved road, paralleling the highway from Mobile, it is a short distance by automobile up the rise the Apaches walked to a fork where access to the hospital's buildings is through a gate to the left, just as it was in the old days. The right branch takes a traveler beside and behind Searcy's buildings, and the brick wall comes into view. Many of the old photographs of incarcerated Chiricahua Apaches were taken nearby, up against this structure. The secluded area where the first tents were raised should be close. Suddenly a hollow where, clearly, the original village was located appears. Eugene Chihuahua was correct: it is indeed low and covered over with heavy branches of tall trees. The air is thick, and curious gnats seem irresistibly attracted to human sweat. On the ground, insects scurry away lest they be trampled. A pale gray sky, barely visible through the leaves, threatens to rain on a picnic table that sits under a tree beside a shooting range. A fifty-gallon drum serves as a receptacle for styrofoam containers and other picnic debris. Now, guards at the mental institution use this spot, certainly once frequented by the prisoners and their keepers, to hone their marksmanship.

According to Arthur Capell, the director of information and community relations at Searcy Hospital, this opening among the trees is in the general region of the Apaches' early settlements. He can't be more specific because no one in a position of authority in the Alabama government is certain of the exact location. In this portion of the clearing the ground is relatively free of undergrowth, but just beyond, where the prisoners' log cabins were erected, it looks impossible to penetrate. The path in front of the Apache homes photographed in the late 1880s is now swallowed up by poison sumac and other less offensive bushes. Staring down the overgrown lane and wanting to enter, the thought of the critters that now call the same place home is prohibitive.

The hot and steamy climate is extremely uncomfortable for someone accustomed to high desert living in the Southwest. Even the act of breathing seems different here—more obvious, harder, wetter. It is decidedly darker than it was on the road just a few minutes ago. Mosquitoes appear and quickly perch on bare faces, arms, and legs. The welts they raise are world class. Ignoring the impediments, however, there is an almost overwhelming sense of *being* in this place, but it feels sad and heavy. Only the dead weight of sorrow is left. And it is practically palpable. Even the ground doesn't hide any artifacts. The whole area was carefully cleaned out, said Capell, when the Apaches left in 1894.

It is a relief, emotionally, to climb back in the air-conditioned vehicle and drive toward the next location, a previously cleared strip of land about half a mile away that held the last Apache prisoner-of-war settlement. Knee-high grasses, vines, and bushes have now filled in this spot, but the dense undergrowth of the earlier campsite is not yet present. This strip of land is about twenty-five feet higher than down below, according to Capell, and sunny. The air moves freely. It feels better, too. Less morose. After the Apaches were transferred, this ground was planted with vegetables to feed the occupants of the military buildings. It is impossible to see the earth beneath the current vegetation, so searching for signs of human habitation cannot be done here either, but it is clear that there was

Geronimo at Mount Vernon Barracks, 1893. Note the handkerchief in his left hand, the ring, the military jacket, and the straw hat. (State of Alabama, Department of Archives and History)

much more space for the Apaches at Mount Vernon than was the case at St. Augustine.

"They had free run of the countryside here," said Capell, describing the difference between incarceration at Mount Vernon and incarceration at Fort Marion. "The only restrictions were that they couldn't leave the village before sunup and they had to be back by sundown. . . . They couldn't go very far . . . they were supervised by the troops." They were prisoners of war—without a war.

✳ ✳ Life and Death at Mount Vernon: The Early Years

Coming under the watchful eye of the military at Mount Vernon was a sometime thing for the Apaches. The military rules and regulations regarding prisoners of war seemed to apply only selectively and erratically, as if the government was confused and unable to come to terms with its actions against the formerly fearsome Chiricahuas. For instance, soon after the prisoners arrived at Mount Vernon, special round-trip excursions on trains to Mount Vernon to see the Apaches were organized in Mobile at a cost of one dollar per adult and fifty cents per child. Train cars were added especially for "colored people." The healthy prisoners of war met the trains, often without their military guards, and sold things that they had made or brought with them from Florida—government-issue blankets, bracelets, moccasins, canes, and so on. Later, after the Fort Pickens prisoners arrived, "Geronimo even sold his autograph."[4] Once again, with official government concurrence, the Apaches were tourist attractions, but by this time the prisoners knew how to exploit their celebrity, having learned these lessons well in Florida.

Insufficient rations, that seemingly endless problem between the prisoners and the government, were again a problem in Alabama. The Apaches, wiser now, supplemented their limited diet by spending some of the tourists' money on food. Oddly, the prisoners were permitted to freely intermingle with local farmers and often bought beef from them to help round out the scanty amount of food issued. Rumor has it that the beef sold to the Apaches by a few unscrupulous farmers was already rotten. This spoiled meat was thought to be the cause of many gastrointestinal disorders among the prisoners. In another unusual action, the army permitted the Apaches to patrol the railroad tracks looking for cows struck by trains on the right-of-way. When a dead cow was found, the prisoners were allowed to haul the carcass back to the camp for food.

Although fish was not part of regular rations in Alabama, pork was. The Apaches once again simply refused to eat it, and the officials refused to provide any beef substitutes to supplement the small amount of coffee, sugar, beans, hominy, salt, pepper, onions, and potatoes already supplied. The situation became so acute so quickly that by July 19, 1887, Major William Sinclair, the officer in charge at Mount Vernon, had to devise a system of barter to fill the prisoners' bellies and keep their strength up. Sinclair so informed the secretary of war, using post surgeon J. H. Patzk's report,[5] which cites numerous health problems previously acquired in Florida, as his reference. The report states that approximately two ounces of the customary ration of flour had been withheld from each prisoner. The total savings per ration period amounted to four pounds of flour, which was then traded to the army stores on the post for seven pounds of potatoes. "No other savings could be made, as the ration of all other articles on which savings might be made is already so small as to be wholly inadequate to supply absolute want and are supplemented by private purchase wherever the Indians can procure money," the doctor reported and Sinclair quoted. "They have never used vinegar," the medical officer's report continued, "as it never has been issued to them; but they may be taught to use it and they are much in need of an anti-scorbutic."[6] Because scurvy was so widespread in the camp, the doctor recommended "the addition of 100 pounds of potatoes and 25 pounds of onions per 100 rations."[7] Major Sinclair agreed verbally and in writing and began a long and concentrated effort within the bureaucracy to bring about changes.

Simultaneously, at least one private attempt was being made to call attention to the rapidly deteriorating physical condition and morale of the prisoners. Sam Bowman, an interpreter stationed at Mount Vernon, expressed his concerns in a letter written on July 26, 1887, to Herbert Welsh of the Indian Rights Association: "There is hardly any improvement in their condition . . . they will never improve at this place . . . the inhabitants tell me that no one but the colored race who are born here can stand it being swampy and malarious . . . and they prophesy an early death to the Indians if they are put to work in the bottom lands."[8] Not associated with either Sinclair's or Welsh's advocacy, however, was a fortuitous shift in medical personnel at the post.

Walter Reed replaced Dr. Patzk as the post surgeon in mid-July 1887, a position he held for the next three years.[9] In his first written medical report, dated August 31, 1887, Reed informed Sinclair that among the prisoners there were "a number of cases of lung bronchial diseases affecting both adults and children, but more especially the latter." One woman, known as the wife of Coonie (Apache women were seldom referred to by name in any of the medical or military documents), had died on August 22 of tuberculosis, as did one child whose name was also not recorded. The wife of Chino died on August 25 of uterine hemorrhage and exhaustion "probably due to malignant disease." Dr. Reed believed "the cases of bronchial disease, largely confined to children under five (5) years of age, were chiefly due to exposure to the wet weather prevalent during the first half of the month." He stated that under his care were a few cases of intermittent fevers which were convalescing, and that three babies had been born during that month. On August 20, a hospital for the prisoners of war was opened inside the wall, but, concluded Reed, it was necessary to have tents on standby to be utilized for isolation and quarantine of serious cases.[10]

When he learned of Major Sinclair's formal efforts through military channels to have the prisoners' rations increased, Reed added his name to the frequent letters of appeal. Nothing helped, and the rations issued to the Chiricahua Apaches remained woefully inadequate. Nonetheless, the people tried to independently provide for themselves and were successful for a time.

In an early letter, Sinclair stated, "As the Government does not furnish these people with sufficient beef, they have been buying cattle, sheep, etc. with the money they brought from St. Augustine [earned by selling their belongings and quartermaster-issued blankets and other nonconsumables to the tourists] but it is believed that their money is almost exhausted as they have no market here for their bows, arrows and trinkets, they have no prospect of earning more."[11] Months after the correspondence was sent, nothing had been done. In another letter, dated September 30, 1887, Sinclair once again recommended that the rations be increased and sounded a note of desperation about the Apache prisoners.

They have sold or pawned about all their private effects; have sold the greater part of the blankets issued to them at St. Augustine, Florida by the Quartermaster Department. Have tried to sell and pawn their crosses and other religious articles [presented to them by missionaries in Florida]. All this has been done to buy food. When they came here they did not beg, their want has reduced them to that, but there are but few people here to beg from and they are mostly poor and have but little to give. It will be readily understood that, not getting sufficient food, they are becoming morose and discontented, and have to be watched more carefully.[12]

Sinclair's letter reflects Dr. Reed's report to him dated the same day. But the statistics were showing a downturn in illnesses and deaths. Reed treated no more than five Apaches per day at sick call during the month of September, a dramatic improvement over the average of twelve per day the previous month. Guardedly optimistic, Reed reported diarrhea, chronic lung diseases, and intermittent fevers as prevailing among his patients. Three children had died in the last thirty days—a ten-month-old who had been ailing from a lung inflammation, a seven-year-old who had chronic diarrhea, and an eighteen-month-old who had tuberculosis. Reed requested an increase in the food allotment, "now issued in too small quantity. I feel sure that a full allowance . . . would be of positive benefit to them." He also recommended that the government issue "onions and potatoes (articles which they have no means of procuring)." [13] The issues of sufficient food and improved health were mutually dependent from a medical perspective and clearly important to the physician. He hoped the continuing appeal for an increase in rations would bring success.

Reed's biographer, William B. Bean, didn't devote many pages of his book to his subject's three years in Alabama, but he did make several important declarations. Stating, "These prisoners were a constant source of embarrassment to the army," and that Reed's concern "over tuberculosis among the captive people became acute," the author added his own opinion about the circumstances at Mount Vernon. This biographer's research and his understanding of the plight of the starving prisoners of war led him to conclude that Dr. Reed "was soon to learn . . . that it was government policy

TABLE 2. *Ailments Reported among the Chiricahua Apaches at Mount Vernon Barracks, Alabama, 1887 (based on a letter from Walter Reed to Major William Sinclair, November 30, 1887).*

Illness	Number of adults	Number of children
Intermittent fevers	9	0
Diarrhea	1	8
Stomach ailments	1	5
Pneumonia	0	4
Acute bronchitis	0	5
Constipation	3	0
Muscular rheumatism	3	0

for these redundant people to be annihilated."[14] Although none of Reed's official letters to his superior officers at Mount Vernon state that particular damaging accusation, he must have been aghast at the seriousness and intractability of the ailments that were taking more and more lives, and at the limited food supply issued to the prisoners.

Table 2 lists the most prevalent diseases treated and the number of Chiricahua Apache patients ailing with them in November 1887. More apparent than real is the absence of illnesses identified as malaria and tuberculosis in the table. However, intermittent fevers are symptomatic of malaria, and pneumonia and bronchitis are affiliated with pulmonary tuberculosis. In his report Dr. Reed listed one adult who died from chronic disease of the liver and lungs. A note of hope was also included. "The ration now issued is adequate in all respects," he wrote.[15] The War Department had finally responded to the months of pleading and increased the Apaches' rations.

The positive effect of sufficient food on the prisoners' health was immediate. Only 38 patients were treated during the entire month of December 1887, as compared with 150 or more per month previously. The type of sickness treated also changed somewhat—from the chronic wasting ailments to acute disorders such as bronchial problems due to the cold and wet weather. However, two Apaches had died: one older woman who had been ill with debility (a mysterious affliction that Reed believed was "latent disease of the lungs") and a one-and-a-half-year-old who had tubercular meningitis. In the first year-end summary of the medical conditions the Apaches suffered as prisoners of war in Alabama, covering the period April 1, 1887, to December 31, 1887, Reed developed the following record:

Total deaths	
Adult males	2
Adult females	10
Children	9
By month	
May	5
June	3
July	4
August	2
September	3
October	1
November	1
December	2
Causes of death	
Consumption	10
Debility/old age	5
Uterine hemorrhage	1
Childbirth	1
Chronic kidney disease	1
Pneumonia	1
Chronic diarrhea	1
Tubercular meningitis	1

No doubt the major cause of death was tuberculosis. While Dr. Reed separated "consumption" from "debility," both ailments were closely related, as was the one death from tubercular meningitis. The chronic kidney disease he mentioned and the pneumonia could also have been affiliated with tuberculosis.

In routine physical examinations of the Apaches, Dr. Reed noted the presence of diseases of a scrofulous type, indicated by enlargement of the lymphatic glands and chronic diseases of the ear, eye, and skin, and commented that he was surprised that the mortality was so low, "given the marked predisposition to . . . diseases" and the fact that the prisoners "pay no attention whatever to the laws of health." His report ends by listing the number of births during the period—sixteen.[16]

It was about this time that two simultaneous occurrences affected the camp. Canvas tents, which had been erected as living quarters for the Chiricahuas, began to rot and otherwise disintegrate because of the climate, and government officials became so alarmed at the contagion and resultant high death rate that the tent village was ordered burned to control the infection. "They replaced the tents with log cabins in the same area . . . for health reasons," said Arthur Capell.[17] Building the new accommodations also gave the able-bodied men productive work to do, thus ameliorating some of the idleness and the brooding attitude that was taking hold with the diseases in the camp.

At the end of 1887, the once mighty and feared Chiricahua Apache nation had been reduced to 348 prisoners at Mount Vernon and 48 prisoners at Fort Pickens. Approximately 100 student prisoners, many of them sick and 6 already dead, were far away at the Carlisle School in Pennsylvania. Those incarcerated at Mount Vernon comprised 70 men, 163 women, and 100 children. Of these, only 30 men were vigorous and in good health, 20 were less so, and 20 others were incapacitated by old age, former wounds, and sicknesses. It is astonishing that only 30 warriors were healthy enough after eight months of incarceration in Florida and Alabama to be considered fit for work. And, remarkably, there were just 17 more Chiricahua men at Fort Pickens who could be added to the list, provided their health was good.

Fifteen warriors were put to work constructing the cabins in alternate shifts. But it wasn't easy. At first the men had no idea how to conserve their energy while working. Their natural impulse was to labor as hard as they could for about an hour, then slump to the ground, exhausted more from the heat and humidity than from actual expenditure of energy. When they learned the way of work, they cut down trees from the woods around the camp and erected seventy-four new living quarters. Debo reported that "each dwelling had two rooms, each ten feet square, with a covered open space between like the settlers' double log cabins. . . . They had earthen floors and no furniture. The Indians slept on the ground or on boards, cooked over open fires, and sat on the ground. The spaces

First prisoner-of-war log-cabin village at Mount Vernon Barracks, ca. 1888. These houses, erected by the healthy men, replaced canvas tents that had deteriorated in the inclement weather. The tree in the center still stands. (State of Alabama, Department of Archives and History)

between the logs were chinked with clay, and a Sibley stove and a circular hearth with no chimney provided some heat. . . . The dwellings were cold and damp in winter, hot and close in summer."[18] Nonetheless, the Apaches' first houses ever were ready for occupancy in January and February 1888, in plenty of time for old friends and family who became new arrivals at Mount Vernon.

Naiche, Geronimo, and the Fort Pickens prisoners were transferred to Alabama on May 13, 1888. As their relatives and friends had done before them, the forty-seven prisoners detrained at Mount Vernon without fanfare and walked the one-half mile up the hill to the wall. There they sat on their bags and stared at the village until a girl, perhaps Geronimo's daughter, came to greet them. Some of the Chiricahuas had blamed Geronimo and his ferocious activities for their incarceration, and so there was an initial coolness toward the newcomers, but everyone was together at long last, more than one year after the initial imprisonment.

The additional Chiricahua Apaches at Mount Vernon increased Dr. Reed's already overburdened caseload, and his May 31 report shows that he had thirty-seven patients under his care. Most ailments were of a "trivial nature," and the largest single sickness was chicken pox, which was affecting twelve of the prisoners. Five people had diarrhea, and five had conjunctivitis. Dr. Reed treated an unusual malady that month: "On the 23rd of May a girl, aged seven, was admitted to sick report with . . . fever which was believed to be measles. As no cases, however, of this disease have been heard of in this vicinity, a positive diagnosis has been withheld. In the meantime, the girl's family has been removed from the main camp and quarantine established."[19] No doubt they were relocated to one of the isolation tents described earlier by the doctor. There was one death in May from tuberculosis, and one birth occurred during the month.

Two months later Reed reported that "the general health of the Indian prisoners of war has been satisfactory. During the month there have been two (2) deaths, one an adult female aged about 50 of general debility and melancholia, and one (1) a female child about five (5) of convulsions. There have been two (2) births during the month."[20]

The prisoners of war quickly became accustomed to the medical services provided by Dr. Reed and learned to consult him when they became sick. In January 1889, the physician treated a large number of Apaches for trivial complaints but reported two deaths, an adult male about forty years of age who had been ill with consumption, and a female child about three years of age who had a tubercular ulceration of the bowel. There had been two births.

The War Department at this time let it be known that it was concerned about the medical maladies that continued to affect the prisoners. Offended by the public declarations of interest, which were often in contrast with reality, Captain John Bourke contacted Herbert Welsh at the Indian Rights Association in Philadelphia. Wrote Bourke, "What I learned was this; that a policy of absolutely-do-nothing was to be carried out . . . either the present do-nothing policy will be continued, or a 'commission' composed of persons who know nothing of the savages, their needs, aspirations and capacity, will be ordered to 'examine and report' and that the 'report' will be prepared right here in Washington."[21]

Of necessity, Dr. Reed remained aloof from much of the growing public and private controversy about the prisoners of war. Administering to their medical needs and keeping up with the expected paperwork was more than a full-time job.

Reed's March report contains detailed information. He had counted the Apaches and stated that the total number was 382, as follows: 77 men, 169 women, 7 boys over age twelve, 4 girls over age twelve, 67 boys under age twelve, and 58 girls under age twelve. He mentioned that George Wratten was on duty at the post and that two women, Vincentine T. Booth and Marion E. Stephens, were teaching and engaged in missionary work. Apache men and women were employed cutting wood, hauling timber, and performing other duties in camp. Reed reported two births that month and two deaths of children due to inflammation of the bowels.

Through all of the ailing and dying, school lessons continued. Teachers Booth and Stephens and their successors, Sophie and Sylvia Shepherd, stayed with the prisoners for as long as the Apaches were incarcerated at Mount Vernon. They used a one-room building furnished by the post to instruct about eighty children, and eventually their parents. In the fall of 1892, enrollment of children and adults was so large that the prisoners built an additional room onto the existing structure to accommodate the pupils. The old warrior Geronimo was one of the foremost advocates of schooling. He made certain that all of the eligible children attended class daily and kept order by patrolling the room with a switch in his hand. Very few students of any age disobeyed.

An official register of prisoners begun around this time was kept on a weekly basis. Not only were men, women, and children enumerated, but information regarding any physical moves was included, and a large space under "Remarks" was available to record additional information. Only occasionally in this material are individuals, male or female, cited by name. The routine method was to refer to the Apaches anonymously; for example, "female child born, male child died." One major exception to the standard procedure was the Apache warrior Lozen. The record specifically names her and shows that "female Lozen died" between June 10 and June 17, 1889. No cause is mentioned, but it is generally agreed that she died from tuberculosis and was buried in an unmarked grave somewhere in the woods surrounding the encampment. Unlike the Florida burial procedures instituted by the military, the Apaches at Mount Vernon were permitted to bury their own in grave sites of their choosing. It is believed that more than 250 Apaches rest anonymously in the Alabama earth, their burial sites known by no one. Along with recording the deaths, the register notes other occurrences, such as transferring one man and two women to school in Pennsylvania, receiving children back from Carlisle, and removing one incorrigible male from the village to prison on Governor's Island, New York.[22]

In the spring, summer, and autumn of 1889, Dr. Reed's reports show increasing numbers of adults and children ill and dying. In April, one adult female died of general debility, and a two-year-old male died of acute tuberculin meningitis. One month later, Reed expressed his concerns in writing about the many youngsters he was treating for acute disorders of the bowels, and pneumonia. Another adult had died of general debility. In July, one baby died from chronic dysentery and an adult male perished from tuberculosis. In August, a one-year-old child died from chronic inflammation of the bowels. Although preventive measures had been instituted, such as building the new uncontaminated homes, burning the infected tents, issuing uncomplicated instructions regarding cleanliness, and daily policing of the village to ensure compliance with sanitary measures, nothing seemed to reverse or even halt the continuing deaths. In September, six Apaches died: two adult females from tuberculosis, one adult female from obstruction of the bowels, one child from convulsions, and two female children from unknown causes.[23]

Reed's summary to Headquarters, Division of the Atlantic, on October 31, 1889, notes 388 prisoners: 81 men, 169 women, 12 boys over twelve, 58 boys under twelve, 10 girls over twelve, and 58 girls under twelve. As a formality, Reed mentioned that George Wratten was on duty at the post and that two teachers—Sophie Shepherd and Marion Stephens—were engaged in teaching and missionary activities. Regarding the main topic of concern, the physician stated that

the health of the Apache Prisoners of War has not been as good as I have heretofore reported. In addition to the usual diseases of the bowels and skin, due to indiscretion in the matter of diet and lack of cleanliness, there has been an unusual number of bronchial affections. I regret, also, to have to report that consumption has again taken hold of the Apaches. Last month, there were two (2) deaths from Consumption, both strong young women, and this month's report shows one (1) death from the same cause (girl, aged 13) and five (5) other cases under treatment; two (2) of the latter having been recently sent from the Carlisle School.[24]

Adding to the misery at Mount Vernon, an overwhelmed Captain Pratt conducted the deplorable practice of sending home from Carlisle the very sick and dying Chiricahua Apache students. Often parents had not heard from their children since they were taken away, and the first contact in years lasted just a few days or weeks at Mount Vernon until the child perished.

In his November 1889 report to the post adjutant, Reed enumerated the causes of five deaths during the previous four weeks: pneumonia, 2 (both young children); consumption, 2 (one adult male and one adult female); poisoning, 1. Wrote Reed, "In the latter case, it is believed that the woman was given an overdose of an Apache medicine, although this could not be positively proven . . . the majority of the deaths have been caused by diseases of the lung. There are under treatment five (5) cases of consumption, all of which will prove fatal."[25]

Two weeks previously, Reed had submitted a long summary to headquarters in New York strongly recommending a change in climate for the Chiricahuas "in order to stop the ravages of pulmonary disease." He cited the "anxiety and alarm" felt by the prisoners because of the many deaths among them, coupled with "mental depression" because of "the belief that the Government does not propose, in the near future, to improve their condition." Reed continued, "I am now convinced that the principal factor in the causation of pulmonary disease amongst the Apaches is the excessive atmospheric moisture which prevails along the Gulf and Atlantic coasts. . . . Already since their arrival they have lost more than one-tenth of their number from pulmonary disease. Add to this the large number of deaths due to the same cause amongst their children at Carlisle, and the mortality from tubercular diseases becomes simply appalling; this too amongst a people who, in Arizona, were remarkably exempt from lung troubles."[26]

Reed's appeal was not overlooked by government officials in

Washington, D.C., who concurred that a change of location to a more healthful climate would be beneficial. An investigation of several sites, including locations in Virginia and North Carolina, began almost immediately. The climate in Virginia somewhat resembled Alabama, but the western woods of North Carolina brought to mind the mountainous terrain the Apaches loved. It seemed to be the perfect choice. Although it was clear to everyone concerned that relocating the Apaches in their homelands of Arizona and New Mexico was the more desirable course and would have positive results insofar as health was concerned, the Southwest was never considered a viable option. Despite almost four years of captivity and the tremendous losses the Apaches had suffered, government officials were loathe to trust that, if returned to their homelands, the Chiricahua Apaches would or could become peaceful Indians. Public opinion there, too, was still fiercely negative. The politics involved with finding another location for the prisoners ultimately resulted in congressional action. In 1890 the Committee on Indian Affairs of the House of Representatives debated the issue for many weeks, giving the prisoners hope. Unfortunately, no action was taken. The Chiricahuas, disappointed and discouraged, remained in the Alabama hollow and came under the supervision of the acting Indian agent, First Lieutenant William Wallace Wotherspoon, in June 1890.

That officer was astonished by the poor environmental conditions in the village, particularly a water pump that often failed and the many log cabins that needed repairs. One of the major problems Wotherspoon saw among the Chiricahua men and women was drunkenness. Depressed, morose, and close to abandoning hope, the Apaches purchased liquor from a few unprincipled neighbors, using the dollars they earned through selling their craftwork at the train station. While the Apaches were still free in Arizona and New Mexico, alcohol had been a destructive factor in their lives, but during incarceration at Fort Marion and Fort Pickens their ability to obtain liquor was limited. The more liberal confinement at Mount Vernon, which included open contact with neighbors, expanded the opportunity to purchase alcohol, and certain Apaches took advantage of it. Gambling, a favorite activity while the Chiricahuas were free, was also out of control at Mount Vernon; losers, frequently women, bet and lost their worldly goods, including wearing apparel,

Chiricahua Apache prisoners of war at Mount Vernon Barracks, ca. 1888. The two women, sitting side by side in the center, facing the photographer, may be Lozen (l.) and Dahteste (r.). Lozen died of tuberculosis at Mount Vernon Barracks in June 1889; Dahteste lived to an old age on the Mescalero Apache Reservation in New Mexico. Interpreter George Wratten stands in background on the right with hand at left trouser pocket. Wratten married Annie, a Chiricahua Apache woman, at Mount Vernon Barracks and became the father of two girls, Amy and Blossom. Very likely this scene depicts gambling. (State of Alabama, Department of Archives and History)

and became even more vulnerable to diseases and the climate without adequate clothing.

Equally hazardous were certain practices of traditional medicine, one of the worrisome activities in the camp addressed by Wotherspoon. A few Chiricahua women were treating patients in the ancient ways, using herbal healing methods that had worked well in their homelands. In Alabama, however, the earth's medicines were unfamiliar and sometimes deadly. Not knowing all the properties of plants growing in the Mount Vernon area, the healers inadvertently caused great harm in a few cases and interfered with Dr. Reed's care of the sick. One incident in particular illustrates the parameters of the problem.

It may have been the fall of 1889 when teachers Marion Stephens and Sophie Shepherd heard that a tragedy had occurred and rushed from the schoolhouse into the village. There they saw a number of women seated on the ground in a circle, weeping and wailing, their faces buried in their hands or knees and heads covered with shawls. In the center of the circle a dead woman lay atop a pile of quilts and blankets. It was obvious to the observers that she hadn't died of a medical malady, but apparently had ingested a poisonous potion prepared by one of the traditional healers. The corpse had been readied for burial: her face was dyed a bright red, and she wore a profusion of beads around her neck, chest, and arms. Her clothes were clean and sandals were strapped to her feet. The deceased's mother was beside the body, dressed in sack clothing, her face and body covered with ashes, according to custom. Deeply affected, the teachers placed a rose on the body. After an elaborate ritual involving the woman's children, the Apache mourners left the body but returned shortly, bringing their most cherished possessions to be buried with their companion. This was a departure from ancient customs that called for only the deceased's possessions to be interred with the body, but the Apache women, it was learned later, were imitating the teachers and wanted to send their belongings into the ground along with the rose. After the burial, everything else the dead woman had owned was burned according to the old ways.

Worried that the Christian customs had been misunderstood, and aghast that most of the material possessions of the Apache women in the camp were interred now in the surrounding woods, a few days after the burial the two Christian teachers asked George Wratten to arrange a meeting. Eighty-three Apache women attended, most with babies in cradleboards. Through Wratten's expert interpretation the Apache women better understood the Anglo customs and were extended an invitation to come to the schoolhouse each Saturday to learn even more.[27] Thereafter, many women attended an adult class and learned to read and write and listened to the Scriptures, another example of the government's duality. In the late 1800s, very few free women were educated, much less Indian women prisoners of war who were not even identified by name in military or civilian documents. Despite this elementary education, however, the practice of traditional medicine among native healers did not stop, and toxic reactions continued. One of Chihuahua's wives, who had been under the care of Dr. Reed for a minor ailment, became ill from poisoning. When she became delirious with fever, which popular plant remedies didn't lower, the physician was summoned. His examination led him to believe that she had been given lethal herbal medicine. The woman died the morning after his house call.

While the doctor continued to treat Apache patients, dramatic physical changes were being made in the Apache camp. The mess hall and kitchen were converted into a hospital that would accommodate an increasing number of prisoners seeking medical help, another facility was built for preparing and eating food, and a nourishing supplement was added to the regular diet. Some of the regular rations were again withheld to trade or sell for milk, eggs, and other special foods for the ailing Apaches. Able-bodied men, growing fewer and fewer, were put to work clearing the land and planting a vegetable garden. Eventually, excess produce grown by the Indians was sold to the army, and the profits were paid as wages to members of the group who gardened, washed the hospital bedclothes, and performed other chores in the village. The extra money also paid for cooking utensils, which formed the beginning of a communal supply of household articles. Eventually, Wotherspoon released a few well-behaved and trustworthy Apaches to work for wages on farms in the surrounding countryside. Geronimo earned about ten dollars per month to enforce discipline among the prisoners and serve as a "justice of the peace." Initially, though, the penalties he levied were too severe; for example, one offender received a hundred years in the guardhouse for being drunk. But with proper instruction, the former terror of the Southwest, now drawing wages for law enforcement activities, became more mellow and sympathetic and conducted his office in a "professional" manner.

Other reforms had been instituted prior to Wotherspoon's arrival, and he endorsed these wholeheartedly. Some were deliberately designed to lift the morale of the prisoners, such as a Christmas party—the first ever for the prisoners of war at Mount Vernon—that was held in 1889. Preparations began in November when Major Sinclair, who had been transferred to Fort Warren, near Boston, met with the Boston Citizenship Committee and other Indian advocacy associations to report on the progress of activities within the Apache village and to share the plans for a Christmas celebration. In the classroom back in Alabama the teachers worked hard to inform their Apache students of all ages about the religious history of Christmas, and military wives donated time and money for the secular side of the event. Major Sinclair and his wife sent four hundred gold and silver cornucopias from Massachusetts.

After breakfast on Christmas Eve morning, the children stood outside the school door, kept out by locked doors and newspapers covering the windows. It was a long day for them, but as soon as dark fell, candles on the tree inside were lighted and the youngsters were permitted to enter. Right beside the children were Naiche and Geronimo, unsure of what all this was about. The tree was holly, covered with red berries, with a white and silver angel perched on the tallest branch. Brightly wrapped presents for the Apache children were all around. Then Santa Claus entered, in the person of George Wratten, speaking Apache. He distributed the gifts and bags of candy before the parents could come in and see their children's presents: "a spinning top, a bag of marbles, a pencil, a slate, a horn, a picture book."[28]

But business as usual also continued. On the day before the party, First Lieutenant Guy Howard of the Twelfth Infantry (also an aide-de-camp to his father, General O. O. Howard, the commander of the Division of the Atlantic) wrote a long letter to the adjutant general about the conditions at Mount Vernon Barracks. He had been instructed by his father to conduct a complete examination and report his findings to the superior officer. After a brief introductory statement in the report, which chronicles the history of the Apache incarceration, Howard devoted a segment to the mortality of the prisoners.

Among the Indians remaining in the south, the following deaths have occurred:

In 1886 (at St. Augustine, Fla.)	18	
" 1887 (at St. Augustine, Fort Pickens and Mount Vernon Barracks, Ala.)	31	
" 1888 (at Mount Vernon Barracks, Ala.)	14	
" 1889 (at Mount Vernon Barracks, Ala. to November 30.)	26	89
Add to this the deaths at Carlisle, Pa.		30
Total deaths in 3½ years		119

There have been numerous births, so that the present number of Apaches is:

At Mount Vernon Barracks, 79 men, 167 women, 142 children.
Total   388
At Governor's Island, N.Y. 2 men
   (undergoing punishment)   2
At Carlisle School   70
Total   460

With a flair for the dramatic, Howard addressed the medical condition of the prisoners:

The three hundred and eighty-eight (79 men, 309 women and children) at Mount Vernon Barracks are now in a condition which needs prompt action to avoid positive inhumanity.

The normal death rate of civilized people is less than 2 per cent per annum. That of these people, including those at school, is more than three times as great, or 6, 8–10 per cent. A number equal to one quarter of those brought east has died in three and a half years. Consumption has fastened itself upon them and has been rapid and always fatal where it has attacked.

A great death rate must be expected, one half of the deaths being of young children whose diseases are aggravated by their parent's neglect of the simplest instructions of physicians and the murderous quackery of old squaws. But the excessive death rate is due to consumption, as have been most of the deaths at Carlisle where proper sanitary precautions have always been taken.

The condition of health and mind of these Indians other than those at Carlisle, precludes the possibility of their improvement and civilization where they are now, for the following reasons:

1st. They are prisoners. Though well fed and well clothed, their labor is prison labor.

2d. Only the men are required to work and that, of course, without remuneration. [This statement is arguable.] Were they paid it would only give the power of purchasing intoxicants and add to their degradation. The women have not enough to do and are without incentive to improvement.

3d. There has been and is much sickness and many deaths with resultant depression.

4th. They have been told that good behavior would secure

action towards permanent homes of their own, and this promise, so long deferred has increased their hopeless feeling. Each year's delay is a great injury to them.

5th. They are a people who have been bred in the mountains and who, as well as the medical officers of the army who have attended them, believe their rapid dying off is due, in great part, to their location in the moist atmosphere of the sea coast.

6th. So many of their children have died away at school that not only have those been grief stricken who have lost their absent ones but all are constantly fearful of taking from them for death at school others of their children.

To summarize then: We are holding as prisoners, with women in idleness tending to vice, a band of savages till they die, in a place and manner that their death is possibly increased by local causes, though we are not now taking their children away from them at school.

He then described the terrain at Mount Vernon, adding, "No military reservation east of the Mississippi River has any better facilities," and, mentioning the dedicated teachers, "the good of these short steps toward education is not apparent without giving the Indian child some better outlook for the future than he now has." Importantly, he cited the Severality Act of February 1887, under which "these Indians would have been entitled, had they been kept on the White Mountain Reservation in Arizona, whenever they should be settled in severality, to about 40,000 acres of farming or 80,000 acres of grazing land for which the United States will receive $50,000.00 to $100,000.00 in money as well as the more rapid industrial development of that territory by the more skillful labor of white immigrants." Here, Guy Howard may have hit on one of the hidden causes of the government's reluctance to return the Apaches to their homelands. Landownership and consequent settlement of the West and Southwest was philosophically and legally considered "manifest destiny," a concept officially promulgated and endorsed by the president and the Congress to favor westward economic expansion of the nation. If the Apaches reoccupied their homelands, obviously the white settlers, reaping the benefits of the government's policy, couldn't.

Howard recommended "that application be made to Congress for the provision of a suitable tract of land and the fitting out of these people with materials and tools to build cabins, with simple farm utensils, cattle and needs, and that they be put on such land by the 1st of March 1890. Another year's delay would be criminal. Land, a portion of which may eventually become each Indian family's own, including the means of going on it, is the fundamental need. That obtained, an industrial school is necessary with school-farm and hospital,"[29] he concluded.

General O. O. Howard endorsed his son's report and sent it up the chain of command to Samuel Breck, the assistant adjutant general. Breck endorsed the document on December 26, 1889, while the Apache children at Mount Vernon were still excited about Christmas, and sent it to Major General J. M. Schofield at headquarters in Washington, D.C. On December 30 Schofield endorsed the report and sent it to Redfield Proctor, the secretary of war. There the matter rested until January 13, 1890, when the material, including the official and impressive endorsements, was sent by Proctor to President Benjamin Harrison. In a letter accompanying the information, Proctor recommended that the Chiricahua Apaches be transferred from Alabama to a tract of land in western North Carolina or to Indian Territory (now part of Oklahoma). When he sent his suggestion, Proctor had already been lobbied by General George Crook, who declared in a long letter that the great number of deaths among the prisoners was due to "homesickness, change of climate, and the dreary monotony of empty lives." Crook concluded his correspondence with a reference to the Apache youngsters. "It would be a mistake," he wrote, "to send the children of these Indians to the school at Carlisle, a place which, from whatever cause it may be, proves so fatal to them. Many of the children die there, and those who return to their people, seem particularly liable to contract consumption, the disease that has taken off so many of them since their removal to the East. The Apaches . . . live in terror lest their children be taken from them and sent to a distant school."[30]

To his credit, the president acted expeditiously. On January 20, 1890, he sent the entire packet of information to the Senate and House of Representatives, adding a few words to the standard letter of transmittal. "I earnestly recommend that the provision be made by law for locating these Indians upon lands in the Indian Territory."[31]

✳ ✳ Life and Death at Mount Vernon: The Later Years

While the bureaucratic process was in motion, Dr. Reed's report dated January 31, 1890, shows two deaths from tuberculosis, three other serious cases of the same ailment under treatment, and "the usual number of afflictions of the bowels and lungs."[32] By June the doctor was so exhausted that he had to take leave, and the Apache village was without a permanent medical officer for the first time in three years. Area physicians attempted to provide care, but they were soon defeated by the medical tragedy. The Indian Rights Association of Philadelphia, still monitoring activities in the Apache camp, stepped in and demanded that the prisoners receive adequate medical attention on a continuing basis. The organization's representatives met with General O. O. Howard at Division of the Atlantic headquarters, and Howard became personally involved. Writing to the adjutant general of the army on September 5, 1890, Howard stated, "I do not know a post in this Division where a medical officer is more needed. It is altogether too much for one medical officer . . . without relief or help."[33] On September 11, 1890, an instruction was issued by J. H. Baxter, the surgeon general of the army, assigning Captain John Cochran, assistant surgeon, U.S. Army, on duty at Fort Adams, Rhode Island, to Mount Vernon Barracks for duty until the return of Captain Walter Reed.[34] Dr. Reed did not return to his post.

Interestingly, during the summer of 1890 Reed wrote an article for a very popular magazine of the day in which he briefly described Chiricahua Apache history and his observations about the prisoners. His words were complimentary, especially when referring to the Apaches' love for their children, which the doctor called a "redeeming characteristic." Added Reed, "Their grief over this compulsory separation [from their children] has been genuine and unabating; and when death has claimed one of their absent children, their intense manifestation of sorrow has touched the hearts of all." Noting their spiritual and healing customs, he wrote:

The belief in a Good and Bad Spirit is well fixed, and it is astonishing to see with what fantastic figures they bedeck the legs, arms, and body of the sick in order to drive away the devil. . . . In referring to the dead the Apache always points upward. The medicine-man, too, before beginning his song to the Good Spirit, rinses his mouth with pure water, thus indicating the belief that "what cometh from within defileth the man." In the absence of remedies, the medicine-men and women are agreed that nothing is so conducive to the recovery of the patient as a good kneading of the abdomen. So that one of the every-day sights of the camp is a half-grown daughter or son dancing, not too tenderly, upon the stomach of his parental ancestor.

In his conclusion Dr. Reed praised his Apache patients and friends, noting, "The sick are always carefully, if not gently, attended by relatives, and when death comes, as come it does very often, they consider it a duty to contribute of their household goods and wearing apparel valuable articles, to enable the dead one to make a good appearance in the next world."[35]

In late November 1890, there were 362 Chiricahuas at Mount Vernon whose lives were endangered from contagion and who would surely become seriously ill if drastic measures to control the deadly infection in their midst were not taken. It was decided that the log cabins down in the hollow had to be burned to the ground and another village constructed on a more elevated level. The new location, not far from the original site, was more healthful—air circulated freely and the sun reached the ground. But it was still damp, wet, and deadly.

Secretary of the Interior John W. Noble submitted a request to Congress in the amount of $41,500 for the fiscal year ending in June 1892, which included appropriations for "support and civilization of the Apache and other Indians that are now, or may be, located at Mount Vernon, Ala., for pay of necessary employees, including a physician, and for the rent of land for the industrial employment of said Indians, including the building of cabins. . . . For pay of an agent at said agency."[36]

The funds were subsequently appropriated, the War Department furnished building materials, and construction of the settlement was begun. Labor was provided by forty-seven somewhat healthy Apache men who had been convinced by Wotherspoon to enlist in Company I (for "Indian"), Twelfth Infantry, a unit he specifically created to provide the warriors with something to do and to put a few dollars in their pockets. More than likely, this was one of the first instances, if not *the* first, of Native American prisoners of war serving as armed soldiers in their own company while still imprisoned. It is also another example of the government's inability to decide what to do with the Apache prisoners. The Chiricahua soldiers were issued official U.S. Army uniforms and weapons and immediately became occupied with regulation army drills and preparations related to building the new village. "There is very little high ground in this coastal area," Arthur Capell told me. "Mount Vernon is the first occasion where there are any hills, and it was selected [as the next Apache camp] because of its height. While there was probably not more than a thirty- to fifty-foot change in height between the first and second sites, the second was elevated and the new village, as far as the surrounding territory was concerned, was much higher."[37]

About eighty small log homes were built by the Apache soldiers, each on a firm foundation, and then painted and furnished with a stove, a bed, and a handmade (by the troops) table and chairs. The homes in the hollow were burned, just as the tents had been burned earlier, to destroy the contagion. The Chiricahua Apaches, at least for the time being, were not moved out of the climate and physical environment that was destroying them, despite all of the pleas and recommendations from civilians, officers, and physicians.

Wotherspoon's report dated May 31, 1891, reflects his opinion about the Chiricahua soldiers. "The effect of allowing them to enlist seems to have been very good and its full benefits are yet to come." He wasn't more specific.

Medical documents reveal that four Apaches died that month: one man, one woman, and two children under twelve years of age. One of the adults died from "old age" and another from "Indian medicine." There were no deaths from tuberculosis; a few Apaches were entering the hospital voluntarily, and permission had been received from the secretary of war to construct additional wards in the hospital building. Resupplying medicines at the hospital in May cost $1.50, and a subsequent report by Wotherspoon to the adjutant general shows the costliest expenditure was $36.56 for 48¾ bushels of sweet potatoes, a necessary part of a healthy diet. The census indicates that 352 prisoners were incarcerated at Mount Vernon Barracks.

Medical reports by the post's new physician are not available, but Wotherspoon's records show that on July 31, 1889, the principal cause of sickness was large quantities of fruit consumed by the prisoners of war. On August 31, infant deaths were due to improper food. A side comment declares, "The Indian garden has produced large crops of tomatoes and melons during the summer besides small vegetables. A large crop of Mexican beans is now in and full planting for winter crops will begin in a few days."[38] The camp was quite active, and idleness seemed a thing of the past. Most everyone was engaged in one chore or another related to improving the general condition of the village. The additions to the hospital were close to completion in August, at a cost of nearly $3,000 for construction and equipment.

In November 1891, the hospital admitted many Apache patients, most of whom were ill because of the exceedingly damp weather. In March 1892, the post was once again without a doctor, and Wotherspoon, in his monthly report, recommended that a surgeon be sent immediately. There was at that time a commanding need for medical visits to the convalescents discharged from the hospital. "These people are much in need of medical supervision," Wotherspoon wrote. "It is difficult to get them to go to the hospital for treatment and it is utterly impossible for one medical officer to give them the attention they should have."[39] Dr. D. J. Spotswood, who lived near Mount Vernon, offered his services at $150 per month plus board and lodging and forage for one horse for three years. His offer was refused by the military, and another doctor/officer, Captain W. C. Borden, was assigned the exhausting task of attending physician to the Apache prisoners of war.

Dr. Borden arrived on April 26, 1892, and quickly became committed to helping the sick and healthy prisoners of war in every way possible. He made rounds on a daily basis, insisting that the homes be sparkling clean. Any found to have even a small amount of dirt or dust were ordered cleaned again, and Dr. Borden reappeared for reinspection. All walls, ceilings, shelves, and floors had to be scrubbed, and the dust collected and burned. There was no rest until each home passed Borden's examination.

Wotherspoon submitted a year-end summary to the commanding officer at Mount Vernon Barracks on July 26, 1892. Thirty-nine prisoners of war (fifteen adults and twenty-five children) had died in the previous twelve months, and six Apache soldiers had died, some from accidental or violent encounters. One of these was a suicide, the first in the camp and an almost unheard-of occurrence in the Apache culture. Geronimo's cousin Fun shot his wife after a domestic dispute. Thinking he had killed her, the warrior left the village and walked the path to the river, about two miles away. Leaning against a tree, he put a weapon to his head and pulled the trigger. A search party found him hours later. Ironically, Fun's wife lived, remarried, and survived the incarceration. The next incident of violence was more complicated. It is believed that Seeltoe, a private in the army, suddenly went mad. He and two other army privates, Zee-lay and Nah-to-ah-jun, had been assigned to guard duty at the jail. Inside were Seeltoe's wife, Belle, and Arnold Kinzhuma, both there for drunkenness. Early one afternoon Belle left the jail to report to the garden where she was assigned to work in a sort of community service activity as part of her punishment. Seeltoe raised his rifle in the air and fired, slamming a bullet into her back. Belle rolled over and over, and Seeltoe shot her again. Nah-to-ah-jun, stationed inside the guardhouse, ran outside, and Seeltoe shot him squarely in the chest. Arnold Kinzhuma looked out the door but pulled back quickly enough to avoid the fourth shot. Zee-lay ran and avoided becoming a target. Seeltoe put the rifle to his head and pulled the trigger, and his hat flew high into the air. He ran, with George Wratten and half the camp after him. Aware that everyone was gaining on him, Seeltoe fell to the ground, took off a shoe, put the rifle to his head again, and pulled the trigger with his toe. This time it worked. Belle, who must have been as hearty as Fun's wife, lived to a ripe old age.

Consigning women to the guardhouse, as in Belle's case, was not an unusual procedure at Mount Vernon, especially when liquor was easily accessible. During the entire course of incarceration at Mount Vernon, at least fourteen Chiricahua Apache women were placed in jail for offenses related to drinking. Their names and ages at the time of punishment are as follows:

Nah-nah-tsee, 39; Zeh-golsh-che-de, 49; Nas-tle, 64; Lie-zha, 44; Bonita, 44; U-go-hin, 54; Zah-nah, 34; Ilth-ton, 39; Tzis-to, 23; Nah-tai-che, 41; Be-sha-de, 25; Nah-zhoo-un, 40; Nah-zissy, 35; and Ke-ah-nun, 37.

Many of these women were ill themselves, had husbands, children, or kinfolk who were ill, or their children had been sent to

Carlisle School. Then, as now, liquor provided temporary refuge from the pain of illness, separation, and incarceration, and fostered aberrant behavior. Ironically, discipline consisted of a period of incarceration in a jail facility within the broader concept of Chiricahua Apache incarceration. The men fared a bit worse when they required chastisement. At least two, Collé and Astoyeh, were so outraged and frustrated at their circumstances that they couldn't contain themselves. After committing acts the army considered punishable, they were sent to a prison on Governor's Island in New York City. There they stayed a short time and then were back among their friends and family at Mount Vernon.

The summer 1892 census shows 343 Chiricahua Apaches remaining in the village, but the count does not include the 47 soldiers in Company I who were being carried on military rolls. Wotherspoon listed the causes of death as follows:

Tuberculosis	27
Capillary bronchitis	1
Croup	2
Asthma	1
Enteritis, chronic	2
Stomatitis	1
Peritonitis	1
Chronic Rheumatism	2
Poisoned by Indian Medicine	1
Inanition[40]	1
Suicide	1
Unknown, infants	2

Sadly, the death rate was still high, and tuberculosis was not really on the wane despite improvements in the Apaches' living quarters and personal sanitation techniques. Wotherspoon stated that he did not believe the Alabama climate had an adverse influence per se, but "the warmth and dampness may make [tuberculosis] more difficult to eradicate. . . . In my opinion, the high death rate amongst these people is due to their low physical condition, to long neglect of sanitary measures, and constant intermarriage and general degeneracy. I doubt if this can be corrected by any change of climate open to them." The "long neglect of sanitary measures," it must be remembered, occurred only in captivity if at all. While free, the

Chiricahua Apaches had cultural customs that dictated actions intended to offset problems with personal and communal hygiene. Wotherspoon's reference to "general degeneracy" is reminiscent of Captain Pratt's conclusion that inherited venereal taint was responsible for the illnesses among the prisoners. Neither opinion is substantive.

Wotherspoon described the efforts made to reduce the mortality rate; for example, abandoning and destroying the old village, building large new houses with good drainage in all directions, building a new hospital and staffing it with a corps of attendants and one matron, and policing the village daily.

The greatest attention has been paid to the cleanness of the houses, they being frequently and minutely inspected. Personal cleanliness has been aided by the construction of a large swimming or bathing tank, and a number of steam bath houses (sweat houses). Tubs, scrubbing boards and soap have been provided for washing of clothing; and whenever a death occurred in any house, it has been closed and carefully disinfected by fumigation.

It is to be noted that a marked decrease in the death rate of the children has occurred under these improved conditions, and that the full benefits of better location, better habitations, and more civilized modes of living and preparing their food have not, as yet, had time to show. . . . I therefore would deprecate any agitation of the question of removing these people for the present. . . . Their health condition is due more to hereditary and physical degeneracy, than to any climatic condition. . . .

Before the completion of the new village, most of the people slept on the ground, or on boards laid upon the ground. They cooked their food on open fires, and habitually sat on the ground. They now all have bedsteads, made by themselves; cook their food for the most part on cooking ranges, and serve it on tables, sitting upon chairs and stools made by themselves.

Attendance at sick call had diminished, and the Chiricahuas,

for the most part, follow the doctor's directions . . . all refuse gathered [is put in] carts and hauled off and burned. . . . All bedding and clothing found not cleaned, and all rags and dirt, are ordered cleaned, if fit for use; burned if not . . . water for village is obtained from four bored wells, varying in depth from 42 to 82 feet. The labor of getting water from this depth by small hand pumps is very great, and the time required so great, that only an inadequate supply is obtained. A large well with some kind of power pump, preferably a simple steam pump, which an Indian could run, with a tank, is very much needed.[41]

In November 1892, one infant died from starvation because the baby's mother, ailing from tuberculosis, was unable to nurse the child, and other food provided to the baby was indigestible. The following month an epidemic of diarrhea raged through the settlement; unusually bad winter weather was blamed. A report dated December 1, 1892, shows there were 332 Chiricahua Apaches at Mount Vernon, many of whom were ill. Two women had died, one from tuberculosis and one who had been ill for a long time, diagnosis unknown. "Her trouble seemed mental," the writer reported, "rather than physical. She and her relatives believe that she was possessed by a devil. This she tried to drive out with indian [sic] medicine, a concoction of herbs gathered from the surrounding woods. Their use resulted, as it almost invariably does, in death from narcotic poisoning . . . in troubles of a mental nature, in which evil spirits play a large part, they think that their own and not the white man's medicine is good." It is obvious from this that traditional healing continued to be practiced, regardless of the outcome.

Other information was included in the report: a short road was being built between the Apache village and the army post, fencing was being repaired, the houses were being painted, and the garden was being cultivated; the soldiers in Company I were drilling, marching, and receiving instruction in field engineering; the women were gambling, and liquor had been found in the camp, obtained from "irresponsible negroes [sic] against whom evidence is being gathered and proceedings will be taken as soon as possible."[42]

W. C. Borden, the medical officer at the post in the summer of 1892, wrote an outstanding article about the Chiricahua Apaches' years of incarceration for *The Boston Medical and Surgical Journal.* A description of the earlier circumstances of Chiricahua incarceration at Fort Marion and during the early days at Mount Vernon introduces the reader to the causes of the medical crises, and Table 3 (reproduced here) provides a comprehensive overview of important vital statistics that supported the narrative.

The information in the table was compiled from statistics derived during the period beginning July 1, 1887, and ending June 30, 1892. To accurately measure the data, Borden separated adults from children at age twelve, as the note to Table I describes. In the narrative, the doctor called attention to the dramatically high birthrate, "nearly double that of civilized communities," for which he identified two causes: great freedom of the union of the sexes and the practice of polygamy. To his credit, he understood the effect warfare and other external conditions had had on the number of Apache men and, consequently, the intense need to birth a large number of babies. The high death rate—a minimum of 48.9, a maximum of 142.5, and a mean of 93.1 per 1,000 living—exceeded the birthrate by 63.

Table 4 from Borden's article (reproduced below) shows the causes of death and the relative frequency of each cause. These statistics reveal that tuberculosis, diarrhea, and malnutrition of children were the greatest causes of the deaths in the period under examination. "Of the total of 180 deaths," reported Borden, "78, or 43⅓ per cent, were caused by tuberculosis alone; while malnutrition of children and diarrheal diseases together caused 49 deaths, or 27⅓ per cent, leaving but 53 deaths or 29⅔ per cent for all other diseases."

The doctor next discussed the diarrheal diseases among the Apache children, noting that of the 39 patients with those ailments, "the large number of 32, or 82 per cent, were of children. These 32 deaths added to the 10 deaths of children from malnutrition account for 42 of the 180 [total] deaths."

One of the causes of infant deaths in the late 1800s, regardless of ethnic background, was improper feeding, according to Dr. Borden. In writing about the special circumstances among the Chiricahua Apaches, he stated:

The improper feeding of children was undoubtedly as common with these Indians previous to their removal from Arizona as it has been since, but other disease-predisposing factors have been added by their change to their present place of abode, which have

TABLE 3. Showing the mean number, according to age and sex, of Apache Indians present at Mount Vernon Barracks, Ala., for each of the five years beginning July 1, 1887, and ending June 30, 1892; the number of deaths according to age and sex; the number of births; and the birth and death rates per 1,000 for the same years. (Reproduced from W. C. Borden, "The Vital Statistics of an Apache Indian Community," Boston Medical and Surgical Journal 139 [July–December 1893]: 5–10.)

Year	Mean number present (corrected for time)				Deaths				Births			Death-rate per 1,000	Birth-rate per 1,000
	Men	Women	Children*	Total	Men	Women	Children*	Total	Males	Females	Total		
1887–88	78	170	118	366	1	11	8	20	9	8	17	54.64	46.44
1888–89	86	179	123	388	2	7	10	19	7	10	17	48.96	43.60
1889–90	92	176	124	392	6	13	24	43	6	28	34	109.69	86.73
1890–91	99	165	107	371	9	11	33	53	10	8	18	142.58	48.51
1891–92	122	169	119	410	10	11	24	45	16	15	31	109.75	75.61
Totals					28	53	99	180	48	69	117		

Mean death-rate for the five years . . . 93.12
Mean birth-rate for the five years . . . 60.19
Excess of deaths over births . . . 63
Excess of female births over male . . . 21
*Under twelve years of age. The division is made at this age, as official record is so kept on account of those over twelve receiving a full ration from the government, while those under that age receive one-half a ration.

helped to produce a high infant mortality. In the hot and moist air of summer, which prevails in Southern Alabama during seven months of the year, putrefactive changes quickly occur; the improperly kept and poorly cooked food of the Indians is apt to take such change, and is, consequently, often given to the children when in anything but the proper condition.

Also cited as a cause of the medical problems was "improper clothing," and the doctor particularly mentioned that "during the first four years the clothing of the children was insufficient to protect them against the ill effects of temperature changes; and this, together with great dampness of the ground from frequent rains, had great effect in producing, or predisposing to, intestinal catarrhs."

He next addressed the effect of tuberculosis on the Chiricahua Apache population. "While the mean death rate of the world from tuberculosis is not far from 2 per 1,000 of living," the doctor wrote, "the average death rate of this community from it has been 40.35." Dr. Borden blamed "taking them suddenly from nomadic life and thrusting them unprepared by previous natural training into a life of quiescence and permanent habitation" as the factor causing vulnerability to tuberculosis.

In a concluding overview he wrote:

For some months previous to their arrival at Mount Vernon Barracks, and during the first four years of their stay there, all the conditions most favorable to the spread of the disease [tuberculosis] existed; and the deaths from it ran as follows: First year 11, second year 4, third year 18, fourth year 18, fifth year 27. Whether the system of disinfection and enforced cleanliness now being carried out in this community together with its bettered condition, will be effective in staying the ravages from this disease remains to be seen, for the unfavorable conditions of changed climate and altered modes of life still remain.[43]

Just as Dr. Borden's article was being prepared for publication, Wotherspoon summarized the status of the Chiricahua Apache prisoners of war in a report dated January 25, 1894. Written in response to a request from the commanding officer at Mount Vernon Barracks, who had been asked for information by the adjutant general of the army, the material Wotherspoon made known was quite

TABLE 4. *Showing the causes of death, the number of deaths from each cause during each year and during the five years, and the percentage of deaths from each cause to the total number of deaths. (Reproduced from W. C. Borden, "The Vital Statistics of an Apache Indian Community," Boston Medical and Surgical Journal 139 [July–December 1893]: 5–10.)*

Causes of death	Number of deaths each year.					Total, 5 yrs	Percent
	'87–88	'88–89	'89–90	'90–91	'91–92		
Tuberculosis	11	4	18	18	27	78	43.33
Scrofula	—	—	—	1	1	1	.55
Chronic rheumatism	—	—	—	—	2	2	1.11
General debility, adults	1	1	—	—	—	2	1.11
Old age	2	4	—	2	—	8	4.44
Malnutrition, children	—	1	3	5	1	10	5.55
Acute diarrhea	—	3	7	13	3	26	14.44
Chronic diarrhea	1	1	5	4	2	13	7.22
Obstruction of bowels	—	1	1	—	—	2	1.11

						Total	%
Peritonitis	1	—	—	3	1		5	2.77
Stomatitis	—	—	—	1	1		2	1.11
Asphyxia of new-born	1	—	1	—	—		2	1.11
Croup	—	—	—	—	2		2	1.11
Capillary bronchitis	—	—	—	1	1		2	1.11
Chronic pleurisy	1	—	—	—	—		1	·55
Pneumonia	1	—	3	—	1		5	2.77
Asthma	—	1	—	—	—		1	·35
Acute nephritis	—	—	—	—	1		1	·55
Chronic nephritis	1	—	1	—	—		2	1.11
Convulsions	—	1	—	—	1		2	1.11
Erysipelas	—	1	—	—	—		1	·55
Poisoned, Ind'n medicine	—	—	2	2	1		5	2.77
Suicide	—	—	—	—	1		1	·55
Unknown, infant	—	—	2	2	2		6	3.33
Totals	20	19	43	53	45		180	100.00

TABLE 5. *Population Statistics for Chiricahua Apaches during Incarceration (based on a report by W. W. Wotherspoon, January 25, 1894).*

| | Total born in captivity | | |
Place	Boys	Girls	Total
St. Augustine, Florida	2	7	9
Fort Pickens, Florida	1	—	1
Mount Vernon, Alabama	68	79	147

			Died during captivity[a]				
			Boys		Girls		
			over 12	under 12	over 12	under 12	
Place	Men	Women	over 12	under 12	over 12	under 12	Tot
St. Augustine, Fla.	1	5		4		4	1
Ft. Pickens, Fla.		1					
Mt. Vernon Barracks	25	66	4	54	6	76	23
Total	26	72	4	58	6	80	24

[a]These figures do not include the widely quoted total of thirty students who perished
Carlisle.

comprehensive. Instead of relying solely on military records, he approached the Apaches for *their* counts, beginning with total births and total deaths in captivity. From what they told him, he produced the information shown in Table 5.

Wotherspoon also compiled the following statistics, which demonstrate how many among the prisoners of war were in fit condition and how many were in poor health:

60 men	able-bodied and healthy
16 men	not able-bodied, being crippled and too old to work
102 women	able-bodied and healthy
47 women	not able-bodied, crippled and too old to work

76 boys	healthy
6 boys	unhealthy
48 girls	healthy
11 girls	unhealthy

The ages of the men ranged from twenty to over ninety; the women were from fifteen to one hundred years; the boys were from newborn to eighteen years; and the girls were from newborn to sixteen years. The forty-seven warriors serving in Company I, Twelfth Infantry, are not included among these statistics.

As of December 31, 1893, Wotherspoon reported 319 prisoners, one of the lowest numbers documented. Of these, 83 were "born in captivity and living, and classified as prisoners of war." Actually, they were children.

The commanding officer also wanted to know the total number of men now surviving of those bearing arms when captured. Wotherspoon responded in a narrative rather than providing numbers:

If the question applies only to those men now prisoners of war, and is not to include the late prisoners of war, who are now enlisted men in Company I, 12th Infantry, then the answer would be that there are eight (8) men now surviving, classed as prisoners of war, who had arms at the time of capture. Three of these belong to Geronimo's band, and include him. Five of them belonged to Chihuahua's band and include him. If the question is intended to include all the Apache Indians, late in confinement at Forts Marion and Pickens, who had arms at the time of capture, then the answer would be: 8 men now classed as prisoners of war, and 10 men, late prisoners, but now enlisted in Company I, 12th Infantry.

. . . If the question is intended to include all Indians now at this post who at any time have borne arms against the United States, then the answer would be that there are now at this post:

29 men classed as prisoners of war who have at some time borne arms against the United States.

26 men, late prisoners, now enlisted men, who have at some time borne arms against the United States, making a total of 55 men who were on the warpath at some time; some few of these many years before 1886.

In his summary Wotherspoon made declarations that put into words what so many people had known for so long but never mentioned: "It may be said of all these prisoners that they have been confined without trial, and are serving without limit to their punishment . . . over one-third are young children who have either been born in captivity or were infants in arms at the date of the capture." He then closed the correspondence with questions regarding the "final disposition" of the Apache prisoners of war,[44] a phrase made even more chilling today by its connotation of the Holocaust in Europe that was to occur fifty years later.

✳ ✳ ✳ The Last Days at Mount Vernon

After years of much bureaucratic ado, a cavalry post at Fort Sill, Oklahoma, was chosen as a more healthful home for the diminished band of Chiricahua Apaches, despite the fact that many influential and well-connected citizens of Mobile objected to the move. The Indians were a popular tourist attraction, and their presence added to the dollars flowing into the local economy. Even the newspaper was worried—about the lack of interesting stories about the prisoners that would result. But being transferred was fine with the Apaches. Skinner stated that in meetings about the pending relocation, Geronimo reiterated that all Apaches wanted to leave Alabama, and that "the weather was too humid and hot, causing many of them to die." Naiche wanted farms for his people. Chihuahua wanted "the wind to blow on him and the sun and moon to shine on him, the same as for other people." Chatto wanted to leave before everyone died. Other headmen were of the same opinion.[45]

In Oklahoma, their prisoner-of-war status would not change. They would still be under the supervision of the military, but they would be physically confined to an area of the country more conducive to their well-being. The site was agreed upon by civilian government officials, the military, civic organizations such as the Indian Rights Committee and the Boston Indian Citizenship Committee, and the Apache people themselves. On September 18, 1894, the action became official and orders for transfer were drawn up by the army. As part of the "closing out" procedures, a list had been prepared with information about some of the prisoners.

According to this military review and evaluation, which is unsigned, the following Chiricahua men had a "disposition to improve" their records: Geronimo; Chihuahua; La-zi-yah; Kay-dah-zinne, soldier; Kay-ih-tah; Bah-ga-do; Nai-che, soldier; Zee-le; Artis; Fatty, soldier; José "First," soldier; Tzo-zonne, soldier; Ruby; Cha-to, soldier; Tiss-nolth-tos, soldier; Na-na, "old and infirm"; Dominick, soldier; Nah-do-zin; Dah-ke-ya, soldier.

The next category addressed was "Apache Indians surviving who were captured by General Miles in 1886, and their families" (remember that the Naiche/Geronimo group surrendered voluntarily; they were never "captured").

GERONIMO. Has been a good man while a prisoner. Age: 60 years. One wife and five children. 1 boy over 12; 1 boy grown and one daughter married. Total number of children 5. His daughter is married to DAH-KE-YA, soldier, and has 2 children. Geronimo also has 2 sisters, 1 is married, the other not. He is Justice of the Peace and does well. Has influence as such.

NAI-CHE. Soldier. A good man since a prisoner. Has two wives, six children under 12; one boy and girl over 12, both at school, the boy at Hampton, the girl at Carlisle. Total children 8. Has two sisters, both are married. His mother is alive and with him.

MANGUS. 1 wife and 2 children under 12. 1 son nearly grown who is married. Mangus has been a good and reliable man since he surrendered.

PERICO. Soldier. Has been an excellent man since his capture. Has 1 wife and 2 children under 12.

YA-NO-ZHA. Soldier. A drinker but harmless. Has one wife but no children.

TISS-NOLTH-TOS. Soldier. A good man but drinks. Has one wife and one child.

LA-ZI-YAH. Can carry a gun but not able to do much hard work; hands crippled. Has one wife.

BE-SHE. Old but ablebodied; industrious. Has 1 wife and 2 daughters, both married.

CHAPO. Geronimo's son. Has returned from Carlisle; is now very sick in the hospital. Character "Fair."

HUNLONA. Now at Carlisle School.

ZHONNE. Now at Carlisle School.

One list comprised the "number of worthy, deserving and reliable men, with good records."

TO-CLANNY. Soldier. Is an excellent man; never been on the warpath. Has done good work as a scout in Arizona.

PERICO. Soldier. A good and reliable man since captured.

GO-KLIZ. Soldier. San Carlos Indian; a good man; has never been on war path. [This man married a Chiricahua woman and spent the years of incarceration at her side, thus becoming one of the prisoners of war.]

MANGUS. A very reliable man.

TOM. Character "Very Good."

BAILTSO. Character "Very Good."

KA-AH-TE-NEY. Character "Excellent."

FRANCIS. Character "Very Good."

CHA-CHU. Character "Good."

COONIE. Character "Excellent." 1st Sergeant, Scout Company, with Captain Maus.

CHINO. Character "Good."

BINDAY. Character "Good."

NAH-NAL-ZHUGGI. Character "Good."

POO-IS-GAH. Character "Good."

NOCHE. Character "Good." Cook for company.

LO-CO. Character "Good." Old and infirm.

The above Indians have shown themselves to be industrious, progressive and reliable.

Those who weren't as praiseworthy were identified as "unreliable" and having "bad characters":

RAMON. Is very mean when drinking; drinks hard.

ASS-TO-YEY. Soldier. A drunkard and a thief.

MARTINE. Soldier. Hard drinker. Beates [sic] his wife, but is a good worker.

SPITTY. Soldier. Drinks hard. Tricky.

ARNOLD KINZHUMA. Soldier. Gets drunk and when drunk is very quarrelsome.

MITHLO. Lazy and good for nothing. Is tricky and gets drunk.

JOLSANNY. A drunkard.

KYZHA. Tricky and unreliable.

All of the above Indians get drunk and often use threats to kill. These men have families as follows:

RAMON. One wife.

ASS-TO-YEY. Two wives and three children.

MARTINE. One wife and two children.

SPITTY. One wife and one child.

ARNOLD KINZHUMA. "Single."

MITHLO. Two wives and three children.

JOLSANNY. Two wives and three children.

KY-ZHA. One wife; no children.

A major category consisted of a list of names of the men who were soldiers and their habits:

1. Tsis-nah. Simple minded, unsettled.
2. Toclanny. Hard worker, very industrious.
3. Naiche. Not industrious.
4. Ka-ah-Te-ney. Fair worker, industrious.
5. Cha-chu. Inclined to be lazy.
6. Anitsa. Sullen, sulky, lazy.
7. Bailtso. Good worker, industrious.
8. Dominick. Sulky.
9. Mangus. An excellent man.
10. Perico. A very reliable man.
11. Noche. Industrious.
12. Tom. Very industrious.
13. Fatty. Very industrious.
14. Too-is-gah. Industrious.
15. Dah-ke-ya. Industrious.
16. Sam Haozous. A musician, character fair.
17. Nice Pas.   "
18. Spitty. Tricky.
19. Kay-dah-zinne. Industrious.
20. Francis. Industrious.
21. Nah-nah-zhugg. An excellent man.
22. Chato. Lazy.
23. Coonie. Lazy.
24. Tis-nolth-tos. Very industrious.
25. Martine. Worthless character.

26. José "First." Industrious.

27. Bin day. Industrious.

28. Eye Lash. A shoe maker, industrious.

29. Mithlo. Lazy and worthless.

30. Ky-zha. Carpenter, character fair.

31. Ass-to-yey. Drunkard and thief. Under sentence in guard-house for one year.

32. Kin-zhuna. Tricky.

33. Tzo-zonne. Industrious.

34. Go-kliz. Industrious.

35. Skuy-yugg. Industrious.

36. Ya-no-zha. Industrious.

37. Gooday. Inclined to be idle.

 4 others.

41 Total Soldiers. All except Cha-chu, Mangus, and Dah-ke-ya, will drink more or less if they get liquor.

The same types of descriptions were applied in another list to those who were not soldiers. They were called "Prisoners."

1.	Geronimo.	Sober, Justice of Peace, well behaved, age about 60.
2.	Lo-co.	Harmless, old and infirm, age about 80.
3.	Nana.	" " age about 94.
4.	Chi-hua-hua.	Able to work, industrious, age 40.
5.	Bish-to-yey.	Old and infirm, age 70.
6.	Ruby.	Rather infirm, character good, age 55.
7.	Zee-le.	Able bodied, eyes bad, character fair, age 45.
8.	La-zi-yah.	Not able to work hard, age 45.
9.	Jolsanny.	Drinks, crippled in arm, age 38.
10.	Es-char-zey.	Sick, age 35.
11.	Chapo.	Sick (son Geronimo) age 35.
12.	Nah-do-zin.	Very industrious, age 40.
13.	Ramon.	A good worker, age 40.
14.	Be-she.	" " 40.
15.	Bah-ga-do.	Lazy, age 35.
16.	Chino.	Industrious, age 45.
17.	Kay-ih-tah.	A good worker, age 40.
18.	Ar-tis.	Fair worker, age 35.

19. Es-kim-inzin.   Character excellent, a farmer.
20. Kin-de-lay.   A hard worker, age 40.
21. Stove-pipe.   Inclined to be idle, age 35.
22. Be-cho-le.   "   " age 35.
23. Chi-qui-to.   Very industrious and faithful, age 70.
24. Curly.   Very industrious, age 38.
25. Tille-chille.   Very industrious, age 40.
26. Nock-e-lah.   Industrious, age 40.

The aggregate number of soldiers and prisoners amounted to sixty-seven (which is disputable). Several Apaches from the San Carlos Reservation, including the last eight in the above list, were at Mount Vernon for disciplinary purposes but were not prisoners. Another southwestern group, Apaches from the White Mountain Reservation in Arizona, were living at Mount Vernon for various reasons.[46]

Pages and pages of summaries of the prisoners' years at Mount Vernon were generated. Some showed that as of January 1, 1894, 157 Chiricahua Apache babies had been born and survived at Mount Vernon. Approximately 250 prisoners of war had died and were buried there, but this number cannot be verified. Arthur Capell believed the figure closer to 300. Thirty-four students had died at Carlisle to that date, many of whom had never returned home, even for a visit; they were buried in Pennsylvania. The total mortality during the period beginning with the transfer of men, women, and children from Fort Marion in April 1887 and including the receipt of the warriors, their wives, and children from Fort Pickens in May 1888, was approximately 284, or a net loss by death, in excess of births, of 127. The death rates by year at Mount Vernon per 1,000 were 1887–88, 54.64; 1888–89, 48.96; 1889–90, 109.69; 1890–91, 142.84. Fully one-half of these deaths were due to tuberculosis. In 1891, after the newest village was constructed on high ground and strict sanitary procedures were observed, the death rate began to fall: 1891–92, 109.75; 1892–93, 80.93; 1893–94, 98.36.

During the 346 remaining prisoners' first year in Oklahoma (1894–95), where the climate was much more healthful, the death rate dropped even more, to 83.05.[47]

Even though the prisoners took their acquired medical conditions with them out of the Deep South, other health disorders would begin to affect them at Fort Sill, including the consequences of melancholia and yearning for those left buried in the Alabama woods. The deceased Chiricahua Apaches remained undisturbed for nearly a century, until timber harvesting on that unmarked site was begun under the auspices of the state of Alabama. The project was halted before too long, however, because of intense and widespread disapproval over disturbing the bones of the Apaches. Once again, a hue and cry from ordinary citizens of various ethnic backgrounds forestalled a political decision that would have adversely affected the Chiricahua Apaches. Once again, a government was embarrassed by its actions toward this small group of people, now long dead, whose ancient bones barely avoided being churned up, cast aside, and casually carted off.

9

Incarceration
in Oklahoma:
Fort Sill

✳︎　✳︎　✳︎

For five years prior to the transfer of the seventy prisoner-of-war families on October 4, 1894, from Alabama to Oklahoma, military and civilian officials investigated potential sites suitable as new quarters of incarceration. In what now might be viewed as a public relations gesture, the federal government also involved certain advocacy organizations in the search for a permanent home for the Apaches. Captain John G. Bourke of the Third Cavalry, a soldier long familiar with Indians, was asked to visit several locations that might be utilized as reservations. On March 14, 1889, in a memo to the newly appointed secretary of war, Redfield Proctor, Bourke identified eight possible places: Santa Rosa Island, Florida, site of Fort Pickens; Mount Vernon Barracks, Alabama, the incarceration site then in use; Fort Livingston, Louisiana, near New Orleans, which was thought to be healthy and free from fever; Fort Riley, Kansas, said to have soil suitable for farming; Fort McPherson, Nebraska, good hay-growing country; Fort Foote, Maryland, on the Potomac, south of Washington, D.C., but malarious; Fort Washington, Maryland, also on the Potomac and also malarious; and Hampton, Virginia, site of the Hampton Normal School.

Bourke recommended Hampton because of the satisfactory climate, the school, the opportunity for the Apaches to sell their farm products at profitable rates, the presence of a garrison at nearby Fort Monroe in case anything untoward happened, and the "stimulus of civilization."[1] C. C. Painter of the Boston Indian Citizenship Committee, an advocacy agency also actively involved in seeking a new location, suggested a farm of "8000 acres near Wilmington, N.C., and a farm near the school at Hampton."[2]

On June 24, 1889, Painter and Bourke, who had connected through bureaucratic channels, traveled to Mount Vernon together to meet with Apache headmen and discuss the issue. Army officers present at the important meeting were Captain C. T. Witherill, the commander of the post; Lieutenant Colonel and Brevet Brigadier General Richard H. Jackson; Assistant Surgeon Walter Reed; and Second Lieutenant Z. B. Vance. Representing the Chiricahuas were Naiche, Geronimo, Chihuahua, Chatto, Ka-e-tennay, the shaman named Ramon, Noche, Toklanni, Martine, Kay-ih-tah, Loco, Nana, Zele, Goth-kly, Guydelkon, Coonie, Patricio, Perico, Dutchy, Fun, Yanohza, Calle, Ta-ni-toe, Bash-ta-yay, Tze-de-tizn, Go-nal-tsis, Juan, Spitty, and Juancinita. George Wratten interpreted the remarks from Apache into English, and Patricio and José (an Apache?) translated from Apache into Spanish. As a courtesy to those present who were bilingual, as were some of the Apaches, the Spanish-to-English translating was done by Bourke.

Painter began by telling the Apaches, "We don't think there is any more room in this country for Indians, but there is room for men: no more land for hunting, but plenty for farming and making your living like the white men do. The old Indian road is all shut up: the white man has built his Railroads across it and the Indian road don't lead anywhere: it don't lead to any more game; it leads only to ruin. The man who wants to follow the Indian trail any longer, goes to death." He offered his organization's support in the form of funds to purchase land east of the Mississippi, "where the white people will be willing for you to come . . . where you can live undisturbed, where you can be men and not Indians. . . . Your choice lies between utter annihilation on the one hand and the white man's civilization on the other."

Several Apache leaders expressed their wish to work for themselves and to receive compensation for their farming labors, a reasonable request, it appears, but apparently one that would not be considered for several more years. One major complaint voiced by the headmen was that they had no money to show for their hard work, and they reiterated that if suitable acreage could be found, they would like to get paid for what they produced. The sly Apaches flattered Painter and Bourke, likened them to brothers, and said how happy they were since becoming like white men. Their statements linked white men with God, and many who spoke agreed that the white way was the right way. Concerns were also expressed, however. Chihuahua referred to his family, saying, "I want the change made for their sake, as I know they'll burn up if they remain here." Loco worried about a son, far away at Carlisle School, stating, "I am getting old and feeble now; my son was taken five years ago to Carlisle School: if we get that farm, I'd like to have him sent back to me." Said Noche, a former scout, to Bourke, "The last time you . . . saw me there were lots of us; now there are very few of us left. In winter time, when the ice freezes, it stays the same size; but, when the hot weather comes, it all melts away; so with us, we have, since you last saw us been melting away like ice in the sun." Others asked for "a home in a snowy country" because "too many died when they lived near the water over at Saint Augustine . . . they were a people born and bred in the mountains . . . and had never been near it [the sea] until within the last three years." The conference ended with a long speech by Chatto in which he compared himself with the seven horses taken from him when he left the San Carlos Reservation in Arizona. "Some horses are bad," he said, "and so are some men; you can't do anything with them." After assuring everyone that he had changed his former ways, he added that he would like to have his horses back "when I am not working any longer for nothing."[3]

Bourke's formal recommendation was made in a nine-page single-spaced letter dated July 5, 1889, to the adjutant general in Washington, D.C. He added his own comments to issues raised by the Apache headmen. In regard to the children at Carlisle, for example, Bourke wrote: "[The Chiricahua] seemed to deplore deeply the terrible mortality at [Carlisle] which had carried off . . . their children. (there was at Mount Vernon, during our visit, a young girl, about fourteen years old, just returned from Carlisle, who seemed to be far advanced in consumption, the seeds of which, I believe, were sewn in the damp, mouldy case-mates of Fort Marion.)"

Forthright in his evaluation of the circumstances of the Apaches' incarceration, Bourke called the processes of interpretation by Wratten and others "the quintessence of idiocy." Why, he asked, "should the Indians not be compelled to speak our language? We send their children to school and teach them at great expense and then return them to their own people, where they see the position of interpreter filled by an American, that is where it isn't filled by an Irishman or a German." Then he separated the Chiricahuas at Mount Vernon into two groups, "those who surrendered in good faith . . . and those who broke their pledges, returned to the war-path, and resumed their former career of rapine and murder," and advised that a distinction be made "when any question of recognition or preferment is to be debated."

Bourke wrote detailed analyses and descriptions of each site he and Painter had visited on their way to and from Mount Vernon and included facts about each, such as the food they were served by Quaker families, the cost of wild strawberries, and the general appearance of residents in areas of the countryside surrounding the potential prison locations. In this carefully crafted report Bourke addressed the four sites he and Painter had visited: the region near the boundaries of Georgia, Florida, and Alabama; Cherokee land in the far western section of North Carolina; Burgaw, a small town twenty-one miles north of Wilmington, North Carolina; and Sherwood Farm in Hampton, Virginia. Bourke rated the Cherokee territory first and the Virginia location second as sites suitable for the Chiricahua Apaches. He also offered his advice, counseling that

> the Chiricahuas should, for a time at least, be kept under military control and a small detachment of troops be kept near them, principally for moral effect, but also as a salutary check upon those who may not yield an unhesitating obedience to the new order of things. . . . Send back the children from Carlisle. . . . Appoint the best one of these children interpreter upon the same salary as is now paid a white man; let the Indians see that the study of our language means something. . . . Let a suitable one of their number act as trader. . . . Let the administration of affairs . . .

be kept under the direct personal supervision of the Secretary of War, or the General of the Army.

The latter suggestion was made because the Apaches, in Bourke's opinion, had great respect for "caste and rank." Bourke's final comment was that "the Chiricahua Apaches can be made self-supporting and law-abiding people in less than three years." [4]

Three months later, when no decision had yet been issued by the government, the Boston Indian Citizenship Committee's representatives wrote to Secretary of War Proctor complaining about the delay and urging prompt action.[5] Little did they know that nothing of substance would be forthcoming for nearly five years.

General Nelson A. Miles, the officer to whom the Naiche/Geronimo band had surrendered in 1886, informally submitted his advice about the same topic to Proctor in an unsolicited letter. Miles wrote that from the day the Apaches "were taken out of my hands and ruthlessly banished to the fever stricken district of Florida, and more than four hundred of them forced into a prison pen of less than an acre of ground . . . I have never been consulted or communicated with concerning the subject." Not allowing what must have been deliberate neglect by the military to stand in his way, Miles stated, "I have always regarded that part of their treatment as cruel and unjust, and the officers who came back after transporting them to Florida openly stated they regarded it as simply brutal." Miles was no fan of the Chiricahuas, however, and urged the utmost caution in relocating the band, believing that

> any effort to move them where there would be any chance of their getting back to the mountains of Mexico or Arizona, will meet, the most earnest protests of the entire populace and press of those territories as well as the entire west . . . the fact should not be lost sight of that they are a body of the most cruel, treacherous savages on the continent. . . . A large number of them are under indictment now for murder and if an effort was ever made to send them back to Arizona, they would immediately be taken out of the hands of the military authorities and tried and hung, or killed without trial.[6]

While "authorities" were offering their opinions, 460 men, women, and children were awaiting an official decision, which was labeled clearly in a letter from Proctor to President Benjamin Harrison in 1890 as a "duty of the Government to remove them to some other point where they can have permanent homes, and pursue some employment tending to their civilization and self-support." Two choices were offered by the secretary of war for the president's consideration: a tract of land in western North Carolina or in one of the nearby states, or a place in Indian Territory. Proctor pointed out that Section 3, Chapter 87, of the Laws of 1879 prohibited the president from removing any tribe of Indians of New Mexico and Arizona to Indian Territory without authorization from Congress, so the option of taking independent action was out. His letter concluded with the recommendation that

> if Congress will grant the necessary authority, . . . these Indians [should] be transferred to Fort Sill in the Indian Territory with a view to their final settlement on the Kiowa, Comanche, and Apache [Kiowa-Apaches were originally members of the great Athapaskan migration to the Southwest, but differentiated themselves from the Chiricahua Apaches through years of separation] Reservation, provided satisfactory negotiations can be consummated with these confederated tribes to that end. The Military Reservation of Fort Sill comprises thirty-six square miles and is located within this Indian Reservation.[7]

After the cavalry post was introduced as a possible future home for the Chiricahuas, Major General George Crook was sent from Headquarters, Division of the Missouri, in Chicago to Indian Territory. He visited Fort Sill and described the area as having "very fertile soil, the surface rolling and the country well watered by numerous perennial streams of clear and limpid water, flowing over sandy and rocky beds without quicksands. The Wichita Mountains near at hand to the North and West of the Post, are well wooded with a growth of different varieties of timber." He cautioned that "the Post has in the past been much troubled with malarial diseases," but added that for the last eighteen months the ailment had been much less prevalent. He recommended that the Apaches be transferred to Fort Sill and believed that "with proper aid and encouragement and wise supervision, these Indians should within a few years become self sustaining."[8] One year of bureaucratic machinations had

Chiricahua Apache wickiup. Fort Sill, 1897. (Smithsonian Institution, National Anthropological Archives)

not moved the sick, suffering, and dying Apaches one inch closer to relocation in a healthier climate.

Five years after it began, the continuing process appeared to be interminable. On September 15, 1894, Captain Marion Maus, an old foe of the Apaches, wrote to Major George W. Davis in the Office of the Secretary of War, reporting on his inquiries regarding the transfer of the prisoners to Fort Sill. He recommended removing the Apaches at once because of the coming winter and stated that it would be absolutely impossible for them to escape from the Oklahoma military reserve, adding,

> The distance to the Mescalero [New Mexico] agency is very long, as you know, and with telegraphic communication and the assistance of the civil authorities I believe they could be easily caught should they make such an attempt. . . . They certainly ought to be moved. Many of them are enfeebled by disease. . . . There is no doubt that the climate at Mount Vernon Barracks is unsuitable for them, although I must admit that they are as well fixed there as they could be under any circumstances and are well cared for. . . . The Indians believe that a change is going to be made and they seem to be very much discontented with the country where they are.[9]

Skinner revealed that "Maus could not understand why the Apaches so badly wanted to leave and start life anew. . . . He would soon learn that they were afraid that everyone would die if they remained in Alabama." Maus was told that 262 Apaches had died since they had been exiled, and his recommendation to his superior, General Nelson Miles, was that all 366 prisoners be transferred to Fort Sill. Miles concurred and informed the new secretary of war, Daniel Lamont, of his recommendation.[10] At long last it appeared that relocation would occur, but would the dying stop?

✻ ✻ ✻ Fort Sill, 1894–1914

In 1894 the Kiowas, Comanches, Kiowa-Apaches (no close relation to the Chiricahuas), Wichitas, and Caddos lived on a reservation known as the Kiowa Agency that included among its vast acreage the countryside surrounding Fort Sill. Because these Plains Indian groups were under the jurisdiction of the Office of Indian Affairs at the Department of the Interior, their medical care was provided by civilian physicians under contract with the government. Fortunately, the civilian authorities kept detailed records that shed light on the medical practices of the later 1800s and early 1900s, and in some cases provide vivid examples of health care, or the lack of it, for Native Americans living on reservations more than one hundred years ago. Into this environment the Apaches stepped, not as equals with their Indian brethren but as prisoners of war under the legal authority of the Department of War, to continue to be medically treated by army physicians. It is a toss-up which was better or worse—health care provided by civilian or military physicians.

The doctors affiliated with the Kiowa Agency were supervised by and reported to the local Indian agent, who served as their conduit to federal officials. When a doctor needed supplies or equipment, the appropriate requisitions, invoices, letters, vouchers, or justifications had to be submitted up through the government's chain of command. For example, Commissioner D. M. Browning, of the Office of Indian Affairs in Washington, D.C., wrote to Captain H. G. Brown, the Indian agent at the Kiowa Agency in Oklahoma, on September 9, 1893. Brown had requested a buggy for the agency physician, who complained about the lack of transportation in the territory. Browning responded that "the Office has uniformly denied applications to purchase buggies, or other conveyances, for the exclusive use of the physician. A physician is not supposed to be 'on the go' all the time, and when he wants a conveyance, there should be enough at the Agency to supply him with one."[11] Request denied. Clearly, if a physician couldn't obtain transportation to visit the homes of ailing Indians, he couldn't render care. Also denied, then, was access to medical care for individuals and families who lived far from the centrally located agency, which was the case with most Native Americans.

Before any purchases for vehicles, surgical equipment, medicines, or health care implements were approved, bureaucratic paperwork required that a standard invoice had to be carefully prepared, identifying the tribe of Indians requiring the supplies, the agency with which they were affiliated, the predesignated order number on packages, the kind of packages (box, carton, tube), the weight of the shipment, the contents in the package, the amount per unit, and the total amount. On January 9, 1894, records show the Kiowa-Apaches at the Kiowa Agency needed 40 bottles of alcohol and 300 dozen corks, at a total cost of $37. Later that year the same tribe placed an order for 4 medical washbasins, 30 quarts of alcohol, 32 ounces of gum arabic, 4 vials of oil of anise, 20 bottles of olive oil, 6 ounces of caustic potash, 4 vials of strychnine, and other medical supplies, altogether costing $89.11. A week later an additional order was made for 48 ounces of acetic acid, 75 pounds of carbolic acid, 32 ounces of citric acid, 8 ounces of blistering cerate, 192 ounces of tincture of opium, 25 sheets of cotton wadding, and 32 ounces of nitrate potassium, at a total cost of $57.53. A full year's [1895] cost of medicines for this large Indian agency of 3,782 Kiowas, Comanches, Kiowa-Apaches, Wichitas, and Caddos, along with 95 employees and their families, cost $1,225.40.[12] There is no record of the cost of the time spent completing the numerous forms necessary to "expedite" the shipments, but it must have been considerable.

Civilian authorities had the right to order that vaccinations be given to reservation Indians, as Commissioner Browning did in a letter to Lieutenant Maury Nichols, the acting Indian agent at the Kiowa Agency, on February 8, 1894. Charles R. Hume was the physician in charge who "endorsed" the contents of this letter on February 14 and began a vaccination program against smallpox shortly thereafter. Unlike officials connected with Indian service, who came and went with regularity, Dr. Hume remained at the agency for several years, and letters in his handwriting indicate the diversity of his responsibilities. In March 1897, for example, he investigated the sanitary conditions at an Anadarko, Oklahoma, hotel, not far from the boundary of the Kiowa Agency's territory. Dr. Hume reported to Major Frank D. Baldwin, the acting Indian agent at the time: "The beds I find to be in a very unsanitary condition. Most of the mattresses are old, dirty, and unfit for use while the bedding is sadly in need of washing, and etc. . . . The drainage from the kitchen is not good . . . everything about the house seems to be in a disorderly condition . . . all the guests at present are Mexicans who smoke and chew and in every other way pollute the atmosphere, so that it is unfit for a white man to endure." In May 1898, Dr. Hume again looked into sanitation problems, writing to Major W. T. Walker, the Indian agent, about the latrines at his Kiowa Agency, particularly the "closet located on the second floor of the administration building." Hume found the bathroom "connected by a leaky pipe with a blind cesspool on the north side of the building. The water supply is inadequate to properly flush it out at all times." In the doctor's opinion, "to preserve the sanitary condition of the building, this closet should be abandoned before further contamination results. Other letters reveal that smallpox was a threat in February 1899 when N. C. Tonner, the assistant commissioner of the Office of Indian Affairs, approved spending fifty dollars to purchase vaccine "if it should be needed by the Kiowa Agency."[13] Whether this episode was cyclical or was a continuation of the 1894 epidemic is unknown. Smallpox can and does occur and recur periodically.

In March 1899, Dr. Hume felt an obligation to intervene and comment on the quality of health care being provided by the military to his neighbors, the prisoners of war at Fort Sill. The physician sent a notarized letter to Walker complaining about the lack of a medical officer there to treat the Chiricahua Apache children. His letter is terse, and the fact that he had it notarized suggests that problems in communication or misunderstandings had occurred earlier. Indications are that Dr. Hume himself felt put upon because his caseload was so large: nearly four thousand Indians at the Kiowa Agency plus the Chiricahua Apache children attending school at Fort Sill. "These children are well known to be particularly susceptible to tubercular trouble and sore eyes . . . four years ago . . . they introduced an epidemic of mumps," he wrote, referring to their arrival at Fort Sill in 1894. Although this letter does not specifically request assistance, its tone is one of exasperation and exhaustion, and it is fair to assume that Dr. Hume, like many physicians who treated the Apaches before him, had asked for help and been denied. Although the consequences of this correspondence are not clear, the doctor took time off shortly after sending the notarized letter and was replaced quickly by another physician, F. Shoemaker.[14] This same situation had occurred in the past in Alabama when Walter Reed, overwhelmed by the medical needs of so many patients, had to leave his post for his own well-being.

Dr. Shoemaker immediately began by visiting an ailing agency Indian family named Meeks. He "found one child, three years of age, suffering with measles, one woman convalescing from measles. . . . In the case of the child there is a tendency to lung complication which makes it unsafe to expose it for several days." Along with treating the sick, making home visits, and meeting personal obligations, Dr. Shoemaker also prepared sanitation reports. For the quarter ending June 30, 1899, he wrote about a severe epidemic of measles in the Kiowa Agency followed by pulmonary complications and

sequelae which resulted in a large mortality among the camp Indians. This mortality from pneumonia and tuberculosis following measles was largely augmented by the fact that in every instance in which it was possible they [the Indians on the reservation] ignored proper treatment until it was too late to save their lives, and first employed their Indian Medicine Men, who are absolutely ignorant of all laws of health and medical treatment. These Medicine Men are quite numerous among the Comanche Indians and, having a strong influence among their people, they are a tremendous detriment to them.

In August 1899, typhoid fever swept through the Kiowa Agency and the immediate vicinity of the Fort Sill military reserve. Impure water was thought to be the cause, and the only remedy was to clean the wells and tanks. Another deadly medical problem, an increased incidence of smallpox, was related, according to Dr. Shoemaker, to the pharmaceutical firm Parke, Davis, and Company, which sent ineffective vaccine against smallpox to the agency. "I am convinced," wrote Dr. Shoemaker, "that the material prepared by Parke, Davis, & Co. is useless. I have seen so many cases, some very ill and one now in the camps that I think will die, that were vaccinated with the tubes and apparently successfully, but without protection." [15]

Dr. Hume was heard from again in the summer of 1900 when he was issued blankets, mattresses, pillows, and tents to maintain a pesthouse for smallpox patients at the Kiowa Agency. It is not clear whether the need for the facility was connected to the ineffective vaccine shipped by the pharmaceutical company. Dr. Hume's records do not suggest a relationship, and he usually was forthright and candid in his letters. Dr. Hume declared in one report that "all articles of bedding, including tents, etc. used during this epidemic of small pox, were by my instructions destroyed by fire as a sanitary precaution." For the quarter ending that same day, June 30, 1900, Dr. Hume wrote a short sanitation report: "The results obtained from the vaccination for the prevention of small-pox and the use of quinine for the treatment of malarial fevers have done a great deal . . . the prevalence of tuberculosis continues without any abatement." [16]

Quanah Parker, a well-known Comanche chief then living on the reservation, wrote a letter to the Indian agent in March 1901. Chief Parker was worried about the outbreaks of smallpox and measles within his tribe, and his letter states that measles had killed a dozen people in the recent past. He had given serious thought to a remedy and was writing to suggest that "if the clothing and bedding and everything that the sick one touches is burned or destroyed, the disease can be avoided to a certain extent" (sanitization procedures that had long been a cultural custom among traditional Chiricahua Apaches). Anticipating the worst, however, the chief went on, "There is a place direct north of Harris & Jas. store, which I want to reserve for a graveyard. Several Indians are buried there already. I spoke to Farmer Igamo about it." Two weeks or so later, the farmer visited Quanah's home to pay a sick call. In a letter to the Indian agent, Igamo wrote, "To-ni-cy is getting over the small-pox and resting well. Quanah keeps her in her room and uses olive-oil on her aflicted [sic] parts." Two days later, Igamo wrote another letter to the same individual, saying, "I was at Quanah's place this morning and find that they are getting along very well. The sick one is improving." [17]

Smallpox was so prevalent among Indian people during the early years of the 1900s that Commissioner of Indian Affairs W. A. Jones thought it wise to issue written directions to all Indian agents. After explaining that it had "only been customary to resort to vaccination when there was some immediate danger of infection," Jones instructed his employees to "direct the [civilian] physician . . . to vaccinate every person on your reservation. Employes [sic] and employes' children must also be vaccinated." And then, in a statement that indicates a prior problem with resistance from the Native Americans, Jones wrote,

The wishes of the Indians should not be considered in this matter. Any objections they may have to the procedure should be overcome by showing them the great need of vaccination and great protection it affords against the disease as to liability to contracting it as well as against death. If these means are found unsuccessful you should try some other method and finally if it becomes necessary, confinement in the guard house or force should be used. These plans for the protection of health and life of these

Indians and of the large white communities surrounding them should not be thwarted through the ignorance or prejudice of a few old Indians.[18]

Thus, the tough-sounding Department of the Interior forced the Indians under its jurisdiction to be vaccinated. The War Department, which was supervising the Apaches, was less emphatic.

Since there were nearly four thousand Kiowas, Comanches, Kiowa-Apaches, Wichitas, and Caddos living at the Kiowa Agency and only one physician, inoculating everyone required a massive effort. Although it took quite some time, the task was accomplished, and medical care subsequently reverted back from prevention by vaccination to an as-needed basis for all ailments.

Problems with sanitation at the agency and in the surrounding towns continued to cause contamination, infection, and illness, especially for women on the reservation, who routinely gave birth in filthy surroundings. The entire situation became so critical, not only at the Kiowa Agency but in all of Indian country, that C. F. Hauke, the acting commissioner of Indian affairs, issued an instruction in late 1912 to all superintendents, stating that "an earnest effort should be made to improve the method of disposal of excreta in Indian country . . . a privy should be constructed for actual use and demonstration purposes. The premises of the field matron, farmer, or day school are suitable places on which to install these. . . . Progressive Indians should be induced to construct sanitary privies in accordance with your directions."[19] In the meantime, diseases such as measles, smallpox, diphtheria, typhoid fever, tuberculosis, malaria, and trachoma were so entrenched in the general Native American population living on the reservations around Fort Sill that erecting a hospital became imperative.

Correspondence about the need for a medical facility to serve the Kiowa Agency had begun in earnest several years earlier, but little progress had been made. One letter between concerned parties referred to the Chiricahua Apaches: "I desire to call attention to the fact that when the Apache Indian Prisoners of War (305 in number) were transferred to Fort Sill, Oklahoma in 1894, the War Department at once provided a suitable hospital for their use. Our Indian population at present amounts to 3992."[20] It is clear that competition for scarce resources in Indian country was occurring, and the

Chiricahua Apaches were definitely a factor to be considered when federal appropriations were made.

❊ ❊ Starting Anew: The Early Years at Fort Sill

Comparisons concerning treatment facilities, while perhaps relevant from a tribal point of view, fail to consider the medical devastation of the Apaches prior to reaching Fort Sill. The military's census for early October 1894 enumerates 259 persons remaining from the original 519 Chiricahuas. This astounding figure reflects a situation experienced by no other Native American group in our nation's history. Nearly 50 percent of the original Apache group had died in eight years.

On a much more mundane, albeit significant, level, the logistics and environmental circumstances of the move to Fort Sill were also unique. A confidential telegram ordered that "any . . . useful material from their houses, the Indian hospital, and the Indian barrack building, that may be no longer required, will be collected, packed, and shipped by the Quartermaster's Department."[21] On the surface this may not appear to be very dramatic, but almost everything usable was made ready for the journey, including doors, window sashes, garden tools, several hundred pounds of clothing, stoves, and the log walls that formed the exteriors of the Apache homes.

As on earlier railroad journeys, the government exploited the prisoners as tourist attractions, designing the route so as to provide citizens with trackside views. The public was informed that the Apaches would take the Southern Pacific Railroad to Houston, the Texas Central to Fort Worth, and then the Rock Island to the end of the line at Rush Springs, Oklahoma.[22] From there they would walk or be carted to Fort Sill, twenty-eight miles away.

The prisoners occupied ten passenger cars, and their baggage was contained in two. A separate trainload of real property was also on its way to Fort Sill. "When moving them from [Mount Vernon] to Oklahoma, they dismantled the second village and loaded it on a train to take to Oklahoma with them. Two hundred cabins. But for some reason it went to New Orleans and the train [carrying the property] was put on a side track. It burned, the village burned. When they got to Fort Sill, they were back in tents."[23] That is not all

Prisoners of war in front of a wickiup on the Fort Sill grounds. From left: Arthur Guydelkon, John Loco, Eustace Fatty, Richard Olsanny, and an unidentified boy. Note the clothing of the men and the dramatic contrast with their living quarters. (Frisco Native American Museum)

of the story. A communication on United States Treasury Department letterhead, dated four years after the transfer, infers that only some of the homes at Mount Vernon were dismantled and loaded onto that ill-fated train. Others remained standing and vacant in the Apache camp. Even though they served no purpose where they were, none had been taken down and shipped to Oklahoma to replace the houses lost in the Louisiana fire. "Those of the Indian houses [at Mount Vernon] which are habitable should rent at $1.50 [per month] each," a letter written to the governor of Alabama stated.[24] While the bureaucracy was still deciding what to do with the Alabama holdings, the Chiricahuas had been settled at Fort Sill for four years and were starting over.

Escorted by the Chiricahua soldiers from Company I, Twelfth Infantry, under the command of Lieutenants Allyn Capron of the

Fifth Infantry and W. Ballou of the Twelfth Infantry, they detrained as planned at Rush Springs. Waiting there to greet them were military personnel who had been specifically assigned certain duties for the occasion. "My grandfather [Loco] told me . . . two things impressed them most: the great pots of food with the Army cooks busy around them and the long lines of Army wagons upon which the people rode to Fort Sill where they were greeted by the Comanches and Kiowas," Raymond Loco recalled.[25] While the wagons served a welcome purpose at the time, the Apaches hated them because they reminded them of coffins, with which they had become too familiar during their stay at Mount Vernon. Said Loco, referring to the alterations made in the wooden conveyances in later years, "Since the Apaches were superstitious of death, they would take the box section off the springs, and ride on the frame."[26]

First, however, basic adjustments at the new location had to be made. Due to the unexpected loss of their Alabama homes, the first winter in Oklahoma, an unusually harsh one, was spent out-of-doors in hastily constructed wickiups made of branches, boards, and tarps provided by the military. Even so, early medical reports indicate that the change from the endless dampness of Florida and Alabama was beneficial.

Charles LeBaron, a private physician from Mobile, accompanied the group to Oklahoma. The day after he arrived, the doctor wrote the first report of the Apaches' health at Fort Sill to the officer in charge of the prisoners, Lieutenant Hugh L. Scott:

There are now in camp the following diseases and disabilities:
> *Tuberculosis*
>> Phthisis Pulmonalis, 6
>> Hip joint disease, 1
>> Lupus, 2
>> Glandular tuberculosis, 1
> *Malaria*
>> Malarial Cachexia, 1
>> Quotidian fever, 2
> *Paralysis*, 1
> *Venereal diseases*
>> Gonorrhoea (male 1, female 1), 2
>> Syphilis (male 1, female 1), 2

Rheumatism
    Dyspepsia, 1
    Indigestion, 1
    Arthritis (chronic), 1
    Conjunctivitis, 1
Injuries
    Sprains, 1
    Sore foot, 1
    Bites (human), 2

Dr. LeBaron noted "only one new case of sickness developed on the trip and this was due to imprudent eating. The sick stood the trip exceedingly well—one birth occurred on the train while passing through Texas (mother and child well)."[27]

On November 1, Ballou wrote a general report to Scott in which he stated, "Vital statistics show no increase of phthisis and most cases of long standing seems [sic] to be held somewhat in abeyance. In my opinion . . . brush arbors that these people so skillfully construct, are far more conductive [sic] to health than houses are—One reason for this is the extreme difficulty met in the attempt to have houses kept ventilated and a second may be found in the fact that the 'vick-i-up' can be burned once a month and its site thoroughly disinfected." Ballou devoted a major portion of his report to one main recommendation—keeping liquor away from the Apaches. He concluded with a census report:

On the rolls (October 1st 1894)
    17 men
    126 women
    70 boys
    46 girls
    Total 259
Born in Oct.
    1 boy
    2 girls
    Total 3
Died in Oct.
    1 girl
On rolls Oct. 31
    17 men

126 women

71 boys

47 girls

Total 261

A medical update submitted by the post surgeon, Fitzhugh Carter, on November 8, 1894, lists seventy-one cases of illness he treated in the first month of incarceration, much of which reflects LeBaron's prior report:

Number	Diagnosis
10	Malarial fever
10	Catarrh, nasal
9	Diarrhea
5	Catarrh, bronchial
5	Scrofula
4	Injuries
4	Phthisis-Pul.
4	Conjunctivitis
4	Rheumatism
3	Abscess
3	Indigestion
2	Lupus
2	Tooth Ache
2	Syphilis
1	Vulvitis
1	Tub. Hip Disease
1	Paralysis
1	Gonorrhea

In his notes Dr. Carter remarked, "A large per centage of the cases are ordinary 'bad colds' (classified as nasal and bronchial catarrh). These have been due probably to the exposure incident to establishing them in camp. The cases of nasal and bronchial catarrh have been confined almost entirely to the younger children."[28]

Because it was important to the army that the Apaches get settled at Fort Sill before winter, George Wratten was asked by the military to provide a list of headmen who could be assigned to separate living arrangements. Each would then take his followers and develop a campsite apart from others, thus imitating, within certain limits, conditions experienced during the days of freedom. Wratten identified the principal leaders, who were then assigned individual sites as follows:

Geronimo: East side of Cache Creek.
Martine: A few hundred yards north of Geronimo.
Perico: A mile south of Geronimo between Cache Creek and Beef Creek. The sawmill, to be used later by the Apaches, was also here.
Chihuahua: A low ridge a little over a mile north of the Old Post.
Noche: Near north boundary, half mile west of Frisco Railroad.
Kaahtenny: Near twin lakes, northwest of Medicine Bluff.
Mangas: Near Wolf Creek.
Toclanny: West of Wolf Creek.
Loco: Near Four Mile Crossing, north of Heyl's Hole.
Naiche: South of Four Mile Crossing.
Chatto: Half a mile west of Four Mile Crossing.
Tom Chiricahua: A mile west of Loco's village.[29]

In these places on the immense military reserve the Apaches rebuilt their lives along with homes made of timber they cut when spring 1895 arrived. Congressional action had resulted in an appropriation to purchase cattle and needed farm implements, so the men not kept busy constructing living quarters were not idle. The children were immediately placed into education facilities, with some attending school in Anadarko, about thirty miles north of the post, and others receiving instruction on the Fort Sill grounds. Eight had been sent from Mount Vernon to be educated at the Normal Institute in Hampton, Virginia, and were suffering the same fate—tuberculosis—as those still in school at Carlisle.

The corresponding secretary of the Boston Indian Citizenship Committee, which was still actively monitoring the government's treatment of the Chiricahuas, wrote to Secretary of War Lamont in February 1895 about some of the children at Hampton. "I am sorry to report," the letter states, "that one of the children is dying of consumption developed by the change of climate, and that two others, Josephine Behado and Vincent Bazine, are pronounced . . . to be too weak in the lungs to remain in safety so far north."[30] No matter

Kaahteny's village on Medicine Bluff Creek, Fort Sill, with storehouse for agricultural implements, ca. 1897. Each house had two rooms connected by a roof, with a breezeway between. (Fort Sill Museum)

where the children went to school, it seemed, they were destined to become ill.

George Wratten was also writing letters, particularly regarding the children at Carlisle. On behalf of the prisoners of war, he addressed Hugh Scott, who had been promoted to captain in 1895, stating that "very earnestly and respectfully they beg that these children be returned to them: Dexter Loco, Rachel Tsi-ta-da, Mabel Nah-rado-kieh, Duncan Balatchu, Oliver Bitchait, Clement Seanilzhay, Naomi Kohten, Dora Chaendee, Lambert Istone, Paul Tee-na-be-kigen, Clay Domieh, Vincent Nah-tail-eh."

Pleading, Wratten described the old men and women, at long last to have homes and livestock of their own, but now too enfeebled to care for this property. To a person, they were counting on their children for assistance. "They are all unable to work," stated the interpreter, "and if their sons and daughters are not returned to them to help them, they will stand a poor chance indeed in the battle for life with the younger and consequently stronger men and women of the tribe. Some of them are very old and have none but these children to depend upon for work. In the case of some of the mothers, it is especially so, as they are entirely alone here, all of their children being at school." Wratten concluded in a passionate tone, "With earnest entreaties, and every prayer that an Indian can utter, they beg of you to do all in your power to have their children returned to them."[31] As this request made its way through military channels, it was given favorable consideration by Scott and subsequently was approved by Lieutenant Colonel E. R. Kellogg, the post commander. A copy was transmitted to the Interior Department on August 6, 1895, but the War Department, also involved in the request, made no recommendation. Eventually these children were released from school and joined their families, for records show that on November 27, 1895, Scott reported receiving five girls and fourteen boys from the Carlisle School.

Amid his many other projects, Scott had time to develop standards by which he hoped to discourage diseases in the separate Apache villages. The manual he prepared contains the following instructions: "The houses . . . and water supply of the Apaches should be frequently inspected—kept in a sanitary condition, the houses fumigated with formaldehyde gas at least once every quarter for tuberculosis germs and the walls whitewashed with . . . sulphuric acid."[32]

On November 1, 1895, J. D. Glennan, the assistant surgeon who provided medical care to the prisoners, wrote a year-end report to the surgeon general. Tables attached as exhibits list the Apaches' ailments according to categories; for example, injuries, infectious diseases, nervous diseases, diseases of the digestive and respiratory systems, genitourinary diseases, diseases of muscles and bones and joints, diseases of the integument (skin), and diseases of the eyes and ears. Six hundred and fifty-five individuals were treated during the year, of which the majority (349) were children; 178 were women, and 128 were men. Below is a summary of the prevailing ailments in selected categories:

> *Injuries*
>> Contusions, 11
> *Infectious diseases*
>> Parotitis (mumps), 55
>> Intermittent fever, quotidian, 47
>> Intermittent fever, tertian, 11

Phthisis pulmonalis, 16
Scrofula, 21
Diseases of the digestive system
Acute indigestion, 37
Constipation, 37
Acute diarrhea, 57
Diseases of the respiratory system
Acute bronchial catarrh, 61
Diseases of the muscles, bones, and joints
Muscular rheumatism, 23
Diseases of the integument
Ulcer, acute, 15
Diseases of the Eye
Acute conjunctivitis, 87

In explaining the figures, Dr. Glennan did not address the incidence of malarial fevers, but he commented on several other afflictions. The digestive disorders, he wrote, were the result of "improper diet and exposure," and eye problems were very common due to "the [prisoners'] manner of living. The conjunctivitis very often seems to be contagious, due possibly to an attenuated gonorrheal virus . . . no case has gone on to the condition of chronic disease and blindness as frequently seen among the Kiowas and Comanches." Of the 55 cases of mumps, "44 were adults, an unusual proportion," Glennan concluded.

"During the year," he added, "twelve children were born and thirteen died. The causes of this mortality are such as obtain among all Indians—bad and improper food and exposure—added to the tubercular infection common among the Apaches. . . . The principal cause of the death rate, and of the diminishing numbers" of all the prisoners, "has been tubercular diseases." Dr. Glennan cited the positive attributes keeping illnesses among the Apache at bay: "They have lived under canvas, and during the greater part of the year, the camp has been on a hill, open to plenty of air and sunshine, well policed, and, as far as possible, cases of phthisis have been isolated and disinfection of sputa practiced."

The physician developed a table describing deaths from tubercular diseases during the years of incarceration (see Table 6). Dr. Glennan commented,

TABLE 6. *Deaths from Tubercular Diseases among the Chiricahua Apaches during Incarceration (based on a report by J. D. Glennan, November 1, 1895).*

Year	Deaths	Rate per 1,000
1887–88	11	30.05
1888–89	4	10.30
1889–90	18	45.92
1890–91	18	48.52
1891–92	27	65.85
1892–93	(not compiled as of report date)	
1893–94	(not compiled as of report date)	
1894–9/95	17	56.47
1895–7/96	4	16.28 (added later)
1895–9/96	6	19.48 (added later)

Many cases of pulmonary tuberculosis do not seem to be originating here. As far as can be determined, only two cases have been under treatment, which were not treated before being removed to this post. Records of cases of pulmonary and laryngeal tuberculosis show that twelve prisoners [ten women and two children] arrived ill with the disease from Mount Vernon, three males were transferred from the Carlisle School in advanced stages of tuberculosis, and two cases were newly diagnosed at Fort Sill. Of these seventeen, ten died and seven were still living at the time of this report.

The practice which prevails at the Carlyle [*sic*] School of retaining students there until in an advanced stage of pulmonary disease, and then sending them back to their people is a bad one. If these cases could be returned to the open air life and dry atmosphere of the western country in the first stage of the disease, many of them would recover. As it is, they return when there is no hope of recovery, only to become a source of infection to their people. Some of them are kept so long that they may not reach their reservations alive. I have seen a boy from Carlyle, dying from phthisis, compelled to travel in a day car until unconscious, and then twenty-eight miles in a stage, kept up under stimulants by the doctor in charge, in an effort to get him on his reservation before death—which was accomplished by a few hours. This is bad in every way. If this school cannot be removed to a climate suitable and natural to the Indian, the students who become infected there, should, at least, be given a chance for life by a prompt return to the western country.

Despite Glennan's strong statements, no changes were made in the status quo regarding the children already attending Carlisle. It is necessary to point out, however, that those youngsters who came of age to be schooled while the Apaches were at Fort Sill attended classes in nearby Anadarko and at a school on the military reserve.

More of Dr. Glennan's computations show the total death rates per one thousand for all diseases during the years 1887–96 as follows:

Year	Total ratio per 1,000
1887–88	54.64
1888–89	48.96
1889–90	109.69
1890–91	142.84
1891–92	109.75
1892–93	80.93
1893–94	98.36
1894–9/95	83.05
1895–7/96	65.14 (added later)
1895–9/96	74.67 (added later)

Information regarding the earlier years was copied from reports issued at Mount Vernon by Dr. W. C. Borden, and then longitudinally expanded to include later years. Dr. Glennan attributed the fall of the death rate between 1892 and 1893 to "sanitary measures inaugurated over two years before."

The birth and death rates for the Chiricahuas' first year at Fort Sill were similarly displayed in a table, as were the causes of death during the same period (see Tables 7 and 8).

Dr. Glennan's report concludes with a positive statement: "I think that their condition already shows the wisdom and humanity of their removal to this territory."[33] The report was excerpted by the surgeon general, George M. Sternburg, and sent on December 11, 1895, to the adjutant general of the army.

TABLE 7. *Birth and Death Rates for Chiricahua Apaches at Fort Sill, Oklahoma (based on a report by J. D. Glennan, November 1, 1895).*

| Date | Born | Number of deaths | | | |
		Men	Women	Children	Total
October 1894	3	—	—	1	1
November 1894	1	—	2	2	4
December 1894	1	—	—	—	—
January 1895	2	1 [a]	—	1	2
February 1895	1	—	—	4	4
March 1895	1	—	2	—	2
April 1895	—	—	2	1	3
May 1895	1	—	2	1	3
June 1895	—	2 [b]	—	—	2
July 1895	—	—	—	—	—
August 1895	1	—	1	1	2
September 1895	1	—	—	2	2
Total	12	3	9	13	25

[a]Student returned from Carlisle School with advanced phthisis.
[b]One a returned Carlisle student.

The need for a burial site was addressed by Scott, who designated a site along Beef Creek, not too far from what would become Geronimo's campsite. In time, some of the Apaches refused to be buried there, including members of the Naiche family, who were instead interred on Signal Mountain. Other Chiricahuas were buried around Twin Lakes, near Medicine Bluff. Initially, the shortage of coffins was offset by the availability of packing boxes and ammunition crates, both of which were abhorred by the Chiricahuas but were utilized until permission to construct more suitable caskets could be obtained.[34]

One year after their incarceration began in Oklahoma, the healthy male prisoners were working the land, running cattle, and growing crops. Prior to this time they'd had no horses, so much of the farm and ranch work was done on foot across nearly seventy thou-

TABLE 8. *Causes of Death in Chiricahua Apaches at Fort Sill, Oklahoma (based on a report by J. D. Glennan, November 1, 1895).*

	Number of deaths			
Diagnosis	Men	Women	Children	Total
Phthisis pulmonalis	2[a]	6	1	9
General tuberculosis	—	—	6	6
Abdominal tuberculosis	—	—	1	1
Laryngeal phthisis	1	—	—	1
Capillary bronchitis	—	—	2	2
Spinal meningitis	—	—	2	2
Chronic diarrhea	—	1	—	1
Secondary syphilis	—	1	—	1
Senile debility	—	1	—	1
Congenital debility	—	—	1	1
Total	3	9	13	25

[a]Carlisle students returned with phthisis in advanced stage.

sand acres. The men's health improved; they regained strength and developed increased resistance to many of the ailments that were affecting their wives and children. However, tuberculosis remained entrenched so deeply among a significant number of the community that not even the outdoors and the return of a portion of their physical prowess a year after leaving Alabama could offset the disastrous consequences of the disease.

By this time everyone had moved out of the wickiups and into a dozen separate villages, totaling sixty-seven permanent log and plank homes built by the Apaches, who first cut and hauled the timber, then shaped it in a sawmill. Additionally, the men were cutting fence poles, digging postholes, and stretching fence wire. After that they constructed reservoirs where the cattle could drink and dug and built earthen dams.

Illnesses were reported to the military by each settlement's headman, after which the patient was examined and hospitalized if necessary in the Apache hospital, a facility specifically erected to care

Chiricahua Apache prisoner-of-war baseball team at Fort Sill. Top row, second from left, James Kaywaykla. Middle row, far left, Sam Kenoi. Front row, left, Sam Haozous; right, Arthur Guydelkon. Chiricahua men were natural athletes and loved baseball, especially when their team beat the soldiers' team. (Frisco Native American Museum)

for the many sick Chiricahuas . . . if they would use it. Initially, there was some reluctance, but Lieutenant Allyn Capron stated to the adjutant general that "these Indians depend nearly as much upon the hospital and doctor, as do whites. Their old way of 'drawing out the devil that caused the illness' by means of Indian medicine—a concoction of herbs gathered from the woods, the use of which almost invariably resulted in death from narcotic poisoning has been generally given up and they now think that the white man's medicine is 'heap good.'"[35] That was a misstatement, or Capron's wishful thinking. Two years after that officer's declaration, Apaches were still dying from lethal plant medicines. For example, in 1898 Chief Naiche's son Paul perished from poisonous substances he ingested while attending a Comanche ritual held on the Fort Sill grounds.

Before that time, though, twenty-two Apaches had died in the first year of incarceration at Fort Sill. Of these, only three died in

Prisoners of war at Fort Sill. Standing, from left: Casper Cailis, James Kaywaykla, James Nicholas, Lawrence Mithlo, Regis Alchintoyeh, Benedict Jozhe, Sr., John Loco, David Chinney (partially obscured). Front row, from left: Albert Seeltoe, Richard Imach, Walter Louie, Watson Mithlo. Lower right: Daniel Nicholas. These men appear to have been working on a hay wagon. (Frisco Native American Museum)

the hospital. Others, according to Scott, "died in their villages without civilized care or medical attendance." At the turn of the year, in January 1897, the hospital was enlarged by three rooms to accommodate the increasing number of patients. The facility was under the control of the post surgeon, a man "who is not entirely in sympathy with the Indians," Scott reported, adding that the doctor had "little time for the Indians."[36] In the same document Scott warned the adjutant general about the developing serious problem of liquor being sold to the Apaches by unscrupulous white men permitted to come onto the military reserve.

The general health of the 299 prisoners was worsening and was, according to Capron, caused by "contact with civilization" and the fact that "these people are so thoroughly saturated with the germs of consumption and scrofula and are so closely intermarried that nothing can save them."[37] Healthy Apaches, however, continued to

Chiricahua Apache prisoner-of-war hospital, Fort Sill, ca. 1905. Ailing Apaches were not treated in Army medical facilities, which were reserved for sick soldiers, their families, and civilians who worked at the post. Thus, the need for a special facility arose and this hospital was erected. (Fort Sill Museum)

run cows and work the land, growing hay and kafir corn. When the herd was of sufficient size, the industrious Chiricahuas sold beef to the military and began to believe they could create a future. The new confidence in their abilities led to a rising incidence of illness in 1899 when an unnamed shaman quietly began urging the prisoners to resist efforts at acculturation. "His appeal was made stronger by his claim that he could cure tuberculosis . . . through the participation of his patients in the Fire Dance. The Chiricahuas believed him and the dances were held more frequently, especially during winter months when the rate of sickness intensified. Masks were used interchangeably by the participants, so many more Apaches died from pneumonia, or tuberculosis," reported William Grosvenor III,[38] a result totally contrary to the purpose of the ceremony and completely disputing the shaman's claim. The dances, an important cultural custom and one of the traits that defines the Apache people, had to be suspended. But still the dying didn't stop.

Geronimo on the grounds of Fort Sill, most likely with members of the Oklahoma National Guard as his escorts. Note his medicine hat, which he wore on special occasions. (H. Henrietta Stockel)

In June 1902, the total number of prisoners of war had decreased to 263. Twenty-two had died in the previous year, while only ten births had occurred. Yet, Scott declared he was pleased with the "low" death rate and attributed it to the fact that the Apaches had been "prohibited from having dances in cold and inclement weather during the past year. Some of their dances . . . were noticed to be followed by episodes of cold and pneumonia and there has been noticeably less of these diseases during the year just passed." A number of infants had died "with intestinal troubles during hot weather of last summer. The Indian women cannot be prevented from feeding their babies condensed milk undiluted and in too large quantities and it is frequently fatal,"[39] he reported.

As ailments continued to ravage the small band, other aspects of their traditional lifeways in the outdoors grew in importance. And some of these pleasures were contradictory. While Eugene Chihuahua thought one of the best things about being at Fort Sill was listening to the cries of the wild animals, and especially to "hear the coyotes sing,"[40] ancient Apache beliefs held that any contact with a coyote, wolf, or fox would cause illness. But should an Apache come across one of these animals during the incarceration at Fort Sill, cultural healing ceremonies to offset the harmful effects of the encounter could be held. The army had no objections as long as the observance did not include any practices that might spread germs. Angie Debo recorded a ritual in which Geronimo, the old shaman, was called upon to cure coyote sickness. "This ceremony was held in an arbor outside Geronimo's house as soon as darkness fell." Geronimo faced east and had the patient in front of him. The man's relatives were in the background, sitting in a semicircle behind the arbor shelter. "In front of Geronimo was a basket tray, holding an eagle feather, an abalone shell, and a bag of pollen." Geronimo started the ceremony by smoking a cigarette he rolled himself and sending the smoke toward each of the four directions. Then he rubbed certain parts of the patient's body with the pollen, praying to the north, south, east, and west at the same time. "Each of his prayers referred to Coyote." Then the famous healer sang and beat his drum with the traditional curved stick of the Chiricahuas. His songs praised Coyote and asked his help in healing the patient before him. Geronimo continued singing each night for four nights, every ceremony a repetition of the one before.

Another of Geronimo's patients was an old woman who had chased a wolf. When the wolf ran into a hole, the woman seized its leg to pull it out. "Then she became violently ill, with her body shaking, her lips twisted, her eyes crossed. Geronimo sang over her and cured her," said Debo, adding, "There is another case of his treating a patient for ghost sickness."[41]

✳ ✳ ✳ Medical Maladies, 1903–1912

But while traditional and scientific medical treatments continued side by side at Fort Sill, so did the unrelenting sickness and death. In the last three months of 1903, for example, 208 prisoners received medical attention for ailments such as malaria, bronchitis, gastritis, and scrofula. Frank Mangus, son of the leader Mangus, died from pulmonary tuberculosis on October 13, 1903, at the age of twenty-seven, just one of many deaths that year from the same ailment. In December, fifty-five cases of scabies[42] developed among

TABLE 9. *Diseases among Civilians and Apaches at Fort Sill, Oklahoma, 1904.*

Ailment	Number of civilians	Number of Apaches
Diphtheria	2	0
Pneumonia	1	2
Catarrh, postnasal	2	0
Bronchitis, acute	1	0
Whooping cough	6	0
Tonsillitis	1	0
Malarial fevers	2	19

the military community and Apaches at Fort Sill, probably the result of soldiers bringing back the infection from a march from Fort Riley, Kansas, in which they occupied campgrounds formerly used by a circus troupe. The cases were all isolated, and the bedding, rooms, and Indian homes fumigated. The Apaches were given sulfur ointment to rub into their oozing sores.

During the first quarter of 1904, scabies continued to be a major complaint, along with malaria, gastritis, constipation, and bronchitis. Keratitis, an inflammation of the cornea of the eye, appeared among the prisoners. Geronimo's wife, thirty-five-year-old Zi-yeh, died of unknown causes in March. Twenty Chiricahua Apaches were hospitalized for various ailments at the end of the same month. During the next three months five more Chiricahuas died from tubercular ailments.

In April, the major ailments treated were malarial fevers, bronchitis, constipation, and scabies. In May, the census was the year's lowest, 218, and malarial fevers continued to be the main complaint, followed by constipation and bronchitis. These ailments plagued the Apaches all through the summer of 1904. In August, baby Rose Chihuahua, the one-year-old daughter of the chief, died from gastroenteritis, and over the next three months approximately fifty prisoners were treated for the same sickness. Malaria and bouts of influenza also sent patients to the doctor for treatment.

A comparison of diseases among the civilians on the post and the Chiricahuas in December 1904 is shown in Table 9.

In the early months of 1905, tuberculosis, malaria, bronchitis, gastroenteritis, constipation, and scabies persisted, joined by pneumonia. The sanitation report for March 1905 mentions "tubercular conditions and occasional outbreaks of scabies among the Apache prisoners of war."[43] Throughout spring and summer, adenitis (swollen glands) infected the villages and added to the miseries caused by the other illnesses. The sanitation report for September states, "Tubercular and skin troubles continue to prevail among the Chiricahua Apache prisoners of war. Pools are oiled weekly and drained where practicable"[44] as a means of keeping the mosquito population under control. No mention is made of the increasing number of patients with malarial fevers. At the end of 1905, many causes of deaths were undetermined, but among those with a clear diagnosis, tuberculosis prevailed.

Conjunctivitis and measles appeared in force in early 1906, the same year a massive undertaking to vaccinate the prisoners against smallpox was accomplished. Although tuberculosis was still the main cause of death, malaria was the major complaint among the Apaches. (Within the ranks of the troops, the predominant ailment in the latter half of the year was syphilis. In warmer weather the soldiers had been on a march to Anadarko, thirty miles away, where, it was determined, they all contracted the venereal disease from one woman!)

Mosquitoes and malaria became a huge problem, and desperate military recommendations were totally inadequate: fill in the sloughs at the rear of the hospital.[45] In August, W. T. Woodall, the assistant surgeon at Fort Sill, recommended that all trenches and depressions be corrected, that all fire buckets be refilled at least once a week and oiled twice as often because numerous mosquito larvae were found in them. All toilets in unoccupied and unused buildings were to have their water traps covered with oil twice a week, and all open vessels and reservoirs were to be emptied of any water or carefully oiled. Earlier, in April and May, Dr. Woodall had complained about the mosquitoes and the useless twelve-gauge mesh screens. Although he requested eighteen-gauge mesh for the soldiers and the Apache prisoners of war, it would not be provided in the near future.

Woodall was eventually replaced by another physician, W. F.

Lewis, who in the first quarter of 1908 faced the same problems with mosquitoes. He ordered all drainage of standing water to be stopped and directed that crude oil be spread on all waterholes to thwart the burgeoning malaria that was wreaking havoc among the Apaches. Another infectious disease of epidemic proportions, influenza, infected the villages in February, and many Chiricahuas were hospitalized, joined by quite a few relatives and friends suffering with mumps and its complications. Heavy spring and summer rains that year caused the creeks to rise and to leave standing water when they receded; again, mosquitoes were everywhere, and by August the screens for the doors and windows had still not arrived. Certain other conditions added to the general distress at the post: twenty-one troublesome Apache prisoners occupied a cell big enough for only ten, and Dr. Lewis, in a letter to the surgeon general, complained that the conditions in the guardhouse were disastrous to everyone's health. At the end of 1908, malaria was once again the predominant disease, according to military records, although the deaths continued to be attributed to tuberculosis.

In March 1909, the lack of adequate screening to protect against mosquitoes was still an issue; some Apache houses had no screens whatever because the older ones had deteriorated. During that year, influenza and typhoid fever were in the fort and the Apache villages, infecting both soldiers and Indians. In the nearby town of Lawton, thirty cases of typhoid fever were documented in July. The only precautions recommended to the Apaches were to air their bedding in the sun at least three hours daily. Twelve months later, the outbreak of typhoid fever had run its course, but officials were still puzzled about the source of the initial contamination. One culprit seriously considered, but never definitely determined, was ice cream sold in Lawton.

In spring and summer of 1910, measles came back again, causing several deaths among children, but pulmonary tuberculosis in patients of all ages was the major killer. Sanitation problems in the summer added to the medical woes, as did major sanitary defects at the post. The vegetable cellar's screen was badly torn, leaking scullery waste filled the cellar, the kitchen doors and the latrine had no screens, and because the garbage cans had no lids, they attracted dozens of flies.

Pneumonia took the lives of several children in the early winter months of 1911, and more adults were victims of tuberculosis. One man died from chronic diarrhea.

Antityphoid vaccinations were started among the Apache prisoners of war in January 1912 but, for unknown reasons, not completed. In February, instructions were issued by Major C. B. Robbins of the Medical Corps at Fort Sill regarding overturned garbage cans, an increasing health hazard at the post. Robbins recommended that "cow proof stands be provided . . . and arrangements be made to prevent the cattle belonging to the Apache Indians from continually roaming throughout the post, around the backs of barracks, and quarters, around the stables, and on the parade grounds, as they do now in the winter months in search of food." Screens were still requested but had not been received by July 1912. Pulmonary tuberculosis continued to be the main cause of death among adults and children.[46]

✳ ✳ ✳ Adjustment and Acculturation, 1904–1914

Against a background of sickness, death, and nearly insurmountable medical obstacles, Captain Farrand Sayre of the Eighth Cavalry succeeded Scott in the summer of 1900 as the officer in charge of the Apache prisoners of war. In August 1904 he wrote an optimistic report about the progress made through the previous fiscal year, which had ended in June. Some physical activities seemed to be going quite well, including farming, which had resulted in large supplies of kafir corn, Indian corn, and 700,000 pounds of hay. Several crops were raised, and the cattle herd had increased from 900 head in 1895 to more than 2,200. Horse and mule raising had begun, and the prisoners were able to purchase farm machinery with the proceeds from sales of beef, hay, and corn to the military.

For recreation, the healthy Apache men and boys had formed three baseball teams and a football team in previous years but hadn't had much success. Sayre reported, however, that in 1904, one of the baseball teams defeated all the troop teams.

But despite the rosier outlook, Sayre was worried about the prisoners' medical status from the very first. "These Indians have lost in numbers every year since they were taken into captivity until this year—but the records of the last five years show a constantly decreasing rate of loss," he wrote. New cases of tuberculosis had decreased, but Sayre was concerned about another possibility: whether the increasing presence of civilians on the reservation would expose the prisoners to alcohol. "On account of the Indians, greater precautions should be observed to prevent the introduction of intoxicating liquor on the reservation than are thought necessary at other posts," Sayre stated.[47] Anyone found selling or giving liquor to the prisoners was prosecuted and fined or sentenced. While these penalties served as deterrents in most cases, there were always a few unscrupulous peddlers willing to tempt the law. Invariably they lost, and alcohol was not readily available to the Apaches at Fort Sill.

Religion began to take hold among the prisoners of war during 1904–7, but not until the first missionary, the Reverend Frank Hall Wright (a Choctaw Indian) of the Reformed (Dutch) Church in America in Oklahoma, overcame the military's opposition.[48] After that, the church sent additional workers to Oklahoma and zealously began instructing the Chiricahuas in Christian ways of worship. The missionaries were extremely successful, and the church counted among its parishioners the leaders Naiche, Noche, Chatto, Jason Betzinez, Benedict Jozhe, James Kaywaykla, Sam Haozous, Quineh, Carlos Keanie, and John Loco. Interpreting was done by James Kaywaykla, a survivor of education at Carlisle, and Amy Imach, daughter of interpreter George Wratten and his Chiricahua wife.

A publication issued in 1906 by the Reformed Church in America describes the church's fieldwork, starting with land acquisition, which was "secured from the Government for a school house and whatever other buildings might be necessary to conduct an educational and religious work among the Apaches." According to church authorities, Rev. Wright and Miss Maud Adkisson won the confidence of the prisoners by the "earnest preaching of the Gospel story." They spent a summer in the villages "visiting the sick, winning the children, teaching the women," and "preparing the way for the work of the teachers." A Sunday school was started, prayer meetings were held, and Bible study was organized. Five buildings were eventually erected by the church for its mission work, and thirty to forty children attended school on the reservation in the church's facilities during the day. The orphanage, also located in the compound, was home to twenty-four children.

Rare photo of children as Mountain Spirit Dancers in Rogers Toklanni's group of dancers, probably at Fort Sill. (Frisco Native American Museum)

The same leaflet includes vignettes about four of the Apache children. Fourteen-year-old Maurice Chatto, son of the warrior and scout, was said to be in frail health and woefully neglected by his mother, who had "fallen into the sin of gambling." His younger brother, Blake Chatto, was so ill that he was unable to attend school, so Maurice taught him at home, reading to him from the Bible. The Chatto children, though, according to the author, had "not yet openly confessed Christ."

David Reno's parents were declared to be "two of the worst old gamblers and Sabbath breakers there are in the tribe. . . . When the two little brothers would come to school, so dirty and neglected that Miss Ewing had to ask that they would come cleaner another day, David would be missing from school the next forenoon," busy bathing his brothers and sisters and washing their clothes. David "united with the church two years ago, and judging by his life, he is an earnest Christian."

Harry Perico, whose father was one of Geronimo's warriors and an army scout, was described as "inclined to cling to the old Indian customs." Harry's mother (not named) "neglects her family and is a notorious gambler." At age twenty, Harry was "now the most promising, and the most progressive grown-up boy in the Apache tribe." After listing many of Harry's admirable qualities, the brief biography concludes by stating, "It is almost impossible to believe that he came out of this degraded home only a few years ago."[49]

The church's activities at Fort Sill were complemented by the Indian Rights Association's (IRA) efforts off the military reserve. Both agencies independently worked toward improving the lives of the prisoners of war, utilizing totally different methods. The IRA fulfilled its mission through political channels, applying the skills of its spokesman, S. M. Brosius, who lobbied in Washington on behalf of providing the prisoners of war with allotments of land that they could work to become self-supporting. Naturally, the plan required that the Chiricahuas be released from incarceration first. Although the IRA realized that the path toward freedom for the Apaches would be long and convoluted, Brosius's first endeavors were encouraging. Because of his influence and political clout, on February 16, 1910, a United States Senate Memorial urged that allotments of acreage be made available to the Chiricahuas and that they be freed. According to the memorial, there were 261 Chiricahuas at the time, "pleading that they may be liberated from bondage." Of these, "250 . . . have been deprived of their liberty for almost a generation without having committed, nor having been charged with committing, any offense against the United States . . . continued serfdom must result in greater despondency and hopelessness . . . the Indians are in a state of bondage."[50]

Brosius was successful, for on March 15, 1910, Senate Bill 6152 authorizing the allotments was introduced and approved by vote. The measure was sent to the House of Representatives, where it was "opposed by the representative from the district within which the military reservation is located. The political influence from the vicinity of the reservation and other forces are being exerted against the allotment of land, for the reason that it is hoped to build up a great military establishment at Fort Sill."[51] The bill failed to pass the House.

During the year that followed, the army investigated the feasi-

Last dance of the Mountain Spirits held at Fort Sill, ca. 1912–1913, before release of the prisoners of war in 1913–1914. Clown at left is Pete Toklanni; dancer is Rogers Toklanni; man on right (stooped over) is Binday, a medicine man. The dance was held near Loco's village at Four Mile Crossing. Binday died in May 1913 on the Mescalero Apache Reservation, the first prisoner of war to perish after their release. (Frisco Native American Museum)

bility of reintroducing the bill, this time with much more political support behind it. Colonel Hugh Scott led the research designed to determine the advantages of allotments at Fort Sill *and* on the Mescalero Reservation in south-central New Mexico. His findings: about 150 prisoners wanted to transfer as free people to Mescalero, and about 90 wanted to stay in Oklahoma and receive the acreage proposed. Scott recommended that legislation be drafted to move the larger group to New Mexico and that an appropriation of $100,000 be granted to fund the effort. He also suggested that when the Chiricahuas arrived at their destination on the Mescalero Reservation they be released from captivity. Oddly, Scott declared that those who decided to remain in Oklahoma would continue as prisoners of war, except for a few who "have trades, are sober, industrious, and are considered by the officer in charge as able to make their way among white men," and that allotments of land would be purchased for them. "If those others who elect to remain at Fort Sill hoping for allotment there, were to be treated in the same way" as those designated to receive special treatment, a report stated, "they would in all likelihood pawn or sell their property in the near future for drink . . . their best chance of survival is with the others who have elected to go with the Mescalero Apaches."[52]

The IRA was immediately critical of Scott's recommendations, especially his idea of releasing some prisoners but not others. The IRA's year-end report stated, "This is so palpably unjust . . . that it should be condemned as unworthy of serious consideration. . . . All friends of these Apache prisoners should petition that the portion of the band desiring to remain at Fort Sill should be allotted lands there and immediately thereafter be relieved as prisoners of war."[53] In the view of the IRA, Scott, once sympathetic to the plight of the Chiricahuas, had changed his mind and was now showing blatant bias.

There are various depictions of the events that occurred while determinations were being made regarding who would stay in Oklahoma and who would go to New Mexico. Turcheneske reported that of the ninety-three prisoners who wanted to remain, "only fourteen would be permitted to do so" because of criteria Scott had developed to apply to all those wishing to continue life in Oklahoma. Hendrina Hospers, a Reformed church missionary among the prisoners of war, told a church official on October 4, 1912, of the presence of a list of names. Fourteen Apaches who didn't gamble or drink and who could run a farm or make a living in the trades were offered a choice. All others *had* to leave for Mescalero. One, Mithlo, was not listed among the favored and wanted to know why. "Col. Scott gruffly told him he was worthless [and] not to say a word. Mithlo had set his heart on staying, is a good worker, [and] has been doing right. He is all broken up over it," Hospers stated. According to Turcheneske, "Not only was it apparent that . . . Scott did not intend to assist the Chiricahuas in attaining freedom, but, as [prisoner of war] Talbot Goody bitterly summed up . . . , there was only one way out—either remove to Mescalero and become free, or remain as prisoners of war at Fort Sill."[54]

After looking closely into the situation, Henry L. Stimson, the new secretary of war in President William H. Taft's administration, transmitted a report to the United States Senate regarding the Apache prisoners of war on March 13, 1912. This information, in response to Senate Resolution 232, dated February 26, 1912, did little more than provide general background on the circumstances of the incarceration since 1886 and enumerate 257 incarcerated individuals—138 males and 119 females. Only 30 of the men were identified as having been engaged in hostilities. The report cites the survivors' names, ages, present condition of health, and general conduct as follows:

Tiss-nolth-tos, age 47; health good; conduct fair.
Calvin Zhonne, age 47; health fair; conduct fair.
Leon Ferico [sic], age 60; health fair; conduct fair.
Beche, age 75; health fair; conduct good.
Yar-no-zha [sic], age 47; health good; conduct fair.
Christian Noiche [sic], age 56; health fair; conduct has been very good for about a year past.

A note added at this point on the list states that "the above six surrendered with Geronimo in 1886," and then the list continues.

Too-is-gah, age 51; health good; conduct fair.
Jasper Kanseah, age 39; health good; conduct good.
Kay-dah-Zinne, age 51; health good; conduct fair.
Nah-do-Zinne, age 51; health good; conduct fair.
Kay-ih-tah, age 51; health good; conduct fair.
Mithlo, age 48; health good; conduct good.
Ky-zah, age 48; health good; conduct fair.
Tah-ni-toe, age 57; health good; conduct fair.
Tse-de-Kisen, age 53; health good; conduct fair.
Martine, age 54; health good; conduct fair.
Binday, age 54; health good; conduct good.
Fatty, age 54; health good; conduct fair.
Dexter Loco, age 48; health good; conduct good.
Harold Dick, age 69; health good; conduct fair.
Paul Gey-dil-Kon, age 52; health good; conduct fair.
Nah-nal-Zhuggie, age 51; health good; conduct fair.
José, age 53; health good; conduct fair.

Kah-ah-te-nai, age 51; health good; conduct fair.

Coonie, age 56; health good; conduct good.

As-toy-eh, age 50; health good; conduct fair.

Tzozonna, age 52; health good; conduct fair.

Jason Betzinez, age 51; health good; conduct good.

Chiricahua Tom, age 62; health good; conduct fair.

Chatto, age 58; health good; conduct fair.

Stimson concluded, "There is no military necessity for continuing to hold these Apache Indians as prisoners of war if provision can be made for their location elsewhere than on the Fort Sill Reservation and if the Indians desire to remove therefrom." [55]

Many meetings were held at Fort Sill among the military and the prisoners of war during these anxious times. At the December 1, 1912, session, Colonel Scott defended his questionable actions by declaring to the Chiricahuas,

> I stated to you . . . that I believed it to be for your best welfare to go to the Mescalero Reservation, and the reasons I gave to you were that many of you have got tuberculosis in your family. Naiche just told me about his wife a few minutes ago. I know that a number of your children have got tuberculosis troubles and that those mountains about Mescalero are some of the best parts of the United States for the cure of that trouble. . . . It is the best chance in the United States to get you rid of the tuberculosis troubles. If you don't get rid of them there it can't be done. [56]

As the release of prisoners became more and more politically complex, support in favor of expeditious action came from many quarters, including officials of the Reformed Church in America. Writing in 1912 about the shameful past years of incarceration, the Reverend Dr. Walter C. Roe stated, "It will literally be true that the iniquity of the fathers is visited upon the children unto the third and fourth generation, if this thing goes on much longer. . . . They must report day by day to the officer in charge for assignment to work, and although perchance their own little field needs tilling, may be ordered out. . . . They may not leave the reservation for more than a few hours without permission. . . . No member of another tribe will marry into their captivity, so that now they must marry 'in and in,' to the detriment of their offspring." After referring to the imprisonment of former Apache army scouts, Dr. Roe asked rhetorically, "Shall innocent babies be born prisoners, and harmless, laughing children grow up in captivity, because their grandfathers fought against or possibly for—think of it, possibly *for*—the United States Government?"[57]

Pressure was building from several quarters simultaneously, and finally, at long last, the ordeal for 187 Chiricahua Apaches came to an end on April 2, 1913. "Upon their arrival at Mescalero Reservation, [they] were released from their status as prisoners of war, and, having been placed under the care of the Interior Department, received their freedom,"[58] wrote Turcheneske. The situation for the 77 Chiricahuas who decided to remain in Oklahoma was less definite.[59]

Allotments of 160 acres each were promised to these Apaches, but no one electing to stay (or selected by the army to stay) received this amount of land. The actual acreages granted ranged between 23 and 158 acres and comprised parcels of land separated by many miles from other Apaches. As the heads of households selected their locations, the military attempted to convince them that having water flow through their properties was undesirable. But the Apaches remembered back nearly three decades to their days of freedom in Arizona and New Mexico when water meant life. "And that is why all of our allotments have creeks or streams running across the land," said Mildred Imach Cleghorn, born a prisoner of war in 1910 at Fort Sill and now the chairperson of the Fort Sill Chiricahua/ Warm Springs Apache Tribe.[60] As a child, her father and his mother had surrendered with Chihuahua; her mother was born at Mount Vernon, the daughter of George Wratten and his Chiricahua wife. Mrs. Cleghorn, who still lives on her 50 acres, gives frequent public lectures in which she recalls her early days of freedom in 1914 when she and her family drove a buggy north about seventeen miles from Fort Sill. As this small Apache family came up over a rise, young Mildred saw her family's property for the first time. Other relatives and friends, however, were not as fortunate.

By December 23, 1920, six to seven years after freedom was achieved, twelve minors and one adult had received neither their promised rations of food (until they could raise a crop) nor their allotments. The adult was Vincent Nahtalish, and his son, Vincent, Jr., was one of the waiting minors, along with Delia Domeah, Theodore Domeah, Davis Mithlo, Garnet Mithlo, Etheline Haozous, Norman Loco, Moses Loco, Geraldine Domeah, Lydia Inez Chinney, Juanita Loco, and Harold Kaywaykla.

In a letter dated December 31, 1920, three Chiricahua Apache men, former prisoners of war and members of the Fort Sill Apache Tribal Committee, wrote an open letter. After a brief one-page history and background of their reason for writing, the men stated:

> It will be seen that thirteen members of the band are entitled to allotments not yet obtained by the Government for them. For the almost seven years which have elapsed since these people were supposed to receive their allotments, they have lost the use or rental which would have been derived from the lands of the minors, and which would have been accruing to the credit of said minors. The rations were not issued nor were they paid in lieu of the failure of their issuance, so there has been real and painful deprivation in this matter. It is true that these Indians are now farming, and are doing creditably, but they had to take money from the sale of their cattle to buy provisions with, which money otherwise could have been invested in stock or needed implements.
>
> WE ARE NOT ASKING ANY FAVORS, BUT ONLY THAT THE PROMISES OF THE GOVERNMENT TO US BE FUL-FILLED BY THIS CONGRESS IF POSSIBLE. Will you, in the name of what is fair and square, do what you can to help us in this matter? We who sign this letter are hard-working farmers, asking only what white men would ask, that we be paid what is owed us, and that we be paid NOW.
>
> Thanking you for your assistance, we are
>
> Jason Betzinez
> James Kaywaykla
> Talbot Goody
> Apache Committee[61]

Thirty-four years after their incarceration began, Chiricahua Apaches were still waiting in vain for the government to fulfill its promises.

✳ ✳ ✳ Explanations: Another Point of View

Towana Spivey, director of the Fort Sill Museum, takes a "balanced perspective" when discussing "the historic situation of the nineteenth century involving the Indians and the government, the agents, the traders, settlers, and whomever might have been affected in a clash or an impact of some kind." Spivey's interpretations of the events that occurred through the entire period of Apache incarceration present an outlook often in stark contrast with that of the Apaches.

In speaking of the Chiricahua Apache families when they reached Florida, Spivey noted, "They were separated. The family unit was broken down. In any society on earth, when the family unity is broken down, and the men, women and children separated, it's very difficult for any kind of society or culture to survive at all. The Chiricahua Apaches became ill, they were distrustful, they wouldn't eat, and they died.

"The story is full of contradictions. On the one hand, they were being treated as VIP's, or tourist attractions. The chambers of commerce in Florida were actively trying to take advantage of the presence of these Indians. Another contradiction is that the photographic record shows these prisoners of war carrying firearms at times. They carried rifles on their saddles." This began at Mount Vernon, when forty-six of the men were enlisted into the Twelfth Infantry's Company I, and continued during the years of confinement at Fort Sill in Troop L of the Seventh Cavalry.

"In Alabama, the men and women were . . . back together again, but the conditions were still not very good. The climate was totally alien to them and they were so far away from home. They had lost touch with their roots, so to speak. . . . When they eventually came to Fort Sill, the Apaches seemed to fit in much better. They adapted. For one thing, the families were reunited."

Spivey believes the military, particularly "people like Hugh L. Scott and Lieutenant [Ernest] Stecker," helped the prisoners assimilate "into society, not as a tribe, but as individuals . . . helped them survive and accomplish goals. At Fort Sill they reestablished their special dances, powwows, family gatherings, and their ceremonies. The government arranged for the Apaches to establish themselves in villages that reflected their own extended families. This allowed the elders, the heads of the families, to regain their sense of pride, their sense of support and continuity that had been lost in Alabama and Florida . . . where the situation was different and the people had died. In Florida some of the burials were done at sea and at the same time they would dispose of the remains, the soldiers would also go to pick up supplies and bring them back. Sometimes the Apaches thought they were eating their own people. The officials were insensitive to the burial situation and insensitive of what they were feeding them. I think in the beginning when they were first removed to Florida the government didn't particularly care what happened to them . . . it was a matter of getting them out of the Southwest for political reasons. After a period of time the government did begin to care and to realize that they couldn't let them just sit there to die and disappear. If there had not been any concern on the government's part, they would have left them in Florida to be mistreated and die.

"The government policy had been shifting and changing for them to end up at Fort Sill. There were people here who were very sensitive to the Apaches' plight. That combination, plus the Apaches' own ability to survive, to adapt, to deal with what's at hand and to overcome a dilemma, was achieved here."

Yet they were constantly supervised, counted twice daily, and still issued rations such as flour, bacon, and other basics, all of which could be obtained because they had ration tags with identifying prisoner-of-war numbers stamped on them. While the Apaches had the freedom to roam the land inside the boundaries of the post, they could not leave the military reservation without an escort. Spivey admitted, "It was a restricted situation, a restricted environment that is unparalleled anywhere else. How do you have prisoners of war if you don't have an official war? The policy of the government toward the Indians was always in a state of flux," and often affected by the lobbying efforts of advocacy organizations such as the Indian Rights Association. "There were judgments being made by the government on a personal level as well," said Spivey. "Conflict was always there within the government on how to deal with the Indians . . . there were conscientious people who cared. There were also those who did not care and sometimes one or the other faction was in control, affecting programs and what happened to the Indians."

Like his colleagues Luis Arana in St. Augustine and Arthur

Capell in Mount Vernon, Spivey did not have much information about the prisoners' health. The topic seems to have been one that didn't generate much paperwork among officials of the day, and detailed medical records were either not kept or were not stored in files that are available today. "We know that a special hospital was set up to treat and deal with the Apaches as part of their being here at Fort Sill," said Spivey. "I don't know why the special hospital was set up apart from the regular hospital facilities. I don't know if there was racism involved, or if there was a very practical reason for it. Health conditions during this period were experiencing great changes among the soldiers and the people who lived here. There were many common diseases from respiratory and stomach problems that resulted from bad water, insects, and from hygiene practices that were not good." After describing the efforts of post surgeon Morris K. Taylor, who was stationed at the post in the mid-1880s, Spivey stated that the doctor "made great strides in eliminating many problems by insisting upon the disposal of garbage and refuse in specific locations and not just taking it out the back door and dumping it somewhere. He insisted on better water, control of the wells, and the source of water. I think the sum total of his efforts were bound to have influenced and benefited the Apaches to some extent. Had they not taken place just a few years earlier, health conditions at the post would have been much, much worse when the Apaches arrived. They [the prisoners] had to build earth closets, specialized latrines or toilets, in certain places away from where the water supply was located. You don't build your toilet upstream from where your source of drinking water is. You don't put the two together," as was done in the courtyard at St. Augustine.

"The relationship of germs to disease was not well understood by most people, even most medical people. We know today that the Native Americans in prehistoric North America experienced certain different health considerations than did the non-Indian cultures when they arrived. There are diseases, for instance," reported Spivey, "which the Native Americans in the early days had a built-in resistance [to] that the white culture did not, and vice versa." Asked to be more specific, Spivey cited "syphilis, a disease that Native Americans experienced but with far less dramatic symptoms or impact on their body than the white people did. We know from the history of syphilis, as an example, that it was taken back to

Europe by Columbus, who himself died of the disease. We hear about diseases such as smallpox and measles that just wiped out whole [Indian] villages, but we don't often hear the reverse of that, where there were some diseases acquired by the white culture from the Native Americans and taken back to Europe. Syphilis caused devastation throughout Europe because they had no immunity or resistance to it, whereas the Native Americans had a certain amount of resistance. We can see in the skeletal record of Native America where syphilis caused abnormal growth situations, and striations on the bone itself." [62]

Despite the illnesses brought to Oklahoma from Alabama, and those subsequently acquired at Fort Sill, Spivey sees the years of incarceration at Fort Sill (1894–1914) as "rebuilding from the depths they had sunk to in the Southeast, gaining ground, building momentum, achieving goals and objectives, recovering, recuperating, and bouncing back. If it had not been for certain non-Indians who cared, the whole thing would not have worked. As good as the Apaches' resiliency was, it would not have been enough and we could have potentially had another bad situation at Fort Sill."

One of the last remaining large parcels of Indian land was opened for settlement in Oklahoma in 1901. Settlers arrived in the Fort Sill area, founded the nearby town of Lawton, and economic dependencies between the town and the fort began to develop. Nonetheless, most of the cavalry left in 1905, and two years later artillery began arriving in significant numbers. In 1910, with war looming in Europe, the federal government realized the advantages of setting up a specialized artillery training center at Fort Sill, and the first School of Fire for Field Artillery was established. This was in direct violation of the promises made to the Apaches; that is, that the Fort Sill Reserve would be their permanent home, an arrangement confirmed by treaty in 1897 with the Plains Indians whose reservation included the site of the Fort Sill Military Reserve. Over twenty-six thousand acres were ceded by the tribes to the United States, and later increased by an additional twelve hundred acres for the permanent settlement of the Apache prisoners of war and for other military purposes.

"Not much thought was given to the Apache situation at first," said Spivey. But, "firing on the ranges commenced and more conflicts developed as the artillery fired into an Apache hay field, cornfield, or where their cattle were grazing. Complaints were generated, disruptions began to occur, and the question began to be asked, 'Who is Fort Sill for, the artillery or the Apaches?' The question went all the way to Washington . . . where Hugh L. Scott, the person who had been so prominent and so helpful with the Apaches during the early period of their settlement here at Fort Sill, was in a position as chief of staff of the army to make some kind of overall command decision about the fate of the post.

"There were other considerations, which, as far as Washington was concerned, were overpowering the Apache problem—economic and political situations . . . people weren't making decisions based on the Apaches at all. They weren't really a factor . . . it was more a question of economics and military requirements, the coming war, and politics. Eventually Scott was prominent in making the final decision [to break promises to the Apaches regarding the Fort Sill homelands]. I don't think he made it by himself, but he certainly had considerable input into Fort Sill being retained as an active military post.

"Then you're left with what happens to the Apaches. The decision was made around 1912 that the Apaches would be given a choice . . . Mescalero or Oklahoma." Those who chose Mescalero, according to Spivey, were given about a year to "gather up their livestock and dispose of them. Supposedly, the proceeds from the sale were to go to support the relocation that was to take place. I've been told, but never heard it verified, that the money did not go for that purpose, that it was either siphoned off for other purposes or it was never forthcoming to the Apaches. I don't know the answer to that.

"One of the other questions that you hear a lot of confusion about is the choice, whether or not they were given the choice to go to Mescalero or move off the post to occupy individual homesteads. I've heard that there was no choice, and decisions were based on a preselected list worked up by the government saying that this person would go to Mescalero and this person would stay in the vicinity. I see no evidence of this, but I've heard this complaint from some of the Apaches. . . . I don't know what the distinct advantage would have been to the government for certain people to stay here and certain people to go there."

When I reminded him of the government's long-lasting paranoia about the Chiricahua Apaches and perhaps a fear that locating all

Leaving Fort Sill as free women for the Mescalero Apache Reservation in New Mexico, early April 1913. Note the blankets and bundles. This train took the newly released prisoners to Tularosa, New Mexico, where the men, women, and children were met by the Mescalero Apaches and welcomed to their new homes. However, it would be approximately one year before these Chiricahuas would be settled permanently on the reservation. (Frisco Native American Museum)

the free Chiricahuas in one place would be just enough to get them back on the warpath, Spivey disagreed. "It was too late. The decision was based on pure choice," he said. "Those who want to go to Mescalero, raise your right hand. Those who want to stay, raise your left hand.

"It was as simple as that. I think the Apache story stands out as an icon. There's no other way to describe it. An icon of adaptation dealing with difficult circumstances, making the best out of the situation that they could. Truly, they are an amazing people."[63]

10

A Collection

of Chiricahua

Voices

Chiricahua Apaches haunt American history. Their own words, interpreted by George Wratten and others and preserved in formal and informal documents, present the most accurate portrayal of the moods and attitudes of the Chiricahuas at the time they lost their freedom. These carefully chosen words of the chiefs and other headmen convey a sense of vulnerability and resignation to fate, and a solicitous and ingratiating attitude totally out of character for the most infamous band of Indians in the United States.

Interviews conducted just a few years later, in 1890, while the band was incarcerated in Alabama amid the morass of sickness and death, show the pragmatism that enabled the Chiricahuas to survive the years of imprisonment, but they also reveal the anger and despair felt by the leaders. Remarkably, hope never died, and the prisoners always continued to look forward to the time when the government would fulfill its promise of only two years of confinement and set them free. Even if it took twenty-seven or more years.

✳ ✳ Naiche, Hereditary Chief and Son of Cochise

[To General George Crook, March 27, 1886, Cañon de los Embudos, Mexico]

"I give you my word, I give you my body. I surrender; I have nothing more to say than that. When I was free, I gave orders, but now I surrender to you. I throw myself at your feet. You now order and I obey. What you tell me to do I do. Now that I have surrendered I am glad. I'll not have to hide behind rocks and mountains; I'll go across the open plain. I'll now sleep well, eat contentedly, and be satisfied, and so will my people. There may be lots of men who have had feelings against us. I will go wherever you may see fit to send us, where no bad talk will be spoken of us. When I was out in the mountains I thought I should never see you again, but I am glad because I now see you and have a talk with you. I think now it is best for us to surrender and not remain out in the mountains like fools, as we have been doing. I have nothing further to say. I surrender to you, and hope you will be kind to us, as you have always been a good friend to the Indians and tried to do what was right for them. I have changed all my thoughts. I surrender to you. Whatever you do to me is right, and all these men here are witnesses that I surrender to you. The day has at last come when I could see you, talk to and surrender to you. . . . You don't lie to me. I hope from this day on you will see that I am in earnest and will believe what I say. . . . I surrender to you, and place myself in your hands. I'll do what you say, but I want you from time to time to talk with me."[1]

[To General George Crook on why he and certain followers changed their minds and didn't surrender in March 1886; January 2, 1890, Mount Vernon Barracks, Alabama]

"I was afraid I was going to be taken off somewhere I didn't like; to some place I didn't know. I thought all who were taken away would die. . . . We were afraid. It was war. Anybody who saw us would kill us, and we did the same thing. We had to if we wanted to live."[2]

[To Colonel Hugh L. Scott, at Fort Sill, Oklahoma, 1911]

"All we want is to be freed and be released as prisoners and given land and homes that we can call our own. This is all we think about. We are thinking the same today as the last time, and that is why we are here now to say these things. . . . Half or more than half of these people talk English. Half or more than half can read and write; they all know how to work. You have held us long enough. We want something else now."[3]

✳ ✳ ✳ Chihuahua, Subchief

[To General George Crook, March 27, 1886,
Cañon de los Embudos, Mexico]

"We are always in danger out here. I hope from this day on we may live better with our families and not do any harm to anybody. I am anxious to behave. I think the sun is looking down upon me and the earth is listening. I am thinking better. It seems to me that I have seen the One who makes the rain and sends the winds; or He must have sent you to this place. I surrender myself to you because I believe in you and you do not deceive us. You must be our God. I am satisfied with all that you do. You must be the one who makes the green pastures, who sends the rain, who commands the winds. You must be the one who sends the fresh fruits that appear on the trees every year. There are many men in the world who are big chiefs and command many people, but you, I think, are the greatest of them all, or you wouldn't come out here to see us. I want you to be a father to me and treat me as your son. I want you to have pity on me. There is no doubt that all you do is right, because all you do is just the same as if God did it. Everything you do is right. So I consider, so I believe you to be. I trust in all you say; you do not deceive. All the things you tell us are facts. I am now in your hands. I place myself at your disposition. I surrender myself to you. Do with me as you please. I shake your hand . . . I want to be right where you are. I have roamed these mountains from water to water. Never have I found the place where I could see my father or my mother, until today I see you, my father. I surrender to you now and I don't want any more bad feeling or bad talk. I am going over to stay with you in your camp. Whenever a man raises anything, even a dog, he thinks well of it and tries to raise it right and treat it well. So I want you to feel towards me and be good to me and don't let people say bad things about me."[4]

[To General George Crook, January 2, 1890,
Mount Vernon Barracks, Alabama]

"I am getting so my limbs feel as if they were asleep. I would like to have some place better than this. I would like to have a place where I could have a farm and go right to work so that my children can have plenty to eat; and I would like to have tools to go right to work with. I have a daughter away at school and two other near relatives. I want to see them soon. Won't you make it so I can see them very soon? I didn't get any of the money that was to be sent to me. I never said anything about it. . . . I am just the same now as when I saw you last going along the same road. There are trees all about. I would like to go where I can see."[5]

✳ ✳ Geronimo, Shaman and Warrior

[To General George Crook, March 25, 1886,
Cañon de los Embudos, Mexico]

"From here on I want to live at peace. Don't believe any bad talk you hear about me. The agents and the interpreters hear that somebody has done wrong, and they blame it all on me. . . . I want good men to be my agents and interpreters; people who will talk right. I want this peace to be legal and good. Whenever I meet you, I talk good to you, and you to me, and peace is soon established. . . . I want to have a good man put over me. While living I want to live well. I know I have to die some time, but even if the heavens were to fall on me, I want to do what is right. I think I am a good man, but in the papers all over the world they say I am a bad man. . . . I never do wrong without a cause. Every day I am thinking how am I to talk to you and to make you believe what I say; and, I think too that you are thinking of what you are to say to me. There is one God looking down on us all. We are all children of the one God. God is listening to me. The sun, the darkness, the winds, are all listening to what we now say."[6]

[To General George Crook, March 27, 1886,
Cañon de los Embudos, Mexico]

"I surrender myself to you . . . I give myself up to you. Do with me what you please. . . . Once I moved about like the wind.

Now I surrender to you and that is all. I don't want any one to say any wrong thing about me in any way. I surrender to you and want to be just as if I were in your pocket. My heart is yours, and I hope yours will be mine. Now I feel like your brother. . . . I was very far from here. Almost nobody could go to that place. But I sent you word I wanted to come in here, and here I am. I have no lies in my heart. Whatever you tell me is true. We are all satisfied of that. I hope the day may come when my word shall be as strong with you as yours is with me. That's all I have to say now, except a few words. I should like to have my wife and daughter come to meet me at Fort Bowie."[7]

[To Lieutenant Hugh L. Scott, August 29, 1893,
Mount Vernon Barracks, Alabama]
"Young men, old men, women, and children all want to get away from here—it is too hot and wet—too many of us die here."[8]

[In 1906, reflecting on life when the Apaches were free]
"When disease or pestilence abounded we were assembled and questioned by our leaders to ascertain what evil we had done, and how Usen could be satisfied. Sometimes sacrifice was deemed necessary. Sometimes the offending one was punished. . . .

"The Indians knew what herbs to use for medicine, how to prepare them, and how to give the medicine. This they had been taught by Usen in the beginning, and each succeeding generation had men who were skilled in the art of healing.

"In gathering the herbs, in preparing them, and in administering the medicine, as much faith was held in prayer as in the actual effects of the medicine. Usually about eight persons worked together in making medicine, and there were forms of prayer and incantations to attend each stage of the process. Four attended to the incantations and four to the preparation of the herbs.

"Some of the Indians were skilled in cutting out bullets, arrow heads, and other missiles with which warriors were wounded. I myself have done much of this, using a common dirk or butcher knife."[9]

[To General George Crook, January 2, 1890,
Mount Vernon Barracks, Alabama]

"I remember all General Crook told me and also all that General Miles told me. He told me how to behave myself. He told me to go back to Camp Apache. I had a farm there. . . . I went back there and made a big farm and worked it. . . . I got a contract for wood . . . and got a good deal of money from it. . . . General Miles told me, '. . . now I'll have to send you away. People don't seem to like you.' I told him there was lots of wood here, and I wanted to stay. He said, 'The Indians at San Carlos and Camp Apache are talking about you all the time, and I had better send you away from here. We will take the train and in one and a quarter days we will go to the place we were talking about and look at it.' We didn't see that land. We were four days on the train and stopped only when we reached Washington. I saw the President and shook hands with him. He told us, 'Do not be afraid to come amongst us; I am the great father of you all. Go back to your farms at Camp Apache and settle down quietly. There nobody will harm you, nobody will say anything to you. Go back there and do just as the commanding officer tells you. Do as he tells you and he will write good letters to me about you.' He told us when we got in the cars it would be about a week before we got home, but when we had been on two days we were stopped [at Fort Leavenworth] and they told us we would not go back to Camp Apache. We were there two months and they told us we would not go back to our homes any more, but would go some place on the coast.

"On the evening of the third day after we got to St. Augustine our people came there from Camp Apache. We were told then we would be in confinement. . . . We were told we would have our stock; we were told this after we had reached the east. What horses we had were finally sold and we got what few dollars were received for them. I had four horses and three mules and received $127 for them. I received pay for my horses but not for the wood I had piled up there. I had about 90 cords of wood for which I never received anything.

"I thought we were coming to a place that was healthy, but you can see for yourself that we are not so many as when you saw us last. A great many have died. We lost more than a hundred. More than fifty have died since leaving St. Augustine. About thirty children have died at Carlisle. Between fifty and a hundred have died here. Chatto had a son and nephew to die at Carlisle. . . . They told me about that big reservation that General Miles told him about, where all the Indians should be together. He said, 'When you get there you will have good farms, horses, cattle, and they will belong to you. Nobody will have anything to do with them but yourself. I am telling you the truth; I am telling you no lie.' When he told me that, I shook hands with him two or three times and said, 'Thank you.' " [10]

✳ ✳ ✳ Kuni (Coonie), Scout

[To General George Crook, January 2, 1890,
Mount Vernon Barracks, Alabama]
"[At White Mountain] there was an Indian, a chief Sanchez, [who] had a talk with the officers and he said the Chiricahuas were no good. He did not want us there and wanted us taken away. [The soldiers] told us the Indians who had gone on to Washington (Chatto, etc.) were waiting there for us." [11]

✳ ✳ ✳ Toklanni, Scout

[To General George Crook, January 2, 1890,
Mount Vernon Barracks, Alabama]
"It was on counting day and . . . some cavalry was going along as if it were going somewhere, but it turned and joined with the infantry and scouts and surrounded the Chiricahuas. After they had counted us and given us tickets, they sent the women home, and told the men they wanted to talk and we went to a tent. They told us nobody would be harmed, but that we were going to be sent away." [12]

Samuel E. Kenoi, Scout

"At Holbrook, Arizona, they loaded us on a train. . . . It was the first time most of us had seen a train. When that train was coming along the river and it whistled, many said it was run by lightning, and they began to pray to the train. I saw many old men and women doing this. They said, 'Bless us, that we may be blessed wherever we go.'

"Lots of the children were running out in the brush. They were afraid of the train. The soldiers had to chase them and get them in. I ran away from them; they had to catch me. I was afraid. I was thinking that they were taking me somewhere to kill me. I was so afraid." [13]

✳ ✳ Chatto, Warrior and Scout

[To General George Crook, January 2, 1890,
Mount Vernon Barracks, Alabama]

"[General Miles] told us also: 'You have good farms at Apache. You have good water, etc., but this is not enough. Go to the Washington country and you can get 20. to 50. a month.' It was some lieutenant who read this letter to us. . . . He told us he would like us to do as we did when we signed the pay-roll, and we all touched the top of the pen. . . . We thought it was good to get 20. to 50. a month." [14]

✳ ✳ Ka-Ah-Tenney, Member of Chatto's Group and Delegate to Washington, D.C.

[To General George Crook, January 2, 1890,
Mount Vernon Barracks, Alabama]

"I was taken to St. Augustine, but tried to be as I always was, and to do what I said to you I would. I like you. I like your talk and try to follow in your footsteps. What do you think of me? . . . I help build roads, dig up roots, build houses, and do work all around here. Leaves fall off the trees and I help to sweep them up. I was working this morning when you came here. I don't know why I work here all the time for nothing. . . . I have children and relatives, lots of them, and I would like to work for them before I get too old to work. I'd like to have a farm well, and would like to have a farm long enough to see the crops get ripe."[15]

> [To Colonel Hugh L. Scott, October 16, 1911,
> Fort Sill, Oklahoma]
> "I want to speak to the Colonel about a brother of mine who was an enlisted man. We was in Alabama and while he was an enlisted man he was murdered somewhere near a railroad. Some soldiers murdered him. He was an enlisted man then and he had some money coming to him and I never knew anything about how much money was coming to him and it has never been paid to anybody and that is what I wanted to ask you about."[16]

Conditions at Fort Sill, while infinitely better than at St. Augustine and Mount Vernon, still presented both medical hardships and those of a different sort, such as the twice daily roll call. Regardless of where on the vast acreage at Fort Sill the Chiricahuas were, they had to appear at designated hours and locations to be counted. Another requirement—that the prisoners farm and ranch on the military reserve—while certainly valid, was impeded by the lack of horses and resulted in the prisoners walking more than seventy thousand acres at Fort Sill to round up the livestock. Too, the first winter, 1895, was very cold, dry, and blustery. The temperature hovered close to zero for long stretches of days and weeks. The government, unprepared to receive the Chiricahuas without housing, had not been able to construct any living quarters for them, and so the people lived in the traditional wickiup dwellings that they had lived in when they were free in southern Arizona and New Mexico. Obviously, winters were different in Oklahoma than they had been in any other place familiar to the Apaches, including Florida and Alabama, yet the prisoners didn't complain.

An excellent eyewitness account of those days at Fort Sill is in an interview conducted in 1976 with a woman who was born a prisoner of war, then was freed and lived in Oklahoma, where she and her husband, also a former prisoner of war, raised their children.

Blossom Haozous, Daughter of George Wratten and His Chiricahua Wife, Annie, Prisoner of War

July 22, 1976

"They were in St. Augustine I don't know how many years. From there they kept dying out and dying out from that dampness. They were right on the water front. So they moved them to Alabama which wasn't much better. It was swampy over there too. So in later years they moved them to Fort Sill.

"After coming to Fort Sill, the Army supplied them with condemned mules . . . that were still useable. The army just had no further use for them so they let the Apaches use them. . . . They gave us rations every five days . . . fresh beef, coffee, sugar, and candles. . . . They usually boiled the meat over the hot coals. They also had dried corn. They'd boil it with beef bones. They made their own bread. It was what people call tortillas now. They flatten it (the dough) out and cook it over the hot coals. They didn't have a grill . . . they made a little rack and put live coals under it. You browned one side and then turned it over and browned the other. They made a rough rack out of bailing wire mostly. Wove it back and forth and then put little legs on or propped it up on rocks to hold it up. The bread would rise a little bit and make bubbles.

"The government just gave us little two room houses with a breeze-way in the middle. We'd cook in one side and sleep in the other. If it was a big family, you used both rooms to eat, cook, and sleep in. . . . Those houses were all board walls and they just put nails in the walls and hung bags [of dried food such as corn] on the walls. That was the only place they had to store it. You just put them in bags and hung them around in the house. Everything you wanted to get out of your way, you hung on the walls.

"In our village there were several houses. About six families lived in that village where we were. They called it Noche's village. . . . We had to go for a quarter of a mile to get water. We used to carry water. One of my chores was that I had to see that the water buckets were full of water all the time. The whole village used that same well. It was quite a ways from the house.

"When my uncle died, he had tuberculosis. They said he had tuberculosis and they had to send him out west. I guess the worse thing they did was to send him out to Mescalero. It was cold up there. It's high altitude. He didn't live too long when they sent him out there.

"I guess we [Blossom and her sister, Amy] were kind of different because our father was white. George Wratten, the interpreter for the Indians. He lived among the Apaches ever since he was fifteen, I think he said. He learned the language and he stayed with them all the time and wherever they were taken as prisoners. . . . My father [who died of tuberculosis contracted while with the Chiricahua Apaches] is buried in the Post Cemetery." [17]

November 11, 1976
"Oklahoma was much better than the swamps in Alabama; the people were much better when they got to Oklahoma." [18]

When the day of the release of the prisoners of war who were going to New Mexico came, it was one of extreme emotion. The Mescalero-bound Apaches were leaving behind their relatives and friends and once again faced an uncertain future.

✳ ✳ ✳ Raymond Loco, Grandson of Chief Loco

November 12, 1976
"The day of separation was a great day of sorrow. There was weeping and wailing, in part due to separation [from kinfolk]. . . . When they were on the train [to Mescalero] they were in a sense of puzzlement. . . . What's going to happen to us? . . . not overjoyed, they were not happy, they were disturbed. . . .

"Freedom as defined by the whites is hard for the Indian to give expression to. He knew only freedom when the buffalo roamed the plains, when the rivers ran clean, and when the grass was green and abundant." [19]

Mildred Cleghorn, Born a Prisoner of War
in 1910 at Fort Sill

[From a story told by her mother, prisoner of war Amy
Wratten Imach, daughter of interpreter George Wratten]
"During the course of their first night spent on the Oklahoma prairie, a whole new generation of Chiricahuas, unaccustomed to such cacaphony, encountered the howls of coyotes plain-
tively echoing about the landscape. Yet there were those among
the Apache prisoners who dimly remembered such doleful cries.
As they began to recall scenes from another misty, distant era, the
emotion evoked by the sounds now unfamiliar except in memory,
must have been too great to contain. Reminded thus of times long
past and places far away, a number of the old women began to cry.
They felt the people had come home at last." [20]

August 8, 1989
"We [prisoners of war] were promised 160 acres apiece [in Okla-
homa] but Uncle Sam doesn't follow through. No one got 160 acres.
The closest they got was 158 acres [allotted to Robert Geronimo],
and the least amount they got was 23; a majority received 80 acres
apiece . . . from day one until today, the government has never kept
its promise. As Indian people, we didn't need black and white to
keep a promise. All we needed was your word. We didn't have to
write it down. . . . When they told Geronimo he was going to be
back in Arizona in two years, he believed. He never did get back." [21]

[From a lecture given November 13, 1991]
"When I look back and see how our people were treated, I
just wonder. . . .
"My father [Richard Imach] was taken prisoner of war when he
was eight or nine years old. He said the climate in Florida was so
bad that many became ill with tuberculosis and fevers. The sanitary
conditions were terrible. When we were little, my uncle Sam Haozous told us about the cistern at St. Augustine. The people would
get so thirsty that they couldn't stand it, so they had to drink the
water, which made them sick.
"He also told us about some paintings in caves in Arizona and we

saw them for the first time in 1986. We stood in front of them and wept, men too, because we all felt like we'd been here before.

"We gave up fifteen million acres of land. We were never, ever, given a chance to have back what was ours. But because Geronimo surrendered, we are living today. He said that if he kept on fighting there would be no more Chiricahuas, that we would be wiped off the face of the earth. The two years of incarceration turned into twenty-seven for those who went to Mescalero, twenty-eight for those who stayed in Oklahoma.

"Many more wanted to live in Oklahoma, but were sent to Mescalero because the powers-that-be believed they couldn't cope with the outside world and live among non-Indians. The allotments we got in Oklahoma were not allowed to be contiguous. The Benedict Johze family lived twelve miles out. My relatives, the Haozous family, were six miles away. It was hard to get from one place to another, but we children used to ride our horses back and forth.

"When the land was being allotted, our people realized that we needed water, so they chose parcels that had creeks or streams running through. The supervisor tried to tell them they should choose solid land, but our people, having come from Arizona and New Mexico, knew the value of water and wanted it somewhere on their land.

"After we were freed, my parents told me 'You have to know a little more than the white man does to be able to compete. You must go to school.' We also have to learn to live with one another. Our people have come a long way because now we have a lot of blonde, blue-eyed grandchildren." [22]

✱ ✱ ✱ Elbys Hugar, Great-granddaughter of Cochise, Granddaughter of Chief Naiche

November 19, 1991
"We don't eat anything that breathes under water." [23]

October 1, 1991

"My dad trained for war, and I think it was Frank Mangus who was in charge. Even though he was directly kin to my dad, Frank treated him just like anybody else. The subchief had to get them up in the morning, and the first thing they did was go down to the river and get a mouthful of water. Sometimes there was a thin sheet of ice over the water and they'd have to break that with a rock and would have to completely cover themselves in the water. Then they'd start up the mountain. The subchief was with them, riding horseback and holding a rawhide whip. If they did anything wrong, they would get whippings. When they got up to the top of the mountain, they were supposed to spit out the water to show that they had gone all the way up there without breathing through their mouths. My dad said sometimes their hair and their G-strings were just frozen. When they got back to camp the women were usually making tortillas and fixing food. They had fires going but the young men were told not to go by the fire, to keep moving around, moving around to get warm without help. And they were taught how to wrestle and how to cut down a thick branch with their knives and then break it over their legs. They had mock battles in which they would use slingshots and real rocks. Anyone who was hit by a rock had to take a whipping with the rawhide whip. It was really rough.

"My dad said he was taught how to run like a cottontail, never straight, from side to side, so he wouldn't be an easy target. All the young boys used to carry black powder up to the men who were fighting in the trees. They would take a round rock and roll it and stay behind it until they reached the warriors. It scared my dad to think back and remember sleeping beside a fire with bags of black powder tied to their belts. The boys also carried water and food to the warriors who were fighting, and when they got there, the men would take off their headbands and hang them in a tree. They ate on the ground while the enemy was shooting at the headbands above them.

"When my people were in hiding, they ate mountain rats that the boys killed. Sometimes as they were walking, they'd see a nice

Sam Haozous in Omaha, Nebraska, at the Trans-Mississippi and Inter-national Exposition of 1898 (World's Fair). Medals were won in foot races with soldiers. Haozous's last wife was Blossom Wratten, daughter of the interpreter. Upon release from incarceration, the Haozous family lived near Apache, Oklahoma, where Sam was a farmer. He loved to sing Chiricahua songs and play his Indian flute. (Frisco Native American Museum)

bone, put it in their bag, and later that evening the marrow would form a little soup if they didn't have anything else to eat.

"Geronimo used to see the soldiers and tell my dad how young they looked. 'They don't know anything about fighting,' he'd say. 'They don't even know how to shoot yet.' Geronimo said the soldiers always gave the Apaches warning because they said 'ready, aim, fire,' and by that time the Apaches had scattered.

"Geronimo called my dad 'cousin,' and my dad knew Geronimo's medicine songs. They went to the exposition in Omaha in 1898 where my dad ran races against other tribes. He used to get up at night and run through the rough country at Fort Sill. A lot of times he just ate crackers and the old army hardtack. Crackers and water because he wanted to keep himself in real good shape. He wore army boots when he practiced running. They were heavy, you know. The army took the boys to Omaha to run and my dad won the 440, the 220, and beat all the tribes that participated. I think it was the Plains tribes. Somebody asked Geronimo if all the warriors ran like that and he said, 'Yeah, everyone runs just like Sam Haozous.' The army brought a big runner from back east to run against my dad, and he just didn't pay any attention. He said as they drew closer and closer together, he could hear him breathing hard, and pretty soon, just as they got close to the finish line, why, this guy collapsed. Just completely collapsed. They hauled him off to the clinic.

"My father was a bugler. When he was a prisoner he played for military funerals, and when we were freed and were little kids in Oklahoma, he had an old bugle. We might be on the creek and he'd take his bugle out and blow it. That's how we knew it was time to come in for lunch.

"He and my mother joined the church while they were prisoners, and he became very different than when he was younger. There were a lot of people who really had hate for what happened. It makes me mad sometimes when I'm reading about it, but I don't carry that with me. It's something that's happened and these are contemporary times now. But every now and then little things happen. . . . I often wonder about the fact that we were the only one of all the Apache groups who stood up and said 'this is my land.' We were the only ones who were brave enough to say 'that's enough.' And we are the only ones who ended up with nothing. The Fort Apache, San Carlos, the Jicarilla Apaches all have big spreads of valuable land where they graze cattle. I always hated that we lost that land at Fort Sill when it was rightly given to us. . . . We didn't get the 160 acres apiece that we were promised. Mom and Dad got 80 acres each. That was all right for a while when you had a good year. But we were just barely making it. I worked the land with my dad. That's the reason I stayed out of school a lot. He was getting old and so I ran that whole farm. That's the reason I never got an early start in my art work. I feel very fortunate that I have succeeded, and I feel badly that my dad, who didn't believe in the arts, couldn't have seen the results. Momma got to see some of the big shows.

"I tried hard to make them happy. One time the tires on Momma's car were bad and she told me she'd had a lot of trouble with it. I said, 'Let's go down and see Malone.' So we did and I said to her, 'Which car do you want?' She said, 'This one's kind of nice.' So I bought that one for her. I paid cash for it right there and she said, 'Oh, no, son, that's too much money.' It's one of those good things I was able to do for her while she was alive. I tried. It made me feel good. I'd give anything in the world if I could have done something like that for my dad. But he didn't live long enough. Right now I could probably buy him a good home and transportation or anything he wanted. But he's not here."[24]

✷ ✷ ✷   Berle Kanseah, Grandson of Jasper Kanseah

November 19, 1991

"When my grandfather and the rest of the Chiricahuas arrived here in Mescalero [from Fort Sill], they told about the train ride and coming up by wagon into the mountains and eventually out into the Whitetail area of the reservation. There they lived first in makeshift homes, tents and so forth, until they got some lumber to build their farm frame homes. On the average, the Apache families had anywhere from thirteen to seventeen acres that could be cultivated, and they fenced off more areas—horse pastures, for instance. The cultivated areas were planted with grain or gardens so when all these were harvested in the fall, the animals were turned back to graze the harvested areas. Everything was done by horseback or wagon. The federal government did help the folks with farming equipment, but not each family was given a plow or things like that.

Sometimes they shared. A piece of equipment would come down the canyon and the families just followed it and helped each other during harvest time.

"Our people were very religious. They tended to their culture and upheld the traditional ways. The children learned from their grandparents and parents and just moved along this way, maintaining their identity. My late father was born a prisoner of war and released in 1913 when he came to Mescalero along with his parents, my grandparents.

"When we were growing up we were told, 'You can always learn English.' Meaning we learned to speak Apache first. Everything was done in the Apache language. It was the cultural way. Everything was given in Apache, everything you did was done in Apache. However, my parents and grandparents regarded education very highly in the Western society's way. Meaning that to make your living today in today's society, you need an education. My grandfather often spoke of 'getting my land back. Give me my land back or pay me for it.' He viewed education as one of the ways that the grandchildren could achieve what he was talking about. I realize now that this matter was much deeper than I realized at the time, this business of 'my land, give me my land back or pay me for it.'

"The Apaches in a way regarded education for the children as the way to make it in today's society as a self-sufficient person. To be a proud person and maintain identity. Also, to hold on to what you have, you need education. Which is the land. The people were a part of the land, so our land base was very important to us. Without our land we feel that we are not the people we could be today. We must maintain a land base which offers us the natural resources that we need to live by and also to maintain our respect, which is within our culture again.

"At the time I heard my grandfather and others speak of this land grab, stealing land and so forth, we took it for granted that this was a common subject. I really couldn't say that my people sounded bitter, but that they were speaking of facts. They stated some things that they wanted their children and grandchildren to absorb and learn about and do something about. It was their land and no one had asked for it. It was just taken.

"In this way our people spoke very strongly because at the time our people were imprisoned, a lot of our culture was lost. A lot of our people were lost due to illnesses because of the areas they were taken into that was foreign to them. Our people were nomadic in nature. We ranged in western New Mexico, eastern Arizona, down into Mexico. Much of that area is semiarid down in the lower elevations, and then they moved back into the mountains, up to six thousand feet or better, all the way up to possibly ten thousand feet elevation. When our people speak of this time, they were a free people and they did not abuse any of the natural resources that were at hand for them to use so that they can live. No, I wouldn't say my grandfather spoke bitterly [of the years of incarceration and what was done to the Chiricahua Apaches]. I would say he spoke very strongly of facts he would want us to learn, to know about. So that in due time we may be the ones through education to do something about some of these atrocities that took place.

"School, for instance. It was a fact that they were taken by force to school, and by force they were introduced to Western clothes and Western-style haircuts. Much of this was humiliation. To lose your hair when you were becoming a teenager was a very tough situation. He spoke of being lonesome. A lot of the students he went there with were lonesome and many were susceptible to diseases because they were down in spirit. The Apaches believe that if you have a strong spirit, you can ward off many of these things. He told us of his training as a cobbler, a shoe repair man. Also spoke of the times when they were assigned to farms and used various automated-type farm equipment. A lot of our boys then were becoming young men, and because they were proud of their background, they were beginning to learn and to become good farmers.

"But then we didn't know in the early to mid-1900s that it would be possible to make your living off an average of fifteen to sixteen acres for farming grain, where the elevation is seven thousand feet, such as at Whitetail here at Mescalero. The season isn't really that long, and when the federal government brought equipment in to harvest, the last families may have had snowfall on their crops already. There really was no intention of going all-out and equipping the families a little bit better so they could purchase their own farm equipment. All in all, I feel that it was a mistake to try to teach our people to farm.

"I remember when I was in school at Mescalero for a little while. My dad worked and we had to live here [instead of at Whitetail] for a short period of time. At recess time we came around the tribal store and there were a lot of old people there to get their groceries and so forth. The old people parted the kids' hair to look at their faces and see if it was a relative, a grandchild, perhaps, from another district. If they found out it was, they would sit and treat the kids to some goodies, however little. They loved the children right there until recess was over and then sent them back to school. This is how our people were caring. It was a time to remember. I feel that many of us took it for granted that it would always be there.

"Personally, I feel that our people were proud originally and knew who they were. They knew their land because they utilized it. They traveled the land, used its resources. Everything in that time was God given. We were taught this way through the Apache language. It is very sacred and many times we have refused to share this area with many people. It's ours, and it's sacred, and it's how we were intended to be, placed here in the Southwest. [We underwent] upheaval, a very serious upheaval, when we were removed from our areas and placed on reservations and eventually ended up being prisoners of war. Thinking about these things, my opinion is not very good of Western society. It's very unfair that we were not considered as equal humans, which we were. We had a right to our land, always left something to regenerate naturally. Some of these things were taken from us when we were taken prisoners of war and relocated. A lot of that was to annihilate, get rid of us so we don't practice our culture again.

"While I feel very strongly about some of these things, our parents and grandparents encouraged education so we can get some of these things changed in the halls of Congress. We must become educated to be just as good as the non-Indian or better. I have to be positive to instill this type of feeling into my children and grandchildren. So somewhere along the line I feel like I'm kind of reliving some of those things that my grandfather taught, and my father taught.

"Our kids are becoming faster and going farther, and when you go farther out, then that takes time and you're not in touch with your people. It makes it even worse when you aren't fluent in your native language, which is Apache, and the gap begins to grow. You have an identity crisis somewhere soon in the near future. We are concerned about this and we are planning, continuing to make plans to tend to our culture and continue our tribal ceremonials, which have to do with our identity. I don't think we are losing, but I think the threat is there. Hopefully, we can gain on it through education. Carefully planned, I think we can do it."[25]

✳ ✳ ✳ Asa Daklugie, Son of Nedni Apache Chief Juh

"I was not in Alabama but I knew most who were. They looked forward as eagerly as I to eventually having a permanent home with assurance that the government would not take it away from us as it had both Cochise's and Victorio's reservations. Both had been promised to them, and to their people in perpetuity. That was done by Executive Order, which is the equivalent to a treaty and is the supreme law of the land. We learned that an Executive Order was as worthless as any other piece of paper. If a man's spoken word is worthless, so is his written one. Who but an Indian ever kept a promise?

". . . we wanted to run cattle. For that purpose the [Mescalero] reservation was ideal. The mountainous area could be grazed during the summer and herds could be driven to the foothills and lower land during the winter.

"Mountains in which to pray, wood, water, grass, abundance of game—and no White Eyes! Best of all, we would live among our own people and worship Ussen according to our own religion. There might be missionaries, but not many; and we need not let them spoil it for us. They meant well and no doubt thought their religion better than ours. Of course White Eyes are not close to Ussen as Apaches are."[26]

11

A Legacy of Death

✳ ✳ ✳

The Chiricahua Apaches who made it through alive to 1913–14 numbered 275 men, women, and children. They were all that remained of 519 captives, who in turn were the descendants of the 930 Apaches registered at the Chiricahua Apache agency less than fifty years earlier. In the late 1870s, these grandparents and parents of the prisoners of war lived within the boundaries of their own agency in Pinery Cañon, Arizona, under the supervision of agent Tom Jeffords. They were a superior bunch—hardy, fertile, skillful, and cunning—the powerful and uncontested rulers of the desert and mountain country they loved so dearly.

They even impressed their agent, Jeffords, a hard-nosed fellow who had been Cochise's personal friend and had spent many years of his life among the Chiricahuas. He knew them well. In an annual report to the commissioner of Indian affairs dated September 1, 1874, Jeffords praised these Apaches highly, stating, "A great many of their traits of character will compare favorably with any class of people." In his experience, the people did not steal from their own, were virtuous, did not lie, and seldom quarreled. The only violence he reported occurred as the result of sudden situations, when the "opponents were perfectly sober." [1]

Just a few months earlier, on July 20, 1874, Jeffords had submitted a general description of an average Apache male within the text of another report. In his characteristic sparse prose, he wrote of an athletic body with many desirable qualities, reflecting good health and a physical condition free from any disabling afflictions: average height: 5′ 8″; average chest measurement: large; limbs: well proportioned, straight; hands/feet: small; muscles: well developed; power of vision: great, better than any race.[2]

In my research I uncovered a questionnaire dated July 25, 1873, regarding the health of the Chiricahuas on their Arizona reservation. In response to the query "About what percentage of sick Indians prefer to rely upon their own Medicine Man?" Jeffords replied, "None. All prefer to be treated by the agency physician." The second question was, "What are some of the most prevalent diseases among them?" Jeffords reported, "Primarily those of the stomach and bowels and it seems to be confined principally to the children, the grown people not however being free from it, due doubtless to their food and mode of living. Affliction of the eyes exist, but to no alarming extent. Syphilis does not exist with them as yet." The questionnaire then asked, "What are some of the most fatal diseases?" Responded Jeffords, "The Indians on this reserve are remarkably free from disease."[3] Thirteen years later, the band was imprisoned and the fatalities from communicable diseases began.

No doubt Jeffords's perceptions were accurate at the time, but to conclude the Apaches would have remained as healthy through the years if incarceration had not occurred is folly. On the contrary, it is fair to assume the obvious—that through continued contact with more and more emigrants settling in the Southwest, the excellent health of the Chiricahuas would have been compromised, although certainly not to the degree it was through imprisonment.

What is not disputable is that when the Apaches were taken forcibly out of their native land, confined in a totally different and unhealthy climate, and imperiled by a variety of unsanitary circumstances they became immediately and wholly susceptible to deadly diseases not confronted in their days of freedom. Yes, the Apaches had been exposed to a limited number of communicable diseases—mainly smallpox and measles—during their experiences with the Mexican authorities and settlers. However, those episodes pale when compared with the enormity of the medical catastrophes that occurred as a result of later encounters with United States government and military personnel.

Many sightseers, Indian advocates, teachers, missionaries, and others carried virulent diseases as well, particularly tuberculosis and malaria. And the imprisoned Apaches were exposed to these ailments each time the general population mingled with them during their confinement. This was particularly true in the South, according to medical writer Ernest Faust, who reported that "by 1850–1860, most of the settled part of the country was highly malarious, although the hot beds of the infection were in the South . . . as prosperity developed in the United States, as land came under more intensive cultivation and the price of quinine was greatly reduced, the heavily endemic territory began to shrink into the area from the coast of Virginia to Central Florida and westward to eastern Oklahoma and Texas."[4] And the east-central coast of Florida was selected as the site of the first Apache prisoner-of-war camp in 1886 by government officials who more than likely were aware of the medical situation but disregarded the clinical implications of their decision.

Admirers of official policy may point out that not a great deal was known in those early days about communicable diseases, but support of governmental actions is indefensible with regard to at least one ailment—malaria. Preventive measures and treatments of the time would have been sufficient to keep contagion among the Apaches to a minimum, but no assistance of any kind, however simple, was offered to help the prisoners survive this ailment or any of the other contagious diseases then flourishing within the Chiricahua camp. Why?

The southwestern United States in the late nineteenth and early twentieth centuries was touted as the most healthful section of the nation for tuberculosis patients. Thousands of coughing, spitting, sneezing, sweating, and shaking easterners and midwesterners, most of recent European descent, moved to the region and set up tent towns outside established cities where the air was pure and where they could rest and recuperate. One wonders how many "lungers," as they were called, knew (or cared) that the land beneath their feet once nourished and nurtured the mighty Chiricahua Apache people. Did they know that the Apaches were coughing, spitting, sneezing, sweating, and shaking too, but couldn't come home to breathe the sweet air again? The prisoners of war remained where they were, poorly fed and clothed amid rain, dankness, illness, and death, while non-Indian patients recovered in the Indians' homelands and hundreds of special medical facilities to care for them sprang up like healing herbs all over the Arizona and New Mexico countryside.

There was no relief in sight for the Apaches until a few advocacy organizations took up the fight and the issue of the suffering prisoners of war exploded publicly. At the conclusion of lengthy bureaucratic machinations, clearly the result of public pressure, the captives were moved. In Alabama, however, the even wetter and more inclement climate caused the prisoners' canvas tent homes, whose walls became soaked with tuberculosis bacilli, to rot. Whether or not the decaying canvas was subsequently made into wearing apparel for the prisoners, as legend tells, is the stuff of frontier myths. It is certain, however, that most of the eighty to one hundred tent homes became so ripe and heavy with infectious diseases that they had to be burned to the ground. But first, log houses were constructed by Apaches who had been convinced to join the military.

Forty-six prisoners of war, comprised of more or less healthy men, were enlisted into the United States Army to give them something to do. These new recruits were permitted to carry guns, to drill, to engage in the war games of the time, and to perform the heavy-duty tasks required to keep the prisoner-of-war camp operating. Those who fell ill with tuberculosis, malaria, or other ailments were released from duty, and others were eventually conscripted to round out the numbers. Even when it was short of soldiers, the company continued its civilian activities and military maneuvers, marching side by side with invisible microscopic murderers capable of killing the soldiers and their loved ones, and plodding through sheeting rainstorms, ankle-deep sucking Alabama mud, and swarms of insects. Hungry, bloodsucking mosquitoes surrounded the Apaches by the millions, always eager to inject misery and to withdraw health through their razor-sharp mouthparts.

The Apaches' log homes in this swamplike setting had no door or window screens to keep the devilish insects out. In their wake, babies died from infected bites that grew into raging septicemias, oozing pustules broke open and ran down the faces and bodies of adults, and deadly malaria flourished. Everyone was sick with one ailment or another.

Not much changed immediately after the Chiricahuas were transferred out of the sopping East to the drier Oklahoma red earth
country. The Apaches continued to cough, spit, sneeze, sweat, and
shake at Fort Sill, still suffering with the diseases acquired in Alabama. Almost three hundred died at Fort Sill. Batches of family
graves in the Apache cemetery today stand as silent witness to the
profane power of contagion. Especially poignant are the graves of
the children.

Along with other grieving parents, Tiss-nolth-tos and his wife Os-
kis-say lost three of their youngsters in rapid succession: Wesley in
1907, Omaha in 1908, and Rufus Jim in 1911. Casper and Josephine
Cailis's five children died in nine years: Oscar in 1900, Julius in
1902, Michael in 1903, Lyle in 1907, and Lucy in 1909. Six of the
Yah-nah-ki and Charlotte LoSahnne family died in seven years:
Clance in 1900, Roland in 1903, Evaline in 1905, Reverend in May
and James in August 1907, and Ethel in 1910. Edwin and Rachel
Yah-no-zha buried six in twelve years: Clyde in 1900, Jewel in 1901,
Kate in March and Thelma in October 1906, Ethel in 1910, and
Cecilia Alice in 1912. Rogers Toklanni and his wife, Siki, watched
five of their children die: Ruth in 1896, Jennie in March and Nor-
man in June 1899, Oliver in 1902, and Lawton in 1911.

Chief Naiche and his three wives buried eight children at Fort
Sill. Three were from his marriage to Nah-de-yole: Peter and Paul
in 1898, and Lena in 1899. Two were from his marriage to E-clah-
heh: Bah-nas-kli in 1901 and May in 1902. Naiche and his third
wife, Ha-o-zinne, saw Jacob die in 1904, Granville in 1905, and
Roscoe in 1910.

The Chihuahua family also seemed particularly hard hit. The
chief and Ilth-gozey lost Mable in 1895, Tom in 1896, Osceola in
1901, and Emily in 1909. Eugene Chihuahua, son of the chief, and
his wife, Viola, had six children die in rapid succession: Tennyson
in 1901, Phillip in 1902, Fanny and Esther in 1903, Rose in 1904,
and Raymond in 1906.

A walk around the Apache cemetery today at Beef Creek on the
post is a heartbreaking experience. Whole families occupy large sections under old, sheltering trees that have watched over these dead
Apaches for nearly a century. Diagonally to the right of the entrance, Chief Naiche's wives and offspring lie in shade most of the

day, although Naiche himself is buried at Mescalero. It is said he died from pneumonia or tuberculosis in 1921, eight years after his arrival in New Mexico at Whitetail, on the Mescalero Reservation. Dorothy Naiche, the chief's daughter with E-cla-heh, is buried off the post in another cemetery in the nearby town of Apache. Her husband, James Kaywaykla, and several of their children and other relatives are buried at the base of a slight slope in the land, not too far from the Naiches. Usually there are flowers at the base of James's marker and those of several of his descendants. The contemporary Kaywayklas, who still live in the Fort Sill area, are quite vigilant in honoring the graves of their parents and grandparents.

Out in the midday sun rest the children of Sam Haozous and his wife, Nellie Gray: son Allyn Capron Haozous, who died on July 16, 1900, and daughter Margaret, who died on January 14, 1901. Nellie is there as well; she died not too long after Margaret, on May 27, 1901. Said Michael Darrow, historian of the contemporary Fort Sill Chiricahua/Warm Springs Apache tribe and grandson of Sam and Blossom Haozous, "In some places you can see entire families that died out. There's hardly anyone alive now who doesn't have relatives buried here."[5]

Some of the Chiricahua Apaches in the cemetery were once students at Carlisle, where tuberculosis was rampant. But it was not only Carlisle; many boarding schools for Indian students across the nation were equally infected. Overcrowding and poor ventilation in most of the schools were the culprits that began the vicious cycle of contagion. Governmental regulations permitted a minimum of 500 cubic feet of air space per pupil in the dormitories, which was adequate during warmer months when windows could be opened. But at Carlisle, for example, long and harsh Pennsylvania winters in overheated rooms exacerbated ailments such as nasopharyngitis and tonsillitis. The sick students' coughing, spitting, sneezing, sweating, and shaking helped to spread ailments such as tuberculosis.

Added to airborne contagion from the flying bacilli were health hazards inherent in the washing facilities at many boarding schools. While running water and separate towels for the pupils were also governed by Indian Office regulations, the use of the towels was frequently unsanitary. In most facilities they were hung up by loops at their corners on rows of nails driven into the walls so close together

A section of the Apache prisoner-of-war cemetery at Fort Sill. More than 300 Chiricahua Apaches are buried here. (H. Henrietta Stockel)

that towels overlapped and infectious organisms were transferred from one to the next. Common drinking cups rested nearby, acting as containers in which millions of infectious germs lived and multiplied.

Toilets contributed to the increasing rate of contagion; they were located in dank basements and were often in a state of disrepair. Outhouses were in use as well, and during the summer they served as breeding places for hundreds of thousands of flies that had easy access to the dormitories and classrooms, but not the kitchens and dining rooms. These facilities were usually well screened with fine-mesh weave.

Considering that about 24 prisoners died at Fort Marion, at least 36 children died at Carlisle, and approximately 250 prisoners died in Alabama in eight years, it is surprising that no more than 300 Chiricahuas died at Fort Sill in two decades. Apparently the peak point of medical fatalities had passed during the period of incarceration in Oklahoma, and a general recovery was slowly beginning. Unfortunately, unsanitary conditions at Fort Sill continued to contribute to the general ill health of most of the prisoners.

In particular, the lack of adequate screens on the doors and windows of the Apaches' homes allowed flies and mosquitoes inside, where they had ready access to foodstuffs and the people themselves. Similar unhealthy conditions among Indian tribes across the nation were so serious that a graphic description of a doctor's visit to an unnamed tribe and patient appeared in a U.S. Senate document, apparently in an effort to convince readers of the oppressive and thankless job the medical branch of the Office of Indian Affairs was required to perform.

After a drive of 14 miles over bad roads, through rain and sleet we arrive. We enter the house; in one room about 12 feet square live from 5 to 10 people; they sleep on dirty blankets or a pile of dirty rags strewed around on the floor, which is covered with grease and filth . . . all the doors and windows are closed to keep out the cold. . . . Dark as it is and cold, every time you move you can hear the flies buzzing as they are driven from their sleeping places. Indeed, some of them have not yet gone to bed and can be dimly seen crawling around over the nostrils and lips of the little sufferer whom the doctor has come to see. . . . He is 5 years old, has had whooping cough for the past three weeks, and now has pneumonia. The poor little fellow is so dirty the doctor hates to touch him. On the same pile of rags is stretched his sister, 12 years old, in the last stages of consumption. If by some miracle the child should survive its present ailments, it would certainly die later of tuberculosis.[6]

Cato Sells, the commissioner of Indian affairs during the early 1900s, was so alarmed by the many reports he received about the unhealthy conditions that he had sanitation instructions printed and distributed to Indian reservations. Labeled "From Breeding Place to Feeding Place," the fliers read, in part:

Flies feast on tuberculosis sputum and other discharges of the sick, and then go direct to your food, to your drink, to the lips of your sleeping child, or perhaps to a small open wound on your hands or face. Germs deposited in milk multiply very fast.

WHAT TO DO TO GET RID OF FLIES.

Screen your windows and doors. Do it early before fly time and keep screens up until snow falls.

Screen all food. Do not eat food that has been in contact
   with flies.
Screen the baby's bed and keep flies away from the baby's
   bottle, the baby's food and the baby's "comforter."
Keep flies away from the sick. Screen the patient's bed. Kill
   every fly that enters the sick room.
Catch the flies as fast as they appear. Use sticky fly paper
   and traps.

ELIMINATE THE BREEDING PLACES OF FLIES.

Sprinkle chloride of lime or kerosene over contents of privy
   vaults and garbage boxes. Keep garbage receptacles tightly
   covered, clean the cans every day, the boxes every week. Keep
   the ground around garbage boxes clean.
Sprinkle chloride of lime over manure piles, old paper, old
   straw, and other refuse of like nature. Keep manure in
   screened pit or vault if possible. Manure should be removed at
   least every week.
Pour kerosene into the drains. Keep sewerage system in good
   order; repair all leaks immediately.
Don't allow dirt to accumulate in corners, behind doors, back of
   radiators, under stoves, etc.
Allow no decaying matter of any sort to accumulate on or near
   your premises.

FLIES IN THE HOME INDICATE A CARELESS HOUSEKEEPER.

REMEMBER: NO DIRT—NO FLIES.[7]

Easier said than done at Fort Sill. For years, various civilians,
Indian agents, and military personnel responsible for the Chiricahuas attempted to procure eighteen-gauge screening (wide-weave
twelve-gauge mesh was issued by the army for use in the Apache
villages). Oddly, the military bureaucracy could not or would not
fulfill a simple request for screens capable of protecting the prisoners, at least minimally, from diseases carried by flying pests. It
was not until almost a decade later, during the later period of incarceration, that a shipment of eighteen-gauge screens was at long
last sent and installed in the windows and doors of homes within
the twelve Apache villages. But by that time flies and mosquitoes
had exacerbated the existing and pervasive unhealthy conditions at
the fort.

In fairness, it must be stated that military and civilian personnel living on the post grounds had equal difficulty obtaining eighteen-gauge screens. However, the consequences of their not having this material were quite different from the results felt by the Apaches. Employees and their families were able to adopt hygienic techniques that helped them avoid contagion, and most non-Indians had partial or total immunity to the communicable diseases fostered by flies, mosquitoes, and a lack of sanitation. The prisoners, on the other hand, were still learning and experimenting with good sanitary habits and incrementally developing resistance to diseases.

While there is no statistically valid comparison of the rates of the Fort Sill personnel's morbidity and mortality due to *any* medical causes with those of the prisoner Apaches, there is documentation that describes all Indians' susceptibility to certain diseases as being higher than non-Indians'. A report from the commissioner of Indian affairs in June 1913 regarding the general pattern of certain diseases among Native American groups states, "Comparative studies plainly show that the prevalence of tuberculosis among Indians is greatly in excess of that among the white race."[8] Another report from the same commissioner, issued simultaneously, addresses the same topic, stating: "It is reported that there are approximately 25,000 Indians suffering from tuberculosis, while available hospital facilities will accommodate but a few hundred. During the last fiscal year, 1,095 Indians were reported as having died from tuberculosis, and this probably represents not more than 75 per cent of the total number who have succumbed to this disease. In order to check and control this condition, a large expenditure of funds will be necessary and the situation is so grave that immediate action should be taken."[9] Like the screens that took so long to arrive at Fort Sill, this 1913 recommendation was too little, too late. But here at least is a hint of another nervous high government official (Commissioner Cato Sells, who issued the "From Breeding Place to Feeding Place" fliers, was the first) stirred to action by his conscience, even if some of the prisoners were just about to be released to begin again—this time at Mescalero.

When they arrived at the Mescalero Apache Reservation on Friday, April 4, 1913, the Chiricahuas were apprehensive and worried about the future. From a secure, protected environment at Fort Sill, where they had established farms and run cows for twenty years, and attempted to recuperate from all that had befallen them, they were suddenly thrust into yet another way of life. Starting over one more time caused quite a bit of nervousness. No doubt their fears were confirmed when they discovered that the government housing they had been promised at Whitetail, a remote site seven thousand feet up a mountain within the reservation's borders, was not ready. The officer in charge of the Apaches, Major George W. Goode, promised that it wouldn't be long before everyone was comfortably settled and murmured all sorts of reassurances. The Chiricahuas believed him and moved into temporary tents erected not far from the agency headquarters to await transfer to their homes.

A month later Goode returned to Mescalero to inspect the progress made by the Apaches in establishing an independent way of life in their new surroundings. Imagine his surprise when he discovered them still encamped. Nothing of any significance regarding the plight of the newcomers had occurred in Goode's absence.

On October 8, 1913, he came back again and found the Apaches in desperate need of heavy clothing. Only blankets and shoes had been distributed since their arrival six months earlier. By that time winter was closing in fast and frantic preparations were being made at Whitetail. Up so high, Whitetail usually felt the full blast of winter earlier in the season than did homesites at lower altitudes. Howling winds, heavy snows, ice, and isolation were routine at Whitetail, even as early as autumn. Also because of the altitude, the growing period was short, and the Apaches had already lost the opportunity to plant and harvest one season of crops as they waited for permission to function on their own. The outlook was bleak for getting everyone settled at Whitetail before the first snow, especially since many houses were only partially constructed, or not even started. And the rough road up the twenty-mile stretch from the agency was not totally ready, nor were the wells or stock tanks.

Although pneumonia was affecting many of the prisoners and there was no health facility to treat them, thirty families were sent to Whitetail to get through the winter as best they could in the half-built homes. Those without adequate shelter, regardless of whether they were sick or well, had to spend the winter in tents, a situation reminiscent of the first days at Fort Sill when the prisoners, recently relocated from the hot and wet Alabama countryside, nearly froze to death in wickiups because their log cabin homes were not

Chiricahua Apache home at Whitetail, Mescalero Apache Reservation, New Mexico, ca. 1915. Lone man in the photo may be Rogers Toklanni. By 1938 most of these houses had deteriorated substantially; the govern-ment was forced to construct new living quarters but provided no insula-tion in the walls or under the floors. (Frisco Native American Museum)

even started. It would be a long time—nearly ten years—before the people at Whitetail were finally settled and trying to become self-sufficient, or even adequately provisioned.

The cemetery at Whitetail claimed a few newcomers in those early years, and many more before the settlement was abandoned in the 1950s. Unlike the Apache cemetery at Fort Sill, there are no rows of military markers in clusters denoting family sections. Tucked away in a secret hiding place, the graveyard at Whitetail isn't visible from the dirt road and doesn't attract tourists as its counterpart in Oklahoma does. Perhaps that's because Geronimo isn't buried at Mescalero, or because not too many visitors find their way to this special place on the reservation. At Whitetail, most of the dead had to depend upon their kin to provide the tombstones, so the sizes and shapes of the monuments vary. Standard granite gravestones, old temporary plastic markers still implanted in the soil, a baby's toys piled atop a tiny unlabeled earthen bump, iron-work fences, and anonymous, elongated mounds form the mosaic of this cemetery.

Asa Daklugie's grave is prominent, as it should be for the leader who survived all the years of incarceration, including schooling at Carlisle. It is noticeable that Chief Naiche's grave is not here; he is buried at another site, one that his family prefers to keep private.

A new grave with fresh and plastic flowers commands attention. It is for one of the original prisoners of war, of whom there are less than a handful still alive at Mescalero. About ten former prisoners live in Oklahoma and range in age from the late seventies to close to one hundred years.

Some of the Kanseahs are buried at the Whitetail cemetery, but the family doesn't know the exact spot. Jasper Kanseah's descen-dants want to search official files or church archives for a map of who lies where because there are so many unmarked graves. Their preliminary efforts to locate records or old descriptions of the ceme-tery have fallen through, just as almost all of the homes at Whitetail have done. Very few are still standing, but dilapidated as they are, the boards hold an overwhelming sense of sadness. And the sense of frustration in the air is practically palpable even today. No wonder.

By spring 1915, two years after the former prisoners of war had arrived at Mescalero, housing had still not been entirely completed. Those homes that had been erected were constructed so shoddily and of such poor materials that James O. Arthur, a Reformed church missionary among the Chiricahua at Whitetail, observed, "When the high winds from the west . . . sweep down the canyon, every crack and knot-hole is discovered to admit the cooling breeze." Arthur also thought the homes a "disgrace to the white men who are responsible for their erection." They were built from green lumber, and the sap oozed each time a carpenter's nail was driven. When the wood dried, the floors, inside ceilings, and walls cracked. And "the knots drop out of the boards."[10] By the end of 1918, houses had to be rebuilt for several families while others were still waiting to have their promised shelters completed.

That wasn't the worst of it at Whitetail. Political procrastination, fires, crop failures, inclement weather, hunger (government rations were stopped in October 1914), continuing illness (7.2 percent of the Apaches on the Mescalero Reservation were tubercular),[11] and

*Warm Springs Apache Rogers Toklanni with wife Siki (daughter of Loco)
in chair, and unidentified woman standing. Although a prisoner of war,
Toklanni proudly wears medals awarded previously by the U.S. government for his service as a scout. (Frisco Native American Museum)*

terrible poverty plagued the Chiricahuas. William A. Light, the agent at Mescalero, discussed openly his fear that many Chiricahuas would die of diseases or starvation. Leader Asa Daklugie was more graphic. "At the present time some of our number are existing on less than white people feed to their dogs," he said.[12] The situation was so serious in 1918 that Major General Hugh L. Scott, former officer in charge of the Apaches at Fort Sill and later army chief of staff, paid a visit to Mescalero in his new role as a member of the Board of Indian Commissioners. Seeing the deplorable situation firsthand, Scott apologized to the Chiricahuas. "I am sorry," he said. "I am responsible for your people moving here." [13] He offered to personally escort anyone who wanted to return to Oklahoma. Several agreed to go, but they may have regretted their decision once they arrived.

In and around the growing farm town of Apache,[14] seventeen miles north of Fort Sill, conditions were not much better. Freedom for the eighty-nine prisoners who had opted to remain in Oklahoma was delayed more than a year after their friends and relatives departed for Mescalero. The allotments of land were so slow in being granted that at the end of 1920, seven years after the majority of Chiricahuas went to New Mexico, several Apaches were still waiting and depending on friends and relatives for shelter and sustenance. In Oklahoma too, starting over caused untold hardships. In particular, the farming and ranching achievements realized by the prisoners during twenty years on the Fort Sill military reserve could not be transferred to the new living arrangement. It is true that the Apaches were paid the proceeds from the sale of their livestock and crops, but beginning anew required initiatives from each family, some of whom were very ill and barely able to suck in air, much less to manage a farm or run cows. No longer could these Oklahomans count on support from friends and relatives, as they had been doing for decades. Now each family was on its own and was struggling for a livelihood. The newly released prisoners were dropped into the middle of an agrarian society that regarded them as suspiciously as the Indians regarded their neighbors. And many of their loved ones, on whom they should have been able to count for cultural, physical, and emotional support, were far away in New Mexico, having their own serious difficulties.

The final separation still exists. Although the two branches of the

Chiricahua Apaches visit back and forth, the chasm between them is so old, and both groups of the contemporary band are so different, that they share only a few similarities. For example, the ancient language is still spoken among a few older Chiricahuas at Mescalero, but those in Oklahoma have practically lost their mother tongue. Happily, there is an effort under way to reintroduce the ancient dialect to tribal members living in and around Apache. It might be possible in the future for many descendants of both branches to talk together again in the language of their ancestors.

Traditional sacred ceremonies in both locations are well attended, but afterward participants return to their homes and retreat back into their family routines. Often, the people do not meet again for many months. The ten-hour drive one way between the sites in New Mexico and Oklahoma is prohibitive except on special occasions.

The younger generations lead busy lives and, with rare exceptions, pay little attention to their historical heritage. A core group of descendants is attempting to revitalize their people by teaching traditional ways and practices, but the task is arduous and thankless. The American mainstream has beckoned, and its benefits are so seductive that many Chiricahua Apaches in both states cannot resist. To return to their old-fashioned roots would require more of a commitment than many care to make.

Illness is still a central concern, but now it is alcoholism and diabetes that kill, rather than tuberculosis and malaria. In a bizarre way, the modern diseases are also contagious, for very few Chiricahuas get by without being touched by one or the other. Too many members of the mighty nation that once roamed and reigned over the southwestern countryside now lie in its hospital beds with swollen livers or gangrenous limbs—or both. Too many others have gone somewhere else and married outside the tribe, to Indians from another group or to non-Indians. Sometimes they come back home for the ceremonies; sometimes they don't. In New Mexico and Oklahoma, the numbers of Chiricahua Apaches are dwindling once again as they did during incarceration. Not many ask why these things happen anymore; the answers are too painful.

The grandchildren of the great ones, now elders themselves, still hold out hope, though. In the sacred circles of their hearts they trust their people will overcome, will survive and grow—just as their parents, grandparents, and other ancestors believed. After all, Naiche and Geronimo surrendered voluntarily to avoid the extermination of the Chiricahuas. If annihilation didn't happen with the army's weapons, and didn't happen with contagious diseases, it won't happen now.

It must not happen now.

AFTERWORD

❋ ❋ ❋ ❋

We may never know whether government officials plotted genocide to destroy the infamous Chiricahua Apaches. Now, more than seventy-five years after the Apaches' final release from incarceration, there are no documents that incriminate specific politicians, military leaders, or bureaucrats; there is no "gun" still "smoking"; and well-respected authors and academicians with nationwide reputations in American history reject even the mention of such an allegation. Instead, many who are well informed and knowledgeable cite only a bumbling bureaucracy that cared little about the fate of these Indians. While that position has logical and objective validity, the counterpoint that has evolved inside the Chiricahua Apache culture, and is discussed only reluctantly, deserves thoughtful consideration.

A vague distress or discontent surfaces among the ten or so survivors of the confinement when the topic of the medical catastrophes they and their relatives suffered arises. Now elders of the tribe, these men and women who were born into captivity and some contemporary descendants of the prisoners of war believe a campaign of annihilation against their families prevailed in the camps, endorsed and supported by consecutive political administrations. It is not difficult to understand and sympathize with this view, but is it realistic? Could the government have really waged such an unconscionable campaign?

Did officials, through sins of omission or sins of commission, approve a policy of extermination? If not, then many sick Chiricahuas died as a result of bureaucratic inertia. Is there a difference between that and genocide? If so, the distinction may be only a definition in a dictionary.

Certainly it would have been a simple matter, once the politics of the situation were resolved, to return the ailing Apaches to health in their homelands. It was a well-known fact that the arid southwestern climate was conducive to healing respiratory diseases such as tuberculosis. As a matter of fact, hundreds, if not thousands, of non-Indians were already recuperating from this illness and others in Arizona and New Mexico. Why not allow the dying prisoners the same opportunity? Each time the issue was raised by either of the two powerful Indian advocacy organizations of the day or by concerned civilian and military officials who dealt directly with the Chiricahuas it was ignored by Washington officialdom. Is this neglect in and of itself genocide? In the minds of many non-Indians who are experts in the history of the American West, no, it is not.

But today's Chiricahuas carry a soul-deep suspicion about the actions of the United States government toward their kinfolk in captivity. One cannot blame them, surely, and when the topic of deliberate extinction is carefully introduced in quiet conversations, a dank and heavy sorrow suddenly joins the circle.

During one of these intensely private moments, an elderly Chiricahua Apache man, his eyes riveted to the ground, murmured low, "Well, after all your investigations, what do you think?"

I waited long seconds out of respect for his prisoner-of-war parents and his siblings who had died in boarding school. Then, "Yes, I believe it happened," I responded softly.

"Will you say it in your book?" he asked, his voice barely a whisper. "No one has done that before."

"I will," I promised.

CHAPTER 1:
PEOPLES, HOMELANDS, AND CULTURAL CUSTOMS

1. Sweeney, *Cochise*, p. 3. The Zunis, one of twenty-five Puebloan groups, were a peaceful and sedentary people who lived in separate villages along the Rio Grande in New Mexico and westward toward Arizona. The Zunis still live in their ancestral homelands and are well known for their traditional, deeply religious ceremonies and for crafting beautiful jewelry.

2. Gunnerson, "Southern Athapaskan Archeology," p. 162.

3. Sweeney, *Cochise*, pp. 4–5. Leaders of these bands were Mangas Coloradas, Nana, Loco, and Victorio of the Chihennes (the Red Paint People), brothers Juan Diego and Juan Jose Compa, and Juh of the Nednis (the Enemy People), Cochise of the Chokonen (the band first referred to as Chiricahua), and Geronimo of the Bedonkohes (the smallest division, assimilated into the other bands in the early 1860s). Inclusion of members of one band into another became a necessity as more and more Apaches fell victim to military actions. For example, Victorio's band was practically annihilated by Mexicans at Tres Castillos in October 1880. The Chihennes who survived did so because they were elsewhere when the attack took place. Those who avoided capture, a life of slavery in Mexico, or death eventually joined with other groups. Victorio's sister Lozen, for example, joined Naiche's group. At the time, Geronimo was already part of the group. For a complete account of the life of Victorio and the battle at Tres Castillos, see Thrapp, *Victorio and the Mimbres Apaches*.

4. Opler, "Chiricahua Apache," p. 401.

5. Griffen, *Apaches at War and Peace*, p. 5.

6. Moorhead, *The Apache Frontier*, p. 4.

7. Hrdlicka, "Psychological and Medical Observations," p. 221. This article has become a classic for researchers interested in several aspects of Native American culture in the days of the Old West. Hrdlicka, a trained scientist who specialized in diseases affecting early Native Americans, spared no detail in his descriptions of the health of members of several tribes.

8. Elmore, "The Shaman and Modern Medicine," p. 41. Although

the statements of Elmore and Hrdlicka were made so long ago that they may seem outdated to more contemporary researchers, these two writers have excellent reputations, and their depictions of Native American societies of the time are quite credible.

9. Gordon, *Medicine Throughout Antiquity*, p. 409.
10. Underhill, "Ceremonial Patterns," p. 35.
11. Gordon, *Medicine Throughout Antiquity*, pp. 407–8.
12. Perrone et al., *Medicine Women*, pp. 3–17.
13. Stockel, *Women of the Apache Nation*, p. 1.
14. Ibid., p. 2.
15. Ibid., p. 3.
16. Thrapp, *The Conquest of Apacheria*, p. x.
17. Hrdlicka, "Psychological and Medical Observations," p. 243.
18. Elmore, "The Shaman and Modern Medicine," p. 41.
19. Farrell, "Mesquite," p. 42.
20. Hrdlicka, "Seven Prehistoric Skulls," p. 355.
21. Gordon, *Medicine Throughout Antiquity*, p. 417.
22. Ibid., p. 418.
23. Opler, "The Concept of Supernatural Power," p. 70. This classic article is an essential part of any research on Apache spirituality.
24. Underhill, "Ceremonial Patterns," p. 40.
25. Skinner, *Geronimo at Fort Pickens*, p. 4. This taboo is also described in several earlier publications. Geronimo himself mentioned it: "There were many fish in the streams, but as we did not eat them, we did not try to catch or kill them. . . . USSEN did not intend snakes, frogs, or fishes to be eaten" (Barrett, *Geronimo: His Own Story*, pp. 79–80). In 1871, John G. Bourke wrote, "Pork and fish were objects of the deepest repugnance to both men and women" (Bourke, *On the Border with Crook*, p. 125). Frederick Schwatka, in an article about Apaches in 1887, commented, "It would almost seem that they had some supernatural dread of water. . . . Fish never enters into their diet . . . and they repel them in a way that can only be based on superstition" (Schwatka, *Among the Apaches*, p. 12). And, in 1938, Frank C. Lockwood wrote of the Apache, "He did not eat bear meat or pork, or the flesh of the turkey" (Lockwood, *The Apache Indians*, p. 46). A more contemporary author, Eve Ball, described this and many different cultural customs in *Indeh: An Apache Odyssey*.
26. Opler, "The Concept of Supernatural Power," p. 65.
27. Perrone et al., *Medicine Women*, pp. 184–86. Chapters 15 and 16 (pp. 169–96) describe witchcraft in healing and three cultural views of witchcraft. Native American, Hispanic, and Anglo-American

cultures each have practiced bewitchment and, in many cases, continue to work evil on their members and others. The authors present a detailed tricultural view of this subject.

28. Worcester, *The Apaches*, p. 3.

CHAPTER 2:
TRADITIONAL APACHE MEDICINES AND HEALING

1. Lynda A. Sanchez, letter to the author, January 7, 1991.
2. Moore, *Medicinal Plants*, pp. 103–4.
3. Griffen, *Apaches at War and Peace*, p. 208.
4. Opler, "An Interpretation," p. 87. This article provides a comprehensive description of the Chiricahua and Mescalero Apache cultures and is an excellent beginning piece for anyone interested in the ethnology and anthropology of the Apache peoples.
5. Hugar, conversation with the author, June 1989.
6. Opler, "An Interpretation," p. 85. Interestingly, people who are thought to be witches do not take these precautions, for becoming involved with the dead in any way is not dangerous to them. As a matter of fact, witches are friendly with ghosts and may practice their craft through this relationship. Witchcraft consists of the intentional use of power for harmful reasons, and a person may be considered to be a witch because of his or her public actions and aberrant personality. According to L. Boyer et al., witches have three principal ways of operating: through magical words or gestures, by calling upon their supernatural power, and by controlling the actions of ghosts ("An Apache Woman's Account"). Today, witches still function within the culture but may be ostracized from the tribe or may be the butt of jokes or gossip. Naturally, they also may be feared.
7. Opler, *An Apache Lifeway*, pp. 230–32.
8. Boyer et al., "An Apache Woman's Account," p. 302. The Boyers have been engaged in a combined anthropological and psychoanalytic study of the Apaches on the Mescalero Apache Reservation in conjunction with others since 1957. Their longest period of continuous residence there lasted for almost fifteen months in 1959–60. They have spent some time at Mescalero during each of the past thirty-four years. Their ultimate purpose is to delineate the interactions among social structure, socialization patterns, and personality organization.
9. Vogel, *American Indian Medicine*, p. 336. Vogel attributed this

remedy to the Mescalero Apaches, the San Carlos, White Mountain, and Jicarilla Apaches. His survey of Apache plant medicines does not include any specifically preferred by the Chiricahuas, which is an unusual omission from this splendid account. However, he did refer to John Bourke's "Medicine Men of the Apache," which contains information about the Chiricahuas.

10. Moore, *Medicinal Plants*, pp. 75–76.

11. The Apache life-style resulted in an unpredictable food supply. When the hunt was successful, food was plenty. When drought was upon the land, food was scarce. Frequently, starvation alternated with gorging, which wreaked havoc on the digestive system and caused a variety of gastrointestinal symptoms that persisted up to and through the years of captivity. One of the major medical complaints by the Apaches during their period of incarceration at Fort Sill (1894–1914) was constipation. The traditional plant remedy, Apache plume, did not grow in the soil of southern Oklahoma.

12. Haley, *Apaches*, p. 77.

13. Officer and Castetter, "Ethnobotany," pp. 24–25. Britton Davis also mentioned this plant in his book *The Truth about Geronimo* (p. 168) as being used as a poultice to treat a gunshot wound. An army surgeon was prepared to amputate the arm of an Apache, Big Dave, but other Apaches present preferred to cover the wound with *yerba de vivora*, change the dressing, and keep the wound dry. Three months later the patient had recovered the use of his arm.

14. Shapard Papers, North Carolina (hereafter cited SPNC), 1st Loco file (1/2), MC-28, Andrews, "Military Surgery among the Apaches," pp. 1–3.

15. Haley, *Apaches*, p. 78.

16. Opler, *An Apache Lifeway*, p. 217.

17. Bourke, "Medicine Men of the Apache," p. 471.

18. Stone, *Medicine among the American Indians*, pp. 35, 37.

19. Opler, *Apache Odyssey*, p. 89.

20. Bourke, "Medicine Men of the Apache," p. 453.

21. Stone, *Medicine among the American Indians*, p. 8; Karolevitz, *Doctors of the Old West*, p. 3.

22. Hrdlicka, "Psychological and Medical Observations," p. 224.

23. Sweeney, *Cochise*, p. 395.

24. Arizona Historical Society (hereafter cited AHS), Al Williamson Collection.

25. Thrapp, *Victorio*, p. 168; AHS, Fred G. Hughes Collection.

26. Edwin R. Sweeney, letter to the author, January 22, 1991.

27. *Annual Report of the Commissioner of Indian Affairs*, 1874, p. 302.

28. SPNC, 1st Loco file (1/2), MC-28, Andrews, "Military Surgery among the Apaches," pp. 3–5.
29. Boyer and Boyer, "Understanding the Individual," pp. 30–31.
30. I have collected *hoddentin* from cattails, a long process. I have also participated in a puberty ceremony by being blessed by the young maiden and blessing her in return. In this, I was guided by her mother in making a circle on the girl's forehead with pollen and, in turn, receiving a similar touch from her. The yellow color of the pollen is quite striking—in my opinion unlike any yellow in the popular color spectrum.
31. Bourke, "Medicine Men of the Apache," p. 502.
32. Stone, *Medicine among the American Indians*, pp. 27–28.
33. Ibid., p. 14.
34. Bourke, "Medicine Men of the Apache," pp. 550–54.
35. Ibid. A very powerful Apache medicine man who lives today at Mescalero wears a medicine cord as described by Bourke (e.g., hanging over the left shoulder and resting on the right hip) when accompanying the *Gah'e*, the Mountain Spirit dancers, by singing sacred songs while they dance.
36. Lockwood, *The Apache Indians*, pp. 63–65.
37. Ball, "Chiricahua Legends," pp. 110–11.
38. Huff, "The Mountain Spirits," pp. 41, 43.

CHAPTER 3:
NEWCOMERS

1. Hrdlicka, "Disease, Medicine, and Surgery," pp. 1161–63. The list of ailments Hrdlicka ruled out among pre-Columbian Native Americans includes rachitis (also known as rickets), tuberculosis, microcephaly, hydrocephaly, plague, cholera, typhus, smallpox, measles, cancer, lepra (leprosy), syphilis, nevi, and mental disorders. Malaria was probably introduced from Africa as well, via slaves. Only Hrdlicka's designation of syphilis as being absent has been disputed.
2. Cortés, *Views from the Apache Frontier*, pp. 56–58.
3. Matson and Schroeder, "Cordero's Description," p. 338.
4. Greenfield, *A History of Public Health*, pp. 7–8. This author also stated that in 1670 a great famine among both Indians and Spanish occurred. During this time, the survivors ate dried animal hides and the straps from their carts. No further information is given.
5. Aberle et al., "The Vital History," pp. 167–70.

6. Griffen, *Apaches at War and Peace*, p. 106.

7. Ibid., p. 89. Edwin Sweeney, Cochise's biographer, saw a photo of one of Geronimo's warriors whose face was pocked with small-pox scars.

8. Ibid., p. 208.

9. University of New Mexico Special Collections (hereafter cited UNMSP), Steck to Collins, November 21, 1857. Michael Steck, son of John and Elizabeth Steck, was born in Hughesville, Pennsylvania, on October 6, 1818. He attended Jefferson Medical College in Philadelphia and was graduated in 1844. Steck practiced medicine in Mifflinville, Pennsylvania, for a number of years and then accepted an appointment from President Millard Fillmore as Indian agent for the Mescalero Apaches in southeastern New Mexico. He was reappointed to this post by President James Buchanan and in 1863 was appointed superintendent of Indian affairs for New Mexico. Steck strongly and bitterly opposed the Navajo Indian policy established by General James Carleton. He "retired" from the Indian Service during this quarrel and engaged in gold mining in New Mexico with Stephen B. Elkins, later U.S. senator from West Virginia, as his partner. Steck was successful in this venture but later lost his fortune in the Williamsport and North Branch Railroad, in which he invested after his return to Pennsylvania. He retired to a farm five miles from Winchester, Virginia, and died there on October 6, 1883.

   Thrapp addressed this poisoning of Apaches by Mexicans in *Victorio and the Mimbres Apaches*, pp. 57–58, and concluded: "Arsenic, next to whiskey, was often the prime civilizing agency. . . . It also was employed by unscrupulous Americans, some in high places."

10. UNMSP, Steck to Collins, September 1857.

11. Ashburn, "How Disease Came," p. 205. This is a series of articles published in several editions of the magazine. Also addressed are the ailments brought by the slave trade, such as malaria. Yellow fever, respiratory disorders, intestinal diseases, venereal diseases, and miscellaneous others are discussed.

12. Crosby, "Conquistador y Pestilencia," p. 337.

13. McNeill, *Plagues and Peoples*, pp. 212–13.

14. Hrdlicka, "Disease, Medicine, and Surgery," pp. 1662–63.

15. Duffy, "Medicine in the West," p. 5.

1. Duffy, "Medicine in the West," pp. 7–10.
2. Magoffin, *Down the Santa Fe Trail*, p. 38.
3. Typhoid fever is a bacterial infection of the digestive system characterized by general weakness, high fever, a rash, chills, sweating, and, in extreme cases, inflammation of the spleen and bones,
   delirium, and intestinal hemorrhage. Treatment today is with antibiotics. Vaccination provides only temporary immunity.

   Griffen, in *Utmost Good Faith*; pp. 309–12, identified typhoid
   fever as one of the illnesses affecting Apaches in the middle to late
   1800s, along with smallpox, measles, various fevers, colds, convulsions, and coughs.
4. UNMSP, document dated October 9, 1864. Steck saved published
   "helpful hints" about what to do for various medical conditions.
   Box 8, item 18, is a loose page from a publication with no date that
   states with authority: "[Headache, Jaundice, Fainting] arise from
   a disordered state of the digestive organs or from the liver. When
   seized with headache, whether accompanied with nausea or not,
   take a dose of Graefenberg Vegetable Pills, bathe the head and skin
   with camphorated spirits, and lie down in a darkened room." For
   jaundice, the publication also recommends Graefenberg Vegetable
   Pills, "one full dose at night . . . and one pill every morning before breakfast for a week." For fainting, "give a dose of pills and
   let the patient keep quiet with very light diet for the day." The advice was signed by "E. Barden, M.D., Eldred, Pa." Also in Box 8,
   item 16 provides suggestions for treating poisoning, impaired digestion, and asthma, along with letters of support for Graefenberg
   Vegetable Pills.
5. The most common type is bronchopneumonia, which involves the
   bronchi and bronchioles. Lobar pneumonia affects the entire
   lobe(s), and hypostatic pneumonia develops in parts of the lung(s)
   in people who are otherwise ill or immobilized, e.g., hospital patients and the elderly. Recovery from most types of pneumonia is
   rapid once appropriate antibiotics are given.
6. Bacterial meningitis can be successfully treated with antibiotics or
   sulfonamides. Viral meningitis does not respond to drugs.
7. Treatment of trachoma is with antibiotics.
8. Tuberculosis is curable with antibiotics. Preventive measures in-

clude screening of vulnerable populations and inoculation. The tuberculin test determines which people need vaccination.

9. *Annual Report of the Commissioner of Indian Affairs*, June 30, 1914, vol. 2, p. 15; June 30, 1913, vol. 2, p. 20.

10. Ibid., June 30, 1913, vol. 1, p. 34.

11. Hrdlicka, "Tuberculosis among Certain Indian Tribes," p. 30. While the circumstances describe Native Americans' living conditions, it must be remembered that in the days before proper sanitation was understood, accepted, and applied, all groups lived under virtually the same unhealthy physical conditions; only the circumstances varied.

12. U.S. Senate, Document 1038 (62–3), p. 40.

13. Haley, *Apaches*, pp. 77–78.

14. Extracted from chinchona bark, quinine is a dangerous drug. Overdoses can cause severe poisoning; symptoms include headache, fever, vomiting, confusion, and damage to the eyes and ears. Treatment of malaria nowadays is with chloroquinine, quinacrine, and chloroguanide.

15. Marc Simmons, "Sure to Cure or Kill," *Santa Fe Reporter*, October 28, 1981.

16. Antibiotic and emetine (a drug) treatment of amebic dysentery is prolonged.

17. Griffen, *Utmost Good Faith*, p. 16.

18. Crosby, "Conquistador y Pestilencia," p. 325.

19. Betzinez, *I Fought with Geronimo*, pp. 45, 47. Silver City is today a picturesque mountain town of about ten thousand in southwestern New Mexico. In the middle of the nineteenth century it was a pleasant, grassy valley called La Ciénega de San Vicente (the marsh of Saint Vincent). In the spring of 1870 silver was discovered and the bonanza began, lasting until 1893. After a brief respite, the town got on with life through a well-developed cattle industry. Metal mines are again the major employer, followed by ranching and agriculture. Silver City is a stone's throw from the famous copper mine discovered by the Apaches before 1800 and in operation since 1804 at Santa Rita del Cobre.

20. Hopkins, *The Eradication of Smallpox*, p. 13.

21. Marc Simmons, "Small Fry, Smallpox," *Santa Fe Reporter*, May 14, 1981. Simmons's columns have been published for years in this newspaper and are one of the most popular ways of learning the history of the area. Collectors who began saving the columns in the middle 1970s now have a rich resource at their fingertips.

22. Greenfield, *A History of Public Health*, p. 11. A document relating

the history of this interesting episode, including details about children transferring the vaccine from arm to arm, is Smith, "Royal Vaccination Expedition," *Transactions of the American Philosophical Society* 64, pt. 1 (1974): 30–40. Bringing the vaccine north into the provinces was truly a heroic effort by the Spanish Empire, regardless of its motivations, which may have been purely economic.

23. New Mexico State Records Center and Archives, Delgado Family Papers, Dinge Collection. Digitalis, long a cardiac staple, is made from an extract of the leaves of the foxglove plant (*Digitalis purpurea*), but it is not known where the Delgado family obtained their supply. Moore (*Los Remedios*) does not identify foxglove as a medicinal plant growing in the Santa Fe area. It is believed Native Americans used foxglove as a cardiac stimulant hundreds of years before digitalis was "introduced" by William Withering in England, about 1778.

24. Opler, *An Apache Lifeway*, pp. 187, 241, 278. Betzinez discussed the dance also, calling it a "fire dance" (p. 93) or a "medicine dance" (p. 179). In the latter reference, he reported that he tried to stop the Apaches from having the dance because he believed tuberculosis was passed from one person to another through the common use of dance masks. From Betzinez's point of view, the medicine dance was one of the causes of the ailment rather than a remedy. His attempts to prohibit the dance didn't endear him to some of the Apaches, nor did many of his other actions, as described candidly by Betzinez in *I Fought with Geronimo*. Jason Betzinez is buried at the Fort Sill Apache Cemetery, not far from Geronimo's grave. His is the only nonmilitary cemetery marker in the entire graveyard.

25. Pijoan, interview with the author, June 27, 1990.

26. Ewers, "The Influence of Epidemics," p. 110.

27. Virgil Vogel, in *American Indian Medicine* (pp. 125, 204–5, 311–12, and 399), listed the varied uses of this medicinal plant: to treat sore eyes, as a tonic, as an astringent used in inflammation of the mucous membranes (thus its effect in cholera), in childbirth, and for jaundice, ulcerated stomach, colds, and sore mouth.

28. The mortality rate for untreated cases of cholera is more than 50 percent. Treatment is through intravenous salt solution and antibiotics. Vaccination is effective for only six to nine months.

29. Vogel, *American Indian Medicine*, p. 396, discussed several tribes' uses of this medicinal plant. Sagebrush was gathered in large quantities by the Shoshonis and the Utes, and the seeds were eaten after adequate preparation. These same two western tribes boiled sagebrush into a tea and drank it to ease a variety of ailments ranging

from canker sores to irregular menstruation to warts. Religious uses included offering the mashed seeds to the spirits for good health. See H. H. Stockel, "Natural Medicines: Native Americans Found a Pharmacy in Desert Flora," *Las Vegas Review Journal*, October 28, 1990, p. 4U.

30. *Cascara sagrada*, according to Vogel, is the most widely used cathartic on earth; it was first discovered by Native Americans and named "sacred bark" by a Spanish priest.

31. As a soak, small pieces of the *osha* root are placed in a large pan of warm water and allowed to steep for a few minutes. The affected body part is submerged until the water cools or until the patient has had enough.

32. Moore, *Los Remedios*, pp. 30, 58, 28, 10, 55, 61, 24, 9.

33. Also called hydrophobia, rabies is transmitted through a bite from an infected mammal. Symptoms appear in ten days to one year and include malaise, very high fever, difficulty in breathing, and painful swallowing. If not treated with injections of rabies vaccine and rabies antiserum, death follows convulsions and paralysis.

34. Dobie, "Madstones and Hydrophobia Skunks," pp. 3–5. This is a fascinating piece of southwestern folklore and history, combining health, illness, superstition, gossip, oral history, medical anthropology, and the author's rich imagination.

35. Marc Simmons, "The Mad Killer," *Santa Fe Reporter*, January 30, 1986. This author's statistics on the mortality rate of those bitten by rabid animals are hard to believe and are in striking contrast with Dobie's (100 percent for Simmons versus 15 percent for Dobie). Although Simmons is an authority on the American Southwest, I'm sure he had doubts about this figure.

36. Woosley, "Fort Burgwin's Hospital," pp. 5–6.

37. Stockel, "Childbirth in the West," pp. 23–27.

38. Duffy, "Medicine in the West," p. 10.

39. Griffen, "Apache Indians," pp. 188, 191.

40. Howard, *This Is the West*, p. 47. Roll call was the preferred method for gathering the Apaches together under peaceful military supervision. It was utilized for many purposes, including distributing rations. After roll call on the San Carlos Apache Reservation, some Chiricahua Apaches were put into wagons and others were made to walk to Holbrook, Arizona, where they boarded trains for Fort Marion, Florida. During incarceration there, Sam Haozous, a child, was hidden in a rain barrel by his relatives so he didn't have to answer roll call. This time, the procedure was used to separate children from their parents and send the youngsters away to school

in Carlisle, Pennsylvania. Sam eventually faced the same ordeal, though.

41. Salmon, "No Hope of Victory," pp. 270–74. This classic article contains Pineda's 1791 report on the Apache frontier. An educated leader, Pineda kept a detailed journal and compiled copious manuscripts which provide insight into the frontier conditions from the perspective of a trained scientist. Elizabeth A. H. John, an independent historian whose area of special interest is Indian history in the trans-Mississippi West and particularly the northern Hispanic borderlands, wrote an article in response to Salmon's ("A Cautionary Exercise in Apache Historiography," *Journal of Arizona History* 25, no. 3 [Autumn 1984]: 301–15) in which she urged great caution in accepting Pineda's information at face value. Her thesis was that Pineda had no basis for reporting on the Apache wars because he went no farther north than Guanajuato, Mexico. She further elaborated in another article written some years later ("Bernardo De Galvez on the Apache Frontier: A Cautionary Note for Gringo Historians," *Journal of Arizona History* 29, no. 4 [Winter 1988]: 427–30). She has now identified Galvez as the author of the work originally attributed to Pineda. To the best of my knowledge, this controversy has been settled.

Regarding the superior physical conditioning of the Apaches and other outstanding qualities, John G. Bourke's *On the Border with Crook*, pp. 123–27, contains an excellent portrayal of Apaches almost a century after "Pineda's" description. Bourke's depiction is a bit more comprehensive, although similarly respectful.

42. Karolevitz, *Doctors of the Old West*, p. 139.

43. Ibid., pp. 169–70.

44. Tasty watercress today grows abundantly in a stream flowing through the former Warm Springs Apache Reservation in New Mexico. It is fair to assume that the Warm Springs people, including leaders Nana, Loco, and Victorio, chewed on watercress.

45. Clary, "The Role of the Army Surgeon," pp. 56–58.

46. Hrdlicka, "Disease, Medicine, and Surgery," p. 1662.

47. Hrdlicka, "Psychological and Medical Observations," p. 191.

48. Gordon, *Medicine Throughout Antiquity*, p. 405.

49. Worcester, "Early Spanish Accounts," p. 310. Gordon C. Baldwin, *The Apache Indians: Raiders of the Southwest* (New York: Four Winds Press, 1978), p. 147, shows a photo of Cut Nose, a Chiricahua woman who paid the public penalty for her actions. She later became a spy for the army against her own people. Many authors have written about the high moral standards of the Chiricahuas, includ-

ing their prohibition against lying, their commendable treatment of children, and their respect for elders. Many of the traditional traits are still observed today.

50. Haley, *Apaches*, p. 77.

51. Opler, *Apache Odyssey*, p. 111.

52. Opler, *An Apache Lifeway*, p. 222.

CHAPTER 5:

INCARCERATION IN FLORIDA: FORT MARION

1. Ball, *Indeh*, p. 99. Mrs. Ball became a close friend of Eugene Chihuahua's during the years she interviewed the old Apaches. He and Asa Daklugie provided her with information that would have been lost to history had she not gained their confidence and respect. Before Eugene Chihuahua died, he asked Mrs. Ball to write his obituary and bake him a pumpkin pie for the journey; she did both. In an interview with me in May 1982, she smiled as she recalled how she placed the pie in his coffin as she and his wife, Jennie, stood beside the casket.

2. Lummis, *Dateline Fort Bowie*, pp. 35–36, 58. The odd farewell dance is described on pp. 125–26.

3. SPNC, 1st Loco file (1 /2), C-49. Like many other Apache names, these names of some members of Chihuahua's band are of doubtful spelling. For example, Goody-goody may have been the ancestor of the Gooday family, Jozhya may have been Johze, Josanan was probably the chief's brother Ulzanna, and Natchez has often been synonymous with Naiche, who may be confused with another Chiricahua named Noche. Some authors believe these individuals were members of the large group sent to Florida directly from the San Carlos Reservation in September 1886. Edwin Sweeney questioned whether these Apaches were part of Chihuahua's group at all.

4. U.S. Senate, Report no. 184 (49-2), pp. 1–2; and U.S. Senate, Report no. 189 (50-1), pp. 1–2. Needing repairs were the lookout towers; the parapet walls; the chapel entrance; the counterscarp wall; and steps to the ditch, which also needed regrading; the breast-height wall of the covered way; the glacis; and the drains in the seawall. Today the parapets are disintegrating in many places on the terreplein, and barriers have been erected to keep tourists from further eroding the fragile coquina.

5. Skinner, *The Apache Rock Crumbles*, p. 55.

6. SPNC, X file 2/3, X-43; Goodman, "Apaches as Prisoners of War," p. 6.
7. Skinner, *The Apache Rock Crumbles*, p. 120.
8. Stockel, *Women of the Apache Nation*, p. 150.
9. U.S. Senate, Exec. Doc. 73 (49-2), pp. 5–6. One child was the four-year-old daughter of Indian woman No. 22 (as women were designated during imprisonment), who was one of the wives of Geronimo. The other child was a fifteen-month-old male, son of woman No. 25. The causes of death were not mentioned in the report, but Langdon did describe both babies as "very feeble."
10. Ibid., p. 6. In this "special report," different from the "monthly report" submitted on August 20, 1886, Langdon made no further mention of the deaths. He described the activities of the women as "cooking their simple meals" and sewing "as the impulse seizes them," assisted in this endeavor by "several charitable ladies of Saint Augustine." There is a conflict regarding this statement and the statement of Herbert Welsh of the Indian Rights Association, who found most Apaches at St. Augustine still wearing the same clothes six months after their arrival. What were the women sewing? Langdon reported they were "making garments for themselves and children." No further information is available to clarify the situation. Reported Langdon, the men "do absolutely nothing . . . they have no work; they cannot hunt, and will not fish, as they seem to have a religious objection to fish as an article of food." This statement verifies that the government had knowledge of the Apaches' prohibitions regarding fish and pork, yet the rations were not modified to accommodate these beliefs.
11. U.S. Senate, Exec. Doc. 83 (51-1), p. 18.
12. U.S. Senate, Exec. Doc. 117 (49-2), p. 67.
13. SPNC, unindexed material, Bourke to Welsh, September 22, 1886. From 1870 until 1886 Captain John G. Bourke served on the staff of General George Crook. He was part of many military campaigns against the Apaches and had personal knowledge of many of the great chiefs and warriors, including Cochise and Geronimo. Also, Bourke was literate, even erudite, and chronicled much information about the Apache wars. His book *On the Border with Crook* is well known and respected, and is in its fifth printing in the paperback edition. It has been widely circulated in many other editions since it first appeared in 1891.
14. U.S. Senate, Exec. Doc. 35 (51-1), p. 34.
15. Darrow, conversation with the author, May 1991.
16. Betzinez, *I Fought with Geronimo*, p. 141.

17. U.S. Senate, Exec. Doc. 35 (51-1), pp. 34–35. More than likely the scouts didn't believe the soldiers who had teased and taunted them many times in the past, especially about their food taboos. One example was provided by Lori Davisson of the Arizona Historical Society, who wrote me on August 21, 1991, that "the soldiers used to get canned seafood, remove the labels, and persuade the scouts to taste the contents. Then they would show them the labels, and the scouts would run outside and vomit!"

18. Skinner, *The Apache Rock Crumbles*, pp. 76–77.

19. Debo, *Geronimo*, p. 300.

20. Cleghorn, conversation with the author, November 1990.

21. Opler, "A Chiricahua Apache's Account," pp. 383–84.

22. SPNC, X file 3/3; Turcheneske, "Release of the Apache Prisoners of War," pp. 18–23. This description of the disgusting physical conditions aboard the train was confirmed by two of Turcheneske's informants, Raymond Loco and Mildred Imach Cleghorn, during separate interviews on November 11, 1976. Cleghorn was born in captivity at Fort Sill on December 11, 1910, and has been chairperson of the Fort Sill Chiricahua/Warm Springs Apache Tribe, located in Apache, Oklahoma, for more than a decade.

23. Ball, *Indeh*, p. 133.

24. Skinner, *The Apache Rock Crumbles*, pp. 78–79.

25. Strover, *National Tribune*, July 24, 1924.

26. U.S. Senate, Exec. Doc. 35 (51-1), p. 37.

27. Readers must once again be reminded that these numbers are approximate and may not be consistent. Also, the treatments of ailments may seem primitive when viewed from our high-tech perspective, but they were state-of-the-art for their time.

28. That well is now capped with concrete and serves as a focal point in the fort's courtyard. Visitors gather there to rest or to wait for the tours conducted by national park rangers to begin.

29. Delgadillo, conversation with the author, November 10, 1990.

30. Tetanus neonatorum is a severe form of infectious tetanus that occurs during the first few days of life and is caused by such factors as unhygienic practices in dressing the umbilical stump and the lack of maternal immunization. Especially noted from Dr. Webb's speech is the ailment's geography: it is present in the Southeast and not at all in the Southwest. If Dr. Webb was correct, it is possible that new Chiricahua Apache mothers washed or cleansed the umbilical area with herbs and potions that grew in the desert and mountain regions where they lived when they were a free people. Even if a similar plant medicine grew in the area near St. Augus-

tine, the Apache women were not able to roam freely to seek plants that could provide natural medicines for their newborns. According to Robert Tully, a retired pediatrician living in Albuquerque, the disease is "highly fatal" and may still be seen in rural sites where "babies continue to be born in barns and the umbilicus is tied off with an old piece of rope." Dr. Tully recalled seeing a case in 1955 or 1957 in the county hospital in San Antonio, Texas.

31. Hrdlicka, "Tuberculosis among Certain Indian Tribes," pp. 30–33.

32. Marasmus causes severe wasting in infants; the body weight may be less than 75 percent of that expected for the age. The infant looks old, pallid, apathetic, lacks skin fat, and has subnormal temperature. Marasmus is due to a number of factors, including bad nutrition, metabolic disorders, repeated vomiting, diarrhea, severe disease of the cardiovascular or genitourinary systems, or chronic bacterial or parasitic diseases, especially in tropical climates. Treatment is specific to the cause(s), but very gentle nursing and nourishment and fluids by gradual steps are appropriate. When asked about marasmus, Dr. Tully (see n. 30, above) defined it as a "wasting away" that could occur "after the baby is taken off the breast. They just go downhill," he said.

33. East, "Apache Prisoners in Fort Marion," pp. 9–13. DeWitt Webb, M.D., L.L.D. (1840–1917), was born in Clinton, New York, and graduated from the College of Physicians and Surgeons of Columbia University in New York City. He then moved with his wife and adopted daughter to St. Augustine, where he pursued a variety of medical and political interests. In 1903 Dr. Webb was elected to the Florida State Legislature, and in 1911–12 he was the mayor of St. Augustine. He was also president of the staff of physicians at Flagler Hospital and superintendent of the Sunday school of Flagler Memorial Church, where he served as an elder. He was a member of Ashlar Lodge, Free and Accepted Masons; and St. Augustine Commandery No. 10, Knights Templar. When his tenure as acting assistant surgeon and medical officer at Fort Marion was over, he went into the Florida Everglades to investigate medical conditions among the Seminoles. Dr. Webb might have been invited to give this speech before the Duchess County, New York, Medical Society because he completed his early schooling in the Duchess County Academy in Poughkeepsie, New York, in 1857.

34. Betzinez, *I Fought with Geronimo*, p. 146. The boy selected a tent near the eastern end of the terreplein. One hundred and thirty tents were lined up, one beside the other, all across the top of the fort. There was barely enough room for a path among them. To be ap-

preciated, these extremely crowded conditions must be compared with the traditional dwelling place, called a wickiup, which was constructed by women from saplings and brush. When the Apaches were free, their wickiups were placed within a reasonable distance to each other—not too close and not too far—depending on the immediate circumstances and conditions; for example, migration, the hunt, ceremonies, trading.

35. Ball, *Indeh*, p. 122. Asa Daklugie, Geronimo's nephew and a survivor of incarceration at Fort Pickens and of education at the Carlisle School, told Mrs. Ball, "No Apache was ever cruel enough to imprison anyone. Only a White Eye was capable of that."

36. Welsh, "The Apache Prisoners at Fort Marion," p. 13.

37. Skinner, conversation with the author, June 21, 1991.

38. Welsh, "The Apache Prisoners at Fort Marion," pp. 11–15, 20, and 20n.

39. Ibid., pp. 14–15.

40. Ibid., p. 20n.

41. Debo, *Geronimo*, p. 324.

42. Bourke, "Medicine Men of the Apache," pp. 582–84.

43. East, "Apache Prisoners in Fort Marion," p. 13. The exact location of this site is unknown, but it is assumed to be near the fort and not across the river.

44. Darrow, conversation with the author, May 1991.

45. Skinner, conversation with the author, June 21, 1991.

46. SPNC, 1st Loco file (1/2), C-53, Shapard interviews with national park rangers stationed at St. Augustine, undated.

47. Arana, conversation with the author, June 17, 1991. Arana's specialty is the era of the Spanish occupation of Florida, and he concentrates on it almost to the exclusion of other aspects of the fort's history. For example, in his vast library there was only one document that provided information about the period of incarceration of the Chiricahua Apaches at Fort Marion, East's "Apache Prisoners in Fort Marion."

CHAPTER 6:
INCARCERATION IN FLORIDA: FORT PICKENS

1. SPNC, 1884–1915 file, folder labeled "Crook Used Autopsies in Trailing Geronimo"; McClintock Collection, unnamed newspaper, column entitled "Around Here," May 17, 1922, by H. S. Hunter, assistant to editor.

2. Davis, *The Truth about Geronimo*, pp. 225–26.
3. Cleghorn, conversation with the author, September 21, 1989.
4. Utley, *A Clash of Cultures*, p. 79. It is not the purpose of this book to present the reader with a history of the military campaigns against the Apaches; Thrapp has done that in *The Conquest of Apacheria*. Rather, to control the scope of my subject, I must make the assumption that readers are familiar with the Apache wars or that they will be interested enough to investigate the events prior to September 1886.
5. U.S. Senate, Exec. Doc. 117 (49-2), p. 4.
6. Ball, "Interpreter for the Apaches," pp. 26–27, 36. George Medhurst Wratten is one of the more prominent "unsung heros" of American history. He spent his adult life in the service of his country as an interpreter for the Apaches, walking a fine line between the government and his friends among the Apaches, of whom there were many. Born in California, Wratten and his family moved to Florence, Arizona, for their health. When he was fourteen years old, George got a job working with the Apaches at the San Carlos Reservation where he became fluent in their unique language. He later became an interpreter for the army and traveled east into incarceration with the Chiricahuas. He lived with the warriors at Fort Pickens and at the Mount Vernon Barracks in Alabama. His first wife was Annie, a Chiricahua woman, with whom he had two daughters. When she left him, he married Bessie Cannon, a Mount Vernon belle, and raised a large family. They went to Fort Sill with the Apaches, where George continued to serve as their interpreter. He died in Oklahoma and is buried in the post cemetery. After his death, his widow and children were left penniless. She begged the government for assistance but was told she would have to wait until decisions were made regarding allotments to the Apaches. She took her family back to Alabama, where some descendants still live. The orders are in U.S. Senate, Exec. Doc. 117 (49-2), p. 6.
7. Ibid., p. 16.
8. Ball, *Indeh*, p. 131.
9. SPNC, 1st Loco file (1/2), C-41, Shapard interview with Raymond Loco, April 18, 1965.
10. SPNC, X file (2/3), X-43; Goodman, "Apaches as Prisoners of War," p. 62. I have been told that the site where the Apaches were held in 1886 is today an empty field that lures artifact hunters.
11. Letter to Davidson signed by a number of constituents, September 14, 1886, National Archives, Letters Received, Adjutant General's Office (AGO), 1881–1889, microcopy M-689.

12. U.S. Senate, Exec. Doc. 117 (49-2), p. 29.

13. Skinner, conversation with the author, June 17, 1991.

14. Fort Pickens fact sheet. Plans to fortify Pensacola Harbor were prepared in 1822, anticipating the choice of Pensacola as the site of the principal navy depot on the Gulf of Mexico. To secure the approaches to the navy yard from foreign invasion, the U.S. Army Corps of Engineers constructed Fort Pickens (1829–34), Fort McRee (1835–39) on the eastern end of Perdido Key, and Fort Barrancas (1839–45) with its advanced redoubt (1845–56) on the mainland. Fort Pickens, the largest of the four, guarded Santa Rosa Island and the entrance to the harbor and was also sited to prevent enemy ships from anchoring in range of the navy yard. In concert with Fort McRee, the two forts' cannons created a crossfire in the narrow channel between Perdido Key and Santa Rosa Island to prevent a hostile fleet from entering the harbor. All local activities related to the Apache prisoners of war at Fort Pickens originated at Fort Barrancas, located on what is now the Pensacola Naval Air Station. Spain first built a fort (*barranca*) on the bluff overlooking Pensacola Bay in 1698. The French briefly occupied the site in 1719. Later the British acquired Pensacola in 1763 and built a naval redoubt (a brick and concrete construction) on the *barranca*. Spain recaptured the area in 1781 and built new fortifications on the *barrancas*. General Andrew Jackson seized the Spanish forts in 1814 and 1818. When Florida was ceded to the United States in 1821, the U.S. Navy selected Pensacola Bay as the site for a navy yard. U.S. Army engineers made plans for the construction of new harbor defenses on the *barrancas*. The Spanish water battery was improved, and Fort Barrancas was built over the ruins of Fort San Carlos between 1839 and 1844. When Florida seceded from the Union in 1861, Confederate soldiers occupied the Pensacola forts area for thirteen months. Union forces reoccupied the sites in 1862. Until 1947, when harbor defenses were declared surplus, Fort Barrancas was used as a coast artillery training area. Its cannons were scrapped in 1900 and the fort became a signal station, small arms range, and storage area.

15. Ogden, interview with the author, June 22, 1991. Through Mary D. Jones, chief of interpretation for the National Park Service's Gulf Islands National Seashore in Gulf Breeze, Florida, David Ogden stated in later correspondence that the winters at Fort Pickens are not uniformly cold and nasty. According to Ogden, a typical winter has spells of mild weather that break up the cold. The weather pattern at Fort Pickens results from cold fronts racing down across

the Great Plains to strike the warmer, moist air mass over the Gulf of Mexico. This usually stalls the cold front, which then drifts back across the coast as a weak, wet, warm front, until the next cold front comes down. Referring to my comments about the varmints that occupy the fort area, Ogden said there are still plenty of poisonous snakes about, although they generally stay out of the fort itself. Like most wildlife in the National Park Service areas, they are protected by law. Ogden had more information about the sanitary practices at Fort Pickens when the Apaches were present; e.g., Army sanitation practices called for digging slit trenches for waste disposal. At Fort Pickens, this was probably done in the ditch outside the main walls.

16. Skinner, conversation with the author, June 21, 1991.

17. Shapard Papers, Alabama (cited hereafter as SPA), Langdon to Commanding Officer, March 3, 1887.

18. Ball, *Indeh*, p. 135. This fact was in a statement made by Daklugie to Ball. Daklugie and Frank Mangus, son of Mangus, were two of the oldest boys to surrender with Mangus and be sent to Fort Pickens. Frank Mangus died a prisoner of war at Fort Sill in 1903.

19. Skinner, conversation with the author, June 21, 1991.

20. Ogden, interview with the author, June 22, 1991.

21. SPNC, unindexed file, IRA 2, Mount Vernon, Langdon to Welsh, June 23, 1887.

22. Bright's Disease is an inflammation of the kidney. Although this ailment and the pneumonia that might have been one of the complications are generally agreed to have caused Ga-aa's death, Debo mentioned in *Geronimo* (p. 334) that she might have died of tuberculosis contracted at Fort Marion.

23. Erysipelas is an infection of the skin and underlying tissues caused by the bacterium *Streptococcus pyogenes*. The affected areas, usually the face and scalp, become inflamed and swollen, and raised patches that may be several inches across develop. The patient has a high temperature. Attacks may recur in certain persons possibly because of a defect in the lymphatic system. Treatment today is with antibiotics.

24. SPA, Langdon to Commanding Officer, August 9, 1887.

25. Ball, *Indeh*, p. 157.

1. Darrow, conversation with the author, May 1991.
2. U.S. Senate, Exec. Doc. 73 (49-2), pp. 2, 5, 7, 11, 13, 16, 17, 19.
3. Cleghorn, conversation with the author, July 16, 1991.
4. Albert, conversation with the author, July 5, 1991. Sister Mary Albert said no records were kept by her forebears about the health or illness of the children. All reports to authorities consisted of educational progress notes recorded by the nuns who taught the children. There is no information in the convent's records about any topic concerning the Apaches other than education, according to Sister Mary Albert, although without a doubt these devoted and pious women were involved in other endeavors and activities with the Chiricahua Apache children as well. Evidence in this regard is contained in Sister Mary Albert's master of arts thesis ("A Study of the Schools Conducted by the Sisters of St. Joseph of the Diocese of St. Augustine, Florida, 1866–1940," University of Florida, 1940), which states on p. 17: "They [the nuns] visited them [the Apaches at Fort Marion], gave them medicine for their sick, and notwithstanding their surly looks and the many rebuffs received, they finally gained their good will." The incident about the new teacher is explained in greater detail in the thesis (p. 18) as follows: "When the Indians saw their new teacher, they betook themselves to the remotest corner of the class room, turned their backs toward her, and with loud voices, in their own dialect, expressed their disapproval of the substitute imposed on them. Occasionally they looked fiercely back at her and pointed menacingly to the door. In vain did the poor postulant with trembling hand lift the pointer. . . . Angry growls were the only response. . . . In one voice the savage yell came, 'We no want that lady for teacher; we like a Sister.' " In her thesis, Sister Mary Albert attributed this anecdote to Sister Euphemia, the young nun to whom the incident happened, and who, as an elderly sister, communicated the experience directly.
5. Ball, *In the Days of Victorio*, pp. 195, 197.
6. Carlisle Indian School Catalog, 1912, p. 29. This document is in the files of the Latter-day Saints Archives in Salt Lake City. It is a ninety-seven-page catalog describing in great detail every activity offered by the school and is impressive in its description of the school's commitment to educating its pupils in many areas of life, including the academic and the vocational. On the last several pages, data concerning the graduates are listed for classes from

1889 to 1910. Very few Apaches are enumerated, and of those, only the name of Vincent Natailish, a member of Warm Springs chief Victorio's family, is easily recognizable.

7. Trennert, "From Carlisle to Phoenix," p. 267. Captain Richard Henry Pratt first came into contact with Native Americans while commanding black soldiers on the post–Civil War frontier. According to Trennert, Pratt's interest in educating children developed as the result of an assignment to supervise a group of Indian prisoners at Fort Marion, long before the Chiricahua Apaches were incarcerated there. Pratt began efforts to transform those prisoners into model citizens by removing their chains and giving them responsibilities, and this convinced him that Indian contact with whites could result in many benefits to the Native Americans. In this article, using the Phoenix, Arizona, school as an example, the author described what could happen to outing systems in institutions that placed their own values before those of the altruistic outing system.

8. Trennert, "Educating Indian Girls," pp. 275, 288–90. This article has as its basis the premise that education for women, especially minority women, was not widely accepted in the late 1800s and that academic instruction combined with vocational training was highly irregular. Training Native American girls in domestic skills at that time would have prepared them for the realities of life outside the school.

9. Worcester, *The Apaches*, p. 329.

10. Ball, *In the Days of Victorio*, pp. 199–200. James Kaywaykla was nine years old when he was sent to Carlisle. In later years he married Dorothy Naiche, daughter of the famous chief. As a ten-year-old, Dorothy had arrived with her mother, E-clah-heh, one of Naiche's wives, at Fort Marion. They were part of Chihuahua's group, the first to be incarcerated. The Kaywaykla descendants live today in Apache, Oklahoma. Debo reported (*Geronimo*, p. 318) that one of the officers said the separation of the children from their confused and frightened families was the most disagreeable task he had ever performed. Desperate mothers hid their smaller children under their skirts.

11. Ball, *Indeh*, p. 149. Most dead Chiricahua Apache children were buried at the Carlisle School. Their parents never saw them again after they were taken away to be educated.

12. Ibid.

13. Betzinez, *I Fought with Geronimo*, pp. 149–59.

14. Hrdlicka, "Tuberculosis among Certain Indian Tribes," pp. 32–35.

While this information may sound routine and ordinary today, it was once the only defense against the disease.

15. Skinner, *The Apache Rock Crumbles*, p. 161.

16. SPA, Pratt to Commissioner of Indian Affairs, May 24, 1889. Pratt's reference to "venereal taint" was a transparent attempt to lay blame for the illness among the Chiricahua Apache children on conditions outside his control. There is no evidence that his statement was taken seriously. Also, his statement about "sifting" the Chiricahuas and "the unhealthy ones disposed of" is chilling, reminiscent of the attitudes of those responsible for the Holocaust in Europe not so long ago.

17. SPA, Pratt to Commissioner of Indian Affairs, May 18, 1889. It is difficult to understand how Pratt could have been so certain of his beliefs, so short-sighted, and so wrong.

18. SPA, Cochran to Assistant Adjutant General, July 1, 1889.

19. SPA, Isabel B. Eustis to Hemenway, January 5, 1888.

20. SPA, Sternburg to Adjutant General, December 11, 1895.

21. Griswold, "Vital Statistics."

22. SPNC, 1st Loco File (1/2), MC-7, "A List of Apache Children Buried at Carlisle Barracks, Penna." Susie Reed, on the supplemental list, may have been the adopted daughter of Walter Reed, the famous surgeon who treated the Apaches for three years at Mount Vernon. Prior to that assignment, Dr. Reed lived and practiced medicine among the Apaches on the San Carlos Reservation in Arizona, where he took a young child into his home and gave her the name Susie (see chapter 8, note 9).

23. SPA, Pratt to Davis, December 13, 1895.

CHAPTER 8:

INCARCERATION IN ALABAMA: MOUNT VERNON

1. Ball, *Indeh*, pp. 138–39, 152–53.

2. *Montgomery* (Alabama) *Advertisor*, April 4, 1902.

3. Pamphlet, Searcy Hospital.

4. Capell, interview with the author, June 24, 1991.

5. SPA, Patzk to Post Adjutant, June 30, 1887. In his first report after arriving at Mount Vernon, the doctor described debility among many prisoners, which, he thought, was "probably the cause of some deaths." He attributed the medical condition to "previous hardships, privation, and especially insufficient feeding," all situations that were again present and which caused the doctor great

concern. He urgently recommended increasing the adult rations to the regular army ration and that of the children in proportion. There is no indication in this letter of the size of the ration that prompted his recommendation, but it obviously was not equal to that of the soldiers. Dr. Patzk vaccinated the Apaches upon their arrival at Mount Vernon, assuring protection against smallpox; however, in the first month of incarceration, three prisoners died—one from debility and one from tuberculosis.

6. An antiscorbutic would help combat scurvy, an ailment that accompanied the Apaches from Fort Marion.

7. SPA, Sinclair to Endicott, August 3, 1887.

8. SPNC, unindexed file, Bowman to Welsh, July 26, 1887.

9. Walter Reed, the bacteriologist renowned for his work with yellow fever, was born in Gloucester County, Virginia, on September 13, 1851. He was educated at the University of Virginia and Bellevue Medical School, graduating in 1870. In 1875 he entered the Medical Corps of the U.S. Army as an assistant surgeon with the rank of lieutenant. Dr. Reed's primary responsibility at Mount Vernon was to reduce the high mortality rate among the Apaches. It is believed that research for his important discovery of the cause of yellow fever began with his work among the ailing Apaches. Earlier, Dr. Reed had served three years (1876–79) at Fort Apache on Arizona's San Carlos/White Mountain Reservation, where he became familiar with several bands of Apaches and saved the life of a young girl, whom he took into his family and named Susie. She was the only Apache at Mount Vernon who was not a prisoner of war. In 1890 Reed was transferred to Baltimore to further study bacteriology. In 1893 he was promoted to major and was made professor of bacteriology and clinical microscopy at the Army Medical School in Washington, D.C. When yellow fever broke out among U.S. troops in Cuba, Dr. Reed became chairman of a committee to investigate its causes and methods of transmission. His observations of many cases of yellow fever led him to discount the popular idea that the disease was transmitted by person-to-person contact. He revived the then-discarded notion that the yellow fever parasite was carried only by certain mosquitoes and proved it by experiments in which some of his coworkers sacrificed their lives. Dr. Reed died in 1902.

10. SPA, Reed to Sinclair, August 31, 1887.

11. SPA, Sinclair to Adjutant General, May 26, 1887.

12. Ibid., September 30, 1887.

13. SPA, Reed to Sinclair, September 30, 1887.

14. Bean, *Walter Reed*, pp. 42–43.

15. SPA, Reed to Sinclair, November 30, 1887.

16. Ibid., December 31, 1887.

17. Capell, interview with the author, June 24, 1991. Legend has it that the infected tent canvas was cut and sewed into clothing for the prisoners, causing much more sickness.

18. Debo, *Geronimo*, pp. 338–39.

19. SPA, Reed to Sinclair, May 31, 1888. By this time measles was well known to the Apaches. It was one of the deadly contagious diseases acquired from the Mexicans more than one hundred years earlier.

20. Ibid., July 31, 1888.

21. SPNC, unindexed file, Bourke to Welsh, January 10, 1889.

22. National Archives Trust Fund, Register of Indian Prisoners, March 1889–November 1894. This document is on microfilm and is a complete list of the numbers of prisoners in Mount Vernon, by categories, e.g., men, women, boys over twelve, boys under twelve, girls over twelve, girls under twelve, and the totals. The census ranges from a high of 390 in early September 1889 to a low of 301 at the end of August 1891.

23. SPA, Reed to Sinclair, April 30, 1889; May 31, 1889; July 31, 1889; August 31, 1889; September 30, 1889. President Grover Cleveland was replaced on March 4, 1889, by the newly elected president, Benjamin Harrison, and his staff. The former secretary of war, William C. Endicott, was replaced by Redfield Proctor on March 5, 1889. The new secretary of the interior was John W. Noble, who took office on March 7, 1889.

24. SPA, Reed to Whipple, October 31, 1889.

25. SPA, Reed to Kellog, November 30, 1889. Here is the first evidence that traditional healing with unfamiliar herbs from Alabama soil was being practiced, an action that must have caused the doctor great consternation, to say nothing of its sometimes tragic impact on the Apaches.

26. SPA, Reed to Whipple, November 18, 1889. The Medical Director's Office at headquarters was headed by C. Sutherland, colonel and surgeon. On November 30, 1889, he concurred with this request, stating in an endorsement that "under all conditions, the climate of the Mount Vernon reservation, while abundantly healthy for troops and citizens as well, is, as far as the Indian prisoners are concerned, absolutely and positively one to which they cannot become inured or habituated, as it is entirely different from that which is natural to them. The recommendation of the Post Surgeon that the prisoners be transferred to a climate possessing less moisture than a Gulf or Atlantic coast station is concurred with."

Assistant Adjutant General William Whipple received Dr. Reed's letter and Dr. Sutherland's endorsement on December 2, 1889.

27. Skinner, *The Apache Rock Crumbles*, pp. 291–92.

28. Christmas card, Searcy Hospital. Operation Santa Claus, the official name for the first celebration, is still in effect today. Donations are requested each Christmas season with a simple entreaty on the hospital's card: "Your donation will give people whose illness oftentimes makes them feel unwanted, unloved, and apart from the outside world, real reason to believe that people in the community still care about them. This reassurance helps many of them in the recovery process. Your friendship really does make a difference." Donors are encouraged to "send a check . . . give a party."

29. SPA, G. Howard to Adjutant General, December 23, 1889.

30. U.S. Senate, Exec. Doc. 35 (51-1), pp. 32–33.

31. Ibid., p. 29.

32. SPA, Reed to Kellog, January 31, 1890.

33. SPA, Howard to Adjutant General, June 24, 1890.

34. Dr. Cochran was familiar with the terrible impact tuberculosis had on the Chiricahua Apaches. In June 1889 he had been sent to the Carlisle School to check on health conditions among the ailing Apache students.

35. Reed, "Geronimo and His Warriors in Captivity," p. 235.

36. U.S. Senate, Exec. Doc. 41 (51-2), p. 3.

37. Capell, interview with the author, June 24, 1991.

38. SPA, Wotherspoon to Woodruff, May 31, 1891.

39. Ibid., July 31, August 31, November 31, 1891; March 31, 1892.

40. Inanition is a condition of exhaustion caused by lack of nutrients in the blood arising through starvation, malnutrition, or intestinal disease.

41. SPA, Wotherspoon to Commanding Officer, July 26, 1892.

42. SPA, incomplete report to the Post Adjutant, December 1, 1892. The final pages of this handwritten report are missing. The writer's longhand style does not resemble any other, and he is unidentified.

43. Borden, "The Vital Statistics of an Apache Indian Community," pp. 7–10.

44. SPA, Wotherspoon to Commanding Officer, January 25, 1894. The status of the soldiers of Company I, 12th Infantry, was never clear. In some documents they are included with the formal count of prisoners; in other materials they are counted separately, as if they were prisoners no longer. There were many questions regarding the fate of these soldiers when their terms of enlistment expired. Would they revert to the formal "prisoner" category? Would they

be free to return to the Southwest, and if so, what would happen to their wives and children? Would the families of the enlisted men remain incarcerated? If the soldiers became free men, could the government restrict them to the eastern United States? How could they earn a living? Would the government be responsible for providing food and clothing after they were discharged from the army? These questions and more fell into the laps of officials affiliated with former president Grover Cleveland's second administration, which took office on March 4, 1893. Hoke Smith became secretary of the interior on the same day and was followed by John Reynolds (assistant secretary), who took office for three days on September 1, 1896. The final secretary of the interior in this administration was David R. Francis, who commenced his duties on September 4, 1896.

45. Skinner, *The Apache Rock Crumbles*, pp. 386–87.
46. SPA, unsigned and undated letter. This document was written in September 1894 because reference was made to Chappo Geronimo. He was officially listed as having been returned from Carlisle, but being very ill. Chappo died in mid-September 1894. These lists were compiled by several persons, and each individual's opinion influenced his evaluation of the particular Apache prisoner of war. The passing reference to Hampton Normal School in Hampton, Virginia, deserves comment. In 1894, when this document was developed, the Chiricahua Apache children were no longer being sent involuntarily to Carlisle in groups. However, five children did attend the institution that year. None of these was returned because of illness, but in 1894, one man already in attendance died and one was sent back to Mount Vernon. The school at Hampton provided an alternative to Carlisle, but only a few children, possibly eight, were sent there. As this report was being written, no children had come back in good or ill health and none attending Hampton had died.
47. *Tuberculosis among the North American Indians*, p. 12.

CHAPTER 9:
INCARCERATION IN OKLAHOMA: FORT SILL

1. SPA, Bourke to Proctor, March 14, 1889.
2. SPA, Painter to Kelton, June 5, 1889.
3. SPA, report by Bourke appended to letter to Adjutant General,

July 5, 1889. This document contains a poignant description of his meeting with the Apache leaders. Bourke quoted them verbatim. The warriors' words brilliantly kept their dignity intact while communicating their desperate situation to representatives of their captors.

4. SPA, Bourke to Adjutant General, July 5, 1889. This letter presents a thorough review of each site—its assets and liabilities—and Bourke's immediate impressions. It is a document worth studying for a depiction of some of America's agrarian countryside in the late 1880s and a serious view of responsibility taken by an army officer.

5. SPA, Davis to Proctor, October 14, 1889.

6. SPA, Miles to Proctor, December 6, 1889.

7. SPA, Proctor to Harrison, January 13, 1890.

8. SPA, Crook to Adjutant General, February 20, 1890.

9. SPA, Maus to Davis, September 15, 1894. Maus was the officer to whom the Chihuahua group surrendered in the spring of 1886.

10. Skinner, *The Apache Rock Crumbles*, p. 387. During the years in which this political decision was being formulated, the Republican administration of President Benjamin Harrison was succeeded by the second election of Democrat Grover Cleveland to the presidency. Daniel Lamont of New York assumed office on March 6, 1893, three days after Cleveland took office, replacing Redfield Proctor.

11. Oklahoma Historical Society, Oklahoma City, Oklahoma (hereafter cited OHS), Browning to Brown, September 9, 1893, National Archives, Record Group 75.

12. OHS, invoices, Kiowa Agency to McKesson and Roberts, New York City, January 9, 1894; to Richard Kny and Company, New York City, September 14, 1894; to the Maltbie Chemical Company in Buffalo, New York, September 21, 1894; to Department of the Interior's Office of Indian Affairs for fiscal year ending June 30, 1895.

13. OHS, letters, Browning to Nichols, February 8, 1894; Hume to Baldwin, March 5, 1897; Hume to Walker, May 24, 1898; Tonner to Walker, February 11, 1899.

14. OHS, letter, Hume to Walker, March 9, 1899.

15. OHS, letters, Shoemaker to Walker, March 29, 1899; Shoemaker to Commissioner of Indian Affairs, July 1899; Shoemaker to Commanding Officer, March 5, 1900. Recall that a similar situation involving the use of traditional medicines occurred among the Chiricahua Apache prisoners of war when they were incarcerated at

Mount Vernon. Dr. Reed and Dr. Shoemaker had the same reaction.

16. OHS, statement and report, Hume to ?, June 30, 1900.
17. OHS, letters, Parker to Randlett, March 12, 1901; Igamo to Randlett, March 27, 1901; Igamo to Randlett, March 29, 1901.
18. OHS, letter, Jones to all U.S. Indian Agents and Bonded Superintendents, August 24, 1901.
19. OHS, letter, Hauke to Superintendents, November 9, 1912.
20. OHS, letter, Stecker to Commissioner of Indian Affairs, April 5, 1910.
21. SPA, confidential telegram from the Adjutant General's Office, Washington, D.C., to the Commanding Officer, Mount Vernon Barracks, undated, unsigned.
22. Skinner, *The Apache Rock Crumbles*, p. 394.
23. Capell, interview with the author, June 24, 1991. Four carloads of the Apaches' property, including clothing, burned in the freight yard of the Louisville and Nashville Railroad. Published accounts stated that the loss occurred through the negligence of the railroad. The number of cabins is disputable. While Capell counted two hundred, other sources said the prisoners were housed in approximately eighty homes in Alabama.
24. SPNC, unindexed material, "Sale of Mt. Vernon, 4/5/1895"; Green to Johnson, May 4, 1898.
25. SPNC, 1st Loco file (1/2), D-6, Shapard interview with Raymond Loco, December 23, 1963.
26. SPNC, 1st Loco file (1/2), D-5, Shapard interview with Raymond Loco, June 20, 1966.
27. SPA, LeBaron to Scott, October 5, 1894. There is no question that these ailments were brought from Alabama. They form a data base from which future comparisons and conclusions can be derived.
28. SPNC, 1st Loco file (1/2), D-14, "Report of Conditions of Apaches upon Arrival at Fort Sill, November 1894." These census data are suspect. Skinner and others believe more than 350 prisoners were transferred, yet Ballou counted the individuals and identified them at the site by age and gender. The difference in numbers is one variable that has plagued and frustrated researchers. It may never be adequately resolved.
29. Betzinez, *I Fought with Geronimo*, p. 167.
30. SPA, Dewey to Lamont, February 21, 1895.
31. SPA, Wratten to Scott, July 25, 1895.
32. SPNC, Hugh L. Scott Papers, undated, "Special Regulations for Government of the Apache Prisoners of War at Fort Sill, Okla-

homa." Scott rose through the military bureaucracy to become army chief of staff when the United States entered World War I. His efforts with the Chiricahua Apache prisoners of war no doubt contributed to the reputation that won him the coveted position.

33. Fort Sill Museum, Apache Prisoner of War Archives (hereafter cited FSMA), Glennan to Sternburg, November 1, 1895. The distinction between the quotidian and tertian intermittent fevers of malaria is based on the duration of the afebrile (fever-free) intervals. Quotidian fevers, the most severe type, occur frequently—from every few hours to every two days. Tertian fevers occur almost every two days. Scrofula is tuberculosis of the lymph nodes, usually in the neck, causing abscesses which may burst through the skin and form running sores. The acute ulcers listed should not be confused with those of the gastrointestinal tract. Instead, the lesions, because they are listed as diseases of the integument, are probably skin disorders. It is of interest to note that figures were added to the statistical tables after the report. Dr. Glennan went back to these numbers more than one year later and penciled in the latest computations.

34. SPNC, 1st Loco file (1/2), D-5, "Fort Sill—Apache Funerals and Burials"; Shapard telephone conversation with Fort Sill museum director Gillett Griswold, March 3, 1972. Polly Lewis Murphy of Lawton, Oklahoma, spent long hours in the Apache cemetery at Fort Sill recording the names on the granite markers and their locations. She produced a report called "So Lingers Memory: Fort Sill Post Cemetery Inventories." Also of interest by Murphy, and self-published, is *Medical Records of Fort Sill, I.T., of Soldiers, Indians, & Civilians. 1873–1880 & 1903–1913.*

35. SPA, Capron to Adjutant General, December 14, 1896. This information may not be accurate. Legend tells that the Apaches thought of the hospital as a "death house" and were reluctant to enter. Evidence in Scott's letter substantiates their resistance (see note 36, below).

36. SPA, Scott to Adjutant General, January 31, 1897.

37. SPA, Capron to Adjutant General, February 28, 1898.

38. SPNC, X file (2/3), Grovesnor, "Structure and Stress," pp. 150–51. Betzinez, in *I Fought with Geronimo*, pp. 175–79, takes credit for having this dance stopped; by his own admission, it didn't endear him to traditional Chiricahuas.

39. SPA, Scott to Adjutant General, June 30, 1902.

40. Ball, *Indeh*, p. 160.

41. Debo, *Geronimo*, pp. 434–35.

42. Scabies is a skin infection caused by mites and spread through contact. Commonly infected areas are the groin, penis, nipples, and the skin between fingers. All clothing and bedding must be disinfested. Twenty-five of the cases during this outbreak were among the military and thirty occurred in the prisoner-of-war villages.

43. FSMA, "Record of Military History, 1903–1913."

44. Ibid.

45. A "slough" is a mudhole or swamp.

46. FSMA, "Record of Medical History, 1903–1913."

47. Ibid.; Sayre to Adjutant General, August 8, 1904. Sayre took an interest in the Apaches' money-making efforts, in particular raising cattle and harvesting hay. The Apaches had been putting their profits into a special fund, and Sayre began adding to these monies in a determined manner. The funds were used to purchase farm implements, vehicles, and horses. He imposed rules on the prisoners, especially one that forbade the dances during cold weather. Sayre was convinced that sharing dance masks spread contagion. And he stopped the gambling, at least overtly. During the early years of the Spanish-American War and during the Philippine insurrection, many of the troops posted at Fort Sill went off to war, leaving Sayre and Troop C, Eighth Cavalry, as the only military personnel guarding the Chiricahuas. Rumors predicted there would be trouble, perhaps even an Indian uprising, but nothing untoward occurred. Sayre was succeeded by Lieutenant George Purrington, who was also interested in the Apache cattle-raising project and in causing the fund to grow. Purrington lifted the ban on dancing and soon afterward two young men died from pneumonia. Major George L. Scott (no relation to Hugh) succeeded Purrington but didn't stay very long because of ill health. It was during this time that liquor became a factor and gambling made a comeback. Major George W. Goode succeeded George L. Scott and remained with the Apaches until they were released in 1913. Goode set rules for the Apaches and made the Apache scouts responsible for carrying out his orders. He controlled gambling and booted the liquor sellers off the reservation. Goode believed that moving the entire group to Mescalero was in their best interests, but when that didn't happen, he worked to help settle those who decided to remain in Oklahoma. He was involved in selling the prisoners' herd of ten thousand cattle to the highest bidders.

48. Harper, "Missionary Work," p. 329. Soldiers blocked the missionary's access to the Apaches, but one pious young enlisted man, wracked with guilt, finally permitted entry to the villages.

49. OHS, Sec. X, Apache Prisoner of War files, microcopy KA-50, "The Missionary Lesson Leaflet," pp. 3–7.

50. U.S. Senate, Doc. 366 (61-2), pp. 1–3.

51. SPNC, unchron., IRA, "Twenty-eighth Annual Report of the Executive Committee of the Indian Rights Association," p. 28. Geronimo died in February 1909 from pneumonia acquired when he got drunk, fell off his horse, and spent a night outdoors in the rain. Up until then, the military never stopped believing that Geronimo could rally the Apaches and return them to the warpath, even after more than twenty years of incarceration.

52. SPNC, unchron., IRA, "Twenty-ninth Annual Report of the Executive Committee of the Indian Rights Association," p. 51.

53. Ibid., p. 52.

54. Turcheneske, " 'It Is Right That They Should Set Us Free,' " pp. 19–20, 13.

55. U.S. Senate, Doc. 432 (62-2), pp. 1–2. Spelling of certain names was incorrect. Ferico is Perico, Yar-no-zha is Yah-no-zha, and Noiche is Naiche.

56. SPNC, Fort Sill Apaches, 1915–present, "Proceedings of Meeting of Apache Prisoners of War with Committee," p. 3. Whether this was Scott's way of getting out of a tight spot may never be known, but if it was, it was cowardly to use a reference to disease to cover up his prior biased statements.

57. Roe, "Apache Prisoners of War," pp. 10–11.

58. Turcheneske, "The United States Congress and the Release," p. 225. This excellent article is a comprehensive study of the situation and spares no details.

59. SPNC, 1st Loco file (1/2), E-35, Census of the Apache Prisoners of War, Fort Sill, Oklahoma, April 1, 1913. Eighty-seven may be a more accurate figure.

60. Cleghorn, "The Fort Sill Apaches: A History of My People" (Lecture presented November 13, 1991, at the Laboratory of Anthropology, Santa Fe, New Mexico).

61. SPNC, Hugh L. Scott Papers, "Asking No Favors but Only a Square Deal for the Ft. Sill Apaches."

62. Spivey's information regarding syphilis being present in pre-Columbian Native Americans is disputed by the anthropological findings of noted physician and paleopathologist Alex Hrdlicka, who insisted, "Notwithstanding some claims to the contrary, there is as yet not a single instance of thoroughly authenticated pre-Columbian syphilis" in the Indian skeletons he examined (Hrdlicka, "Disease, Medicine, and Surgery among the Ameri-

can Aborigines," p. 1662). A contemporary authority on American Indian medicine, Virgil J. Vogel, stated, "It is noteworthy that within the area which now comprises the United States, no explorer has reported from observation the presence of the [venereal] diseases among Indians prior to the contact with whites" (*American Indian Medicine*, pp. 152–53). Specific to Apaches, Ed Sweeney, in correspondence, cited National Archives, microcopy 234, roll 561, Letters Received, Office of Indian Affairs, 1824–1881, Report from Henry Duane, physician, Southern Apache Indians to B. M. Thomas, Agent, June 30, 1873. Dr. Duane reported treating 4 cases of certain intermittent fever, 7 cases of acute diarrhea, 78 cases of whooping cough, 4 cases of chronic rheumatism, 4 cases of conjunctivitis, 11 cases of inflammation of the lungs, 6 cases of inflammation of the pleura, 4 simple fractures, 4 gunshot wounds, 5 incised wounds, and 2 lacerated wounds.

Continuing his report on Victorio's band of Warm Springs Apaches, Dr. Duane stated, "The number of deaths has been 3— one from whooping cough complicated with pneumonia and two from gunshot wounds. All the children have been suffering from whooping cough. The Apaches are a hardy race with good constitution, consequently much of the diseases are light, readily amenable to remedies. They are virtuous, no taint of syphilis among them. All the cases of gunshot wounds, incised and lacerated wounds, have had their origin in drunkenness . . . from tiswin made from corn. Recommend that flour or bread be issued instead of corn." Today virtually all scholars concede that Hrdlicka was incorrect.

63. Spivey, interview with the author, September 20, 1991.

CHAPTER 10:
A COLLECTION OF CHIRICAHUA VOICES

1. U.S. Senate, Exec. Doc. 88 (51-1), p. 16.
2. U.S. Senate, Exec. Doc. 35 (51-1), p. 33.
3. Debo, *Geronimo*, p. 447.
4. U.S. Senate, Exec. Doc. 88 (51-1), p. 15.
5. U.S. Senate, Exec. Doc. 35 (51-1), p. 36.
6. U.S. Senate, Exec. Doc. 88 (51-1), p. 12.
7. Ibid., p. 17.
8. Debo, *Geronimo*, p. 360.
9. Barrett, *Geronimo*, pp. 77, 73–74.
10. U.S. Senate, Exec. Doc. 35 (51-1), pp. 35–36.

11. Ibid., p. 35.

12. Ibid., p. 35.

13. Opler, "A Chiricahua's Account," p. 382.

14. U.S. Senate, Exec. Doc. 35 (51-1), p. 34.

15. Ibid., p. 36.

16. SPNC, Hugh L. Scott Papers, "Proceeding of Conference with Apache Prisoners of War," p. 21.

17. Haozous, interview with Pat O'Brien, July 22, 1976. Bicentennial Oral History Program for the U.S. Army and Fort Sill Museum, Fort Sill, Oklahoma.

18. Turcheneske, "The Apache Prisoners of War," p. 41.

19. Ibid., p. 263, 283.

20. Ibid., p. 30. Mildred Cleghorn was voted the 1989 Indian of the Year and is at the time of this writing the chairperson of the Fort Sill Chiricahua/Warm Springs Apache tribe.

21. Cleghorn, interview with the author, August 8, 1989.

22. Cleghorn lecture, November 13, 1991. This presentation was held at the Laboratory of Anthropology's auditorium in Santa Fe to a standing-room-only audience. Mrs. Cleghorn's lectures are quite popular across the Southwest.

23. Hugar, conversation with the author, November 19, 1991. As frequently happens, many of the Chiricahua Apache people have valid personal reasons for refusing to discuss what they know through oral history about the events that transpired among their prisoner-of-war ancestors. After very diplomatically explaining her feelings, Mrs. Hugar, who was the curator of the Mescalero Apache Cultural Museum, declined to say anything else.

24. Houser, interview with the author, October 1, 1991. Allan Houser was born on June 30, 1914, near Apache, Oklahoma, on land allotted to his parents, Sam and Blossom Haozous. His surname means "Pulling Roots" in Chiricahua Apache. As a pupil of Dorothy Dunn's in the 1930s at the Santa Fe Indian School, he received the arts and crafts award in 1936. In 1940 Houser was commissioned to create a World War II sculpture honoring American Indian casualties. He was a founding instructor at the Institute of American Indian Art in Santa Fe in the 1960s, where he taught until 1975. Houser's paintings and sculptures have been collected by Europeans and Americans, and his works are exhibited in the Heard Museum in Phoenix; the Philbrook Art Center in Tulsa; the Denver Art Museum; the Museum of Northern Arizona at Flagstaff; the Linden Museum in Stuttgart, Germany; the Fine Arts Museum and the Museum of Indian Arts and Culture of the Museum of

New Mexico; and the United States Mission to the United Nations in New York. Exhibits of his works have been held at the Grand Palais in Paris and at the Kunstlerhaus in Vienna. On April 16, 1991, a copy of a 1988 bronze sculpture entitled *Sacred Rain Arrow* was installed at the United States Senate in Washington, D.C. This powerful sculpture bears the inscription "Dedicated to the American Indian." Said Senator Daniel Inouye (D-Hawaii) of the work: "In my view, the placement of *Sacred Rain Arrow* in the United States Senate will be the first real monument to the Indian people in the Capitol of the United States" (*Focus/Santa Fe*, June–July 1991, p. 23).

25. Kanseah, interview with the author, November 19, 1991. At the time of this writing Kanseah is chairman of the Chiricahua Apache group on the Mescalero Reservation and a member of the Mescalero Apache Tribal Council. Berle Kanseah's grandfather, Jasper, was a nephew of Geronimo and the youngest member of the Naiche/Geronimo band when surrender occurred in September 1886. At age thirteen, Jasper was orphaned and served an apprenticeship as Geronimo's horseholder. When the warriors galloped into the stronghold, often chased by the military, they had to dismount quickly and take up firing positions. Young boys known as horseholders took the horses and immediately led them away from the shooters. Jasper was educated at Carlisle, survived tuberculosis, and came to Mescalero with his family in 1913. In his later years he served as a school bus driver and chief of police on the reservation.

26. Ball, *Indeh*, p. 184. Asa Daklugie, a former student at Carlisle, was a leader of the Chiricahua Apaches after they arrived at Mescalero in 1913.

CHAPTER 11:
A LEGACY OF DEATH

1. Annual Report, Jeffords to Commissioner E. P. Smith, September 1, 1874.
2. Correspondence with Edwin Sweeney, November 17, 1991.
3. Ibid.
4. Faust, "Clinical and Public Health Aspects of Malaria in the United States," p. 199.
5. *Lawton Constitution* (Lawton, Oklahoma), September 21, 1990.
6. U.S. Senate, Doc. 1038 (62-3), p. 70.

7. OHS, Record Group 75, National Archives, "From Breeding Place to Feeding Place."
8. *Report of the Commissioner of Indian Affairs*, June 30, 1913, vol. 2, p. 20.
9. Ibid., vol. 1, p. 34.
10. Turcheneske, "Disaster at White Tail," p. 123.
11. U.S. Senate, Doc. 1038 (62-3), p. 44.
12. Turcheneske, "Disaster at White Tail," p. 125.
13. Ibid.
14. OHS, Indian Pioneer History Collection, interviews by Raymond Jantz, investigator, vol. 109, p. 149, January 4, 1938, Pete M. Levite: "In 1901, there were four hardware stores, six saloons, five grocery stores, and three mixed stock stores. School was held in several different places. At first . . . in a two-room vacant house located in the eastern part of the business district. Then it was changed to the upper story of the building that is the Smith Pharmacy. In 1902 the people erected a school building. . . . The first church services . . . were held in a tent." Vol. 91, p. 303, January 3, 1938, John J. Flood: "When I came to Apache [on January 21, 1901] there were no buildings . . . just shacks. The town first started at Richards Spur, which is ten miles south of the present townsite . . . then moved. . . . After moving, a bank was started, called the Crow Bank or Apache State Bank. In 1902 I helped haul stone to build the bank building. . . . In 1907 I went to work at the cotton gin. The old settlers around Apache are . . . I. W. Crow, Judge Ward, G. H. Black, Dennis Carney, Jim Lay, Ed Heriff, Ollie Felt, Jim Head, John Wagon, Chas. Conel, Bob Collins, Dr. Blair, Dr. Bendar." Vol. 74, p. 373, Jessie Whalen Hines: "Apache had the first automatic telephone system I came across in 1907."

    During 1901, a huge drawing for land was held in El Reno, Oklahoma. Lucky participants received acreage in the Kiowa-Comanche country southwest of El Reno, which included the site that became the town of Apache. The old-timers quoted above and others formed the majority of the early population. Many of the eighty-nine Chiricahua Apache individuals and families moved to Apache, but some were assigned allotments in nearby towns.

✴ BIBLIOGRAPHY

BOOKS

Ball, Eve. *In the Days of Victorio*. Tucson: University of Arizona
Press, 1970.
―――. *Indeh: An Apache Odyssey*. Provo: Brigham Young University
Press, 1980.
Barrett, S. M. *Geronimo: His Own Story*. New York: Ballantine Books,
1971.
Bean, William B. *Walter Reed: A Biography*. Charlottesville: University
Press of Virginia, 1982.
Betzinez, Jason, with Wilbur Sturtevant Nye. *I Fought with Geronimo*.
Lincoln and London: University of Nebraska Press, 1987.
Bourke, John G. *On the Border with Crook*. 6th ed. Fourth Bison Book
Printing. Lincoln: University of Nebraska Press, 1971.
Cortés, José. *Views from the Apache Frontier: Report on the North-
ern Provinces of New Spain*. Ed. Elizabeth A. H. John, trans. John
Wheat. Norman: University of Oklahoma Press, 1989.
Davis, Britton. *The Truth about Geronimo*. Lincoln: University of
Nebraska Press, 1929.
Debo, Angie. *Geronimo: The Man, His Time, His Place*. Norman:
University of Oklahoma Press, 1976.
Gordon, Benjamin Lee. *Medicine Throughout Antiquity*. Philadelphia:
F. A. Davis Company, 1949.
Greenfield, Myrtle. *A History of Public Health in New Mexico*. Albu-
querque: University of New Mexico Press, 1962.
Griffen, William B. *Apaches at War and Peace: The Janos Presidio,
1750–1858*. Albuquerque: University of New Mexico Press, 1988.
―――. *Utmost Good Faith: Patterns of Apache-Mexican Hostilities
in Northern Chihuahua Border Warfare, 1821–1843*. Albuquerque:
University of New Mexico Press, 1988.
Haley, James L. *Apaches: A History and Culture Portrait*. New York:
Doubleday and Company, 1983.
Hopkins, Jack W. *The Eradication of Smallpox: Organizational Learn-
ing and Innovation in International Health*. Boulder, Colo.: West-
view Press, 1989.
Howard, Robert W. *This Is the West*. New York: Rand McNally, 1957.

Karolevitz, Robert F. *Doctors of the Old West.* Seattle: Superior Publishing Company, 1967.

Lockwood, Frank C. *The Apache Indians.* Lincoln and London: University of Nebraska Press, 1987.

Lummis, Charles Fletcher. *Dateline Fort Bowie.* Norman: University of Oklahoma Press, 1979.

McNeill, William H. *Plagues and Peoples.* Garden City, N.Y.: Anchor Press/Doubleday, 1976.

Magoffin, Susan. *Down the Santa Fe Trail and into Mexico: The Diary of Susan Shelby Magoffin 1846–1847.* Ed. Stella M. Drumm. Lincoln and London: University of Nebraska Press, 1982.

Moore, Michael. *Los Remedios: Traditional Herbal Remedies of the Southwest.* Santa Fe: Red Crane Books, 1990.

———. *Medicinal Plants of the Desert and Canyon West.* Santa Fe: Museum of New Mexico Press, 1989.

Moorhead, Max. *The Apache Frontier: Jacobo Ugarte and Spanish-Indian Relations in Northern New Spain, 1769–1791.* Norman: University of Oklahoma Press, 1968.

Opler, Morris. *An Apache Lifeway.* New York: Cooper Square Publishers, 1965.

———. *Apache Odyssey: A Journey Between Two Worlds.* New York: Irvington Publishers, 1983.

Perrone, Bobette, H. Henrietta Stockel, and Victoria Kreuger. *Medicine Women, Curanderas, and Women Doctors.* Norman: University of Oklahoma Press, 1989.

Schwatka, Frederick. *Among the Apaches.* Palmer Lake, Colo.: Filter Press, 1974.

Skinner, Woodward B. *The Apache Rock Crumbles: The Captivity of Geronimo's People.* Pensacola: Skinner Publications, 1987.

———. *Geronimo at Fort Pickens.* Pensacola: Skinner Publications, 1981.

Stockel, H. Henrietta. *Women of the Apache Nation: Voices of Truth.* Reno: University of Nevada Press, 1991.

Stone, Eric. *Medicine among the American Indians.* New York: Hafner Publishing Company, 1962.

Sweeney, Edwin R. *Cochise: Chiricahua Apache Chief.* Norman: University of Oklahoma Press, 1991.

Thrapp, Dan L. *The Conquest of Apacheria.* Norman: University of Oklahoma Press, 1967.

———. *Victorio and the Mimbres Apaches.* Norman: University of Oklahoma Press, 1974.

Utley, Robert M. *A Clash of Cultures: Fort Bowie and the Chiricahua Apaches.* Washington, D.C.: National Park Service, 1977.

Vogel, Virgil. *American Indian Medicine.* Norman: University of Oklahoma Press, 1970.

Worcester, Donald E. *The Apaches: Eagles of the Southwest.* Norman: University of Oklahoma Press, 1979.

ARTICLES AND DISSERTATIONS

Aberle, S. J., J. H. Watkins, and E. H. Pitney. "The Vital History of San Juan Pueblo." *Human Biology* 12, no. 2 (May 1940): 141–87.

Ashburn, P. M. "How Disease Came with the White Man." *Hygeia* 14 (March–July 1936): 205–7, 310–12, 438–40, 514–16, 636–37.

Ball, Eve, as told to her by Eustace Fatty, an Apache. "Chiricahua Legends." *Western Folklore* 15 (April 1956): 110–12.

———. "Interpreter for the Apaches." *True West* (November–December 1971): 26–27, 36.

Borden, W. C. "The Vital Statistics of an Apache Indian Community." *Boston Medical and Surgical Journal* 139 (July–December 1893): 5–10.

Bourke, John Gregory. "The Medicine Men of the Apache." In Bureau of Ethnology, *Ninth Annual Report*, 1887–88. Glorieta, N.M.: The Rio Grande Press, 1983.

Boyer, L. Bryce, and Ruth M. Boyer. "Understanding the Individual Through Folklore." *Contemporary Psychoanalysis* 13: (1977) 30–51. Abstracted in *Transcultural Psychiatric Research Review* 14 (1977): 209–10.

Boyer, L. Bryce, Ruth M. Boyer, and George A. DeVos. "An Apache Woman's Account of Her Recent Acquisition of the Shamanistic Status." *Journal of Psychoanalytic Anthropology* 5 (1982): 299–331.

Clary, David A. "The Role of the Army Surgeon in the West: Daniel Wiesel at Fort Davis, Texas, 1868–1872." *Western Historical Quarterly* 3, no. 1 (January 1972): 53–66.

Crosby, Alfred W. "Conquistador y Pestilencia: The First New World Pandemic and the Fall of the Great Indian Empires." *Hispanic American Historical Review* 47 (1967): 321–37.

Dobie, J. Frank. "Madstones and Hydrophobia Skunks." In *Madstones and Twisters*, ed. Mody C. Boatright, Wilson M. Hudson, and Allen Maxwell, pp. 3–17. Dallas: Southern Methodist University Press, 1958.

Duffy, John. "Medicine in the West: An Historical Overview." *Journal of the West* 21, no. 3 (1982): 5–14.

East, Omega G. "Apache Prisoners in Fort Marion, 1886–1887." *El Escribano* 6, no. 3, (July 1969).

Elmore, Francis H. "The Shaman and Modern Medicine." *El Palacio* 42 (1937): 39–47.

Ewers, John C. "The Influence of Epidemics on the Indian Populations and Cultures of Texas." *Plains Anthropologist* 18, no. 60 (1973): 104–15.

Farrell, Dennis B. "Mesquite." *Arizona Highways* (October 1989): 42–45.

Faust, Ernest Carroll. "Clinical and Public Health Aspects of Malaria in the United States from an Historical Perspective." *American Journal of Tropical Medicine* 25 (1945): 185–201.

Goodman, David Michael. "Apaches as Prisoners of War: 1886–1894." Ph.D. diss., Texas Christian University, 1968.

Griffen, William B. "Apache Indians and Northern Mexican Peace Establishments." In *Southwestern Culture History: Collected Papers in Honor of Albert H. Schroeder*, ed. Albert H. Land, pp. 188–92. Papers of the Archeological Society of New Mexico, no. 10, 1985.

Griswold, Gillett. "The Fort Sill Apaches: Their Vital Statistics, Tribal Origins, Antecedents." U.S. Army and Missile Center Museum Archives. Fort Sill, Oklahoma, 1970.

Gunnerson, James H. "Southern Athapaskan Archeology." In *Handbook of North American Indians*. Vol. 9, pp. 162–69. Washington, D.C.: Smithsonian Institution Press, 1979.

Harper, Richard H. "The Missionary Work of the Reformed (Dutch) Church in America, in Oklahoma. Part II: Comanches and Apaches." *Chronicles of Oklahoma* 18, no. 4 (December 1940): 383–47.

Hrdlicka, Alex. "Disease, Medicine, and Surgery among the American Aborigines." *Journal of the American Medical Association* 99, no. 20 (November 12, 1932): 1661–62.

———. "Psychological and Medical Observations of the Indians of the Southwest." *Bureau of American Ethnology Bulletin* (Washington, D.C.) 32 (1908): 231–53.

———. "Seven Prehistoric Skulls with Complete Absence of the External Auditory Meatus." *American Journal of Physical Anthropology* 17, no. 3 (1933): 355–77.

———. "Tuberculosis among Certain Indian Tribes of the United States." *Bureau of American Ethnology Bulletin* (Washington, D.C.) 42 (1909): 28–32.

Huff, J. Wesley. "The Mountain Spirits Dance at Gallup." *New Mexico Magazine* (July 1948): 13–15, 41, 43.

Matson, Daniel S., and Albert H. Schroeder, eds. "Cordero's Description of the Apache—1796." *New Mexico Historical Review* 32 (October 1957): 335–36.

Officer, James E., and Edward F. Castetter. "The Ethnobotany of the Chiricahua and Mescalero Apaches." *Ethnobiological Studies in the American Southwest* 7 (1936): 1–63.

Opler, Morris E. "Chiricahua Apache." *Handbook of North American Indians.* Vol. 10, pp. 401–18. Washington, D.C.: Smithsonian Institution Press, 1983.

———. "A Chiricahua Apache's Account of the Geronimo Campaign of 1886." *New Mexico Historical Review* 13, no. 4 (October 1938): 360–86.

———. "The Concept of Supernatural Power among the Chiricahua and Mescalero Apaches." *American Anthropologist* 37, no. 1 (January–March 1935): 65–70.

———. "An Interpretation of Ambivalence of Two American Indian Tribes." *Journal of Social Psychology* 7 (1936): 82–115.

Reed, Walter. "Geronimo and His Warriors in Captivity." *The Illustrated American*, August 16, 1890, pp. 231–35.

Roe, Walter C. "Apache Prisoners of War." *Southern Workman* (April 1912): 3–12.

Salmon, Roberto Mario, trans. and ed. "No Hope of Victory: Pineda's 1791 Report on the Apache Frontier." *Journal of Arizona History* 20, no. 3 (Autumn 1979): 269–82.

Stockel, H. Henrietta. "Childbirth in the Old West." *Childbirth Educator* 9, no. 2 (Winter 1989–90): 22–27.

Trennert, Robert A. "Educating Indian Girls at Nonreservation Boarding Schools, 1878–1920." *Western Historical Quarterly* 13, no. 3 (July 1982): 271–90.

———. "From Carlisle to Phoenix: The Rise and Fall of the Indian Outing System, 1878–1930." *Pacific Historical Review* 52, no. 3 (August 1983): 267–91.

Tuberculosis among the North American Indians. National Tuberculosis Association, Committee on Tuberculosis among the North American Indians. Washington, D.C.: Government Printing Office, 1923.

Turcheneske, John Anthony, Jr. "The Apache Prisoners of War at Fort Sill, 1894–1914." Ph.D. diss., University of New Mexico, 1978.

———. "Disaster at White Tail: The Fort Sill Apaches' First Ten

Years at Mescalero, 1913–1923." *New Mexico Historical Review* 53, no. 2 (April 1978): 109–32.

———. " 'It Is Right That They Should Set Us Free': The Role of the War and Interior Departments in the Release of the Apache Prisoners of War, 1909–1913." *Red River Valley Historical Review* 4, no. 3 (Summer 1979): 4–32.

———. "The United States Congress and the Release of the Apache Prisoners of War at Fort Sill." *Chronicles of Oklahoma* 54 (Summer 1976): 199–226.

Underhill, Ruth M. "Ceremonial Patterns in the Greater Southwest." *Monographs of the American Ethnological Society* 13, pp. 35–60. Seattle: University of Washington Press, 1948.

Welsh, Herbert. "The Apache Prisoners at Fort Marion." Unpublished manuscript, n.d.

Woosley, Anne I. "Fort Burgwin's Hospital." *El Palacio* 86, no. 1 (Spring 1980): 3–7, 36–39.

Worcester, Donald E. "Early Spanish Accounts of the Apache Indians." *American Anthropologist*, n.s., 43 (1941): 308–12.

GOVERNMENT DOCUMENTS

National Archives. Letters Received, Adjutant General's Office, 1881–1889, microcopy M-689.

National Archives Trust Fund. Register of Indian Prisoners. 389 Army Continental Commands, part 5.

United States Department of the Interior. *Annual Reports of the Commissioner of Indian Affairs*, 1873–1914.

United States Senate. Document 366. Vol. 5657, 61st Cong., 2d sess.

———. Document 432. Vol. 6175, 62d Cong., 2d sess.

———. Document 1038. Vol. 25, 62d Cong., 3d sess.

———. Executive Document 73. Vol. 2358, 49th Cong., 2d sess.

———. Executive Document 117. Vol. 2358, 49th Cong., 2d sess.

———. Executive Document 83. Vol. 2682, 51st Cong., 1st sess.

———. Executive Document 35. Vol. 2686, 51st Cong., 1st sess.

———. Executive Document 88. Vol. 2686, 51st Cong., 1st sess.

———. Executive Document 41. 51st Cong., 2d sess.

———. Report no. 184. Vol. 2358, 49th Cong., 2d sess.

———. Report no. 189. Vol. 2519, 50th Cong., 1st sess.

Arizona Historical Society, Tucson. Fred Hughes, Loomis Langdon, and Al Williamson Collections.

Fort Sill Museum, Fort Sill, Oklahoma. The Glennan Collection and the Apache Prisoner of War Archives.

Frisco Native American Museum, Frisco, North Carolina. John Shapard, Jr., Papers.

New Mexico State Records Center and Archives, Santa Fe. Dingee Collection, Delgado Family Papers.

Oklahoma Historical Society, Oklahoma City, Oklahoma. Record Group 75, National Archives; Indian Pioneer History Collection.

Searcy Hospital, Mount Vernon, Alabama. John Shapard, Jr., Papers.

University of New Mexico, Special Collections, Albuquerque. Michael Steck Papers.

MISCELLANEOUS PUBLICATIONS

Carlisle Indian School Catalog. 1912.
Christmas Card. Searcy Hospital, Mount Vernon, Alabama.
Fact Sheet. Fort Pickens.
Pamphlet. Searcy Hospital, Mount Vernon, Alabama.

Brown, Capt. H. G., 193
Browning, D. M., 193
Bullis, Clarence, 29
Bull roarers, 25

Calle, 186
Capell, Arthur, 141, 143, 149, 165, 183, 231–32
Capron, Lt. Allyn, 200–201, 212
Carleton, Gen. James, 282n9
Carlisle School: choice of, 113–15, 118, 297n7; correspondence with parents, 129–31; curriculum, 118–19; deaths of children, 123, 131–36, 154, 208–9, 297n11; diet, 123; disease in, xx, xxi, 112, 262–63; and Fort Sill transfer, 187–88, 205–6; outing system, 119–22; separation from parents, 126–29; tuberculosis, xxi, 112, 123, 124–26, 298n16, 301n34
Carson, Kit, 55
Carter, Fitzhugh, 203
Cascara sagrada, 53, 286n30
Castetter, Edward F., 20
Catholic church, 35–36, 50–51
Cattails, 24–25
Chamomile, 54
Chatto, 73–76, 186, 187, 221, 243
Chatto, Blake, 222
Chatto, Maurice, 222
Cheyenne, 57
Chihuahua, 69, 137, 186, 187; interview with, 238–39; surrender of, xviii, 63–64, 65

Chihuahua, Eugene, 64, 78, 137, 215, 288n1
Chihuahua, Rose, 217
Children: deaths of, 72, 82, 83–84, 261–62, 289n9; education, 114, 115–18, 152, 296n4; at Fort Sill, 204; Hampton Normal School, 204–5; marasmus, 85, 291n32; nursing, 70–71; U.S. government policies, xx, xxi, 113–14. *See also* Carlisle School; *specific topics*
Chinney, Lydia Inez, 229
Chiskio, 130–31
Cholera, 52–53, 285n28
Cleghorn, Mildred Imach, xviii, 78, 93–94, 116, 228, 247–48, 290n22
Cleveland, Grover, 68, 95, 139
Climate, xxi, 258, 259–60, 275; Fort Marion, 81, 82, 87; Fort Pickens, 101–2, 294–95n15; Mount Vernon, 137–38, 154–55, 300n26
Clothing, 26, 27
Cochise, 22
Cochran, Capt. John J., 127–29, 163, 301n34
Collé, 168
Coloradas, Mangas, 277n3
Common cold, 31, 53–54
Compa, Juan Jose, 277n3
Contagious diseases, 38–40, 258–59, 266; eastern United States, 41–42; and mobile Apache life-style, 32, 33–35, 36–37; and Pueblo peoples,

Glennan, Capt. J. D., 131–32, 206–9

Goldenseal, 53, 285n27

Go-nal-tsis, 186

Goode, Maj. George W., 267, 306n47

Goody, Talbot, 225, 229

Gordon, Benjamin, 5, 9, 10, 60

Goth-kly, 186

Griffen, William B., 3, 37, 50, 58

Grosvenor, William, III, 214

Guydelkon, Arthur, 186, 200, 212

Haley, James, 19

Hampton Normal School, 185–86, 204–5, 302n46

Ha-o-zinne, 98–99

Haozous, Blossom Wratten, 71, 245–46

Haozous, Etheline, 228–29

Haozous, Sam, 71, 76, 115, 212, 221, 250, 286–87n40

Harrison, Benjamin, 162, 190

Hauke, C. F., 198

Healing: Apache beliefs about, 4–5, 6, 8; and Catholic church, 36, 50–51; *curanderismo*, xxii, 31, 53–55; importance of, xvii; medical treatment of prisoners, 80–81, 103, 145, 192–99, 211–13, 305n35; military physicians, 55–56, 59–60, 192–93; pioneer healing arts, xxii, 55–56, 58–60, 283n4. *See also* Native American healing arts

Heat exhaustion, 82

Herbalists, 19, 22

Hispanic healing arts. *See Curanderismo*

Hoddentin, 24–25, 49, 281n30

Hopis, 57

Hospers, Hendrina, 225

Houser, Allan, 249, 251–52, 309–10n24

Howard, Gen. O. O., 96, 159, 163

Howard, Lt. Guy, 159–62

Hrdlicka, Alex, 4–5, 9, 22, 32, 39–40, 46–47, 60, 84, 85, 124–25, 281n1

Huff, J. Wesley, 29

Hugar, Elbys Naiche, 15, 248

Hughes, Fred G., 23

Hume, Charles R., 194, 195

Igamo, 197

Imach, Amy, 221

Imach, Richard, 78, 125

Inanition, 168, 301n40

Incarceration: breakup of families, 69–70, 97, 100, 108–9, 230; as compassionate, xix; and denial of access to healing arts, 61–62, 89, 290–91n30; and dysentery, 49; enlistment of prisoners, 164–65, 260, 301–2n44; as genocide, 274–75; government reluctance to end, xviii, 93–94, 100, 161; official naming, xx, 130; psychological effects of, 86, 230, 292n35; public opinion, 86–87, 89, 107–8, 155, 178, 184, 260; release from, xviii,

Nana, 186
Native American healing arts:
    Apache beliefs, 4–5, 12;
    death taboos, 15–17, 279n6;
    denial of access to, 61–62, 89,
    290–91n30; Fort Sill, 212,
    214–16, 305n38; herbalists,
    19, 22; and legends, 6, 8, 28–
    29; and moral standards,
    60–61, 287–88n49; Mount
    Vernon, 154, 156–58, 300n25;
    natural remedies, xxii, 4, 9,
    14–15, 19–22, 47, 49, 89,
    285n23; pregnancy and
    childbirth, 57; Reed's article,
    163–64; rituals, xvii, 11–12,
    19, 25–26; sacred objects, 25–
    26; and smallpox, 51–52; and
    tuberculosis, 47, 49; and
    venereal diseases, 60–61. *See
    also* Shamans
Neuralgia, 83
New York World, 107
Nichols, Maury, 194
Noble, John W., 164
Noche, 186, 187, 221, 241–42
Notalq, 48

Officer, James E., 20
Ogden, David, 102, 294–95n15
Olsanny, Richard, 200
Opatas, 3
Opium, 56
Opler, Morris, 3, 12, 16, 21,
    22, 61
Osha, 54, 286n31
Os-kis-say, 261

Overcrowding, 72, 86, 219,
    291–92n34
Owls, 16–17

Painter, C. C., 186–87
Parker, Quanah, 197
Patricio, 186
Patzk, J. H., 144, 145,
    298–99n5
Peña, Mary, 21
Perico, 109, 111, 186
Perico, Harry, 223
Perrone, Bobette, 6, 12
Pimas, 8
Pioneers: dangers to, 42–45;
    and Eastern contagious
    diseases, 41–42; healing arts,
    xxii, 55–56, 58–60, 283n4
Pneumonia, 45, 220, 283n5
Poisoning, 37–38, 282n9
Pork, 11, 70, 144
Pratt, Capt. R. H., 113–14, 125–
    26, 134, 297n7, 298n16. *See
    also* Carlisle School
Pregnancy and childbirth,
    56–57
Proctor, Redfield, 162, 185,
    189, 190
Pueblo peoples, 11, 34–36
Purrington, Lt. George, 306n47

Quaking aspen, 22
Quineh, 221
Quinine, 39, 49, 284n14

Rabies, 54–55, 286n33, 35
Ramon, 89, 186
Rations, 57–58

xx–xxi, 178, 274–75
Upshaw, A. B., 114
Ussen, 12
Utes, 285–86n29

Vaccination, 49–50, 51, 194,
  195, 197–98,
  284–85n22, 299n5
Vance, Lt. Z. B., 186
VanEtten, Teresa Pijoan, 52
Venereal diseases, 45–46,
  60–61, 307–8n62
Victorio, 277n3, 287n44
Viruses, 49–52. *See also*
  Contagious diseases
Vogel, Virgil, 19

Walker, Maj. W. T., 194
Warfare, 4, 277n3
Watercress, 287n44
Water supply, 82, 290n28
Webb, DeWitt, 80–81, 82, 83,
  84, 85, 291n33
Wells, George, 111
Welsh, Herbert, 75, 86–89, 108,
  109, 144, 151, 289n10
Whitetail, 267–69, 271
Whittlesey, E., 113
Wiesel, Daniel, 60
Williamson, Al, 22–23

Willow, 22
Witches, 12–13, 22–23, 279n6
Witherill, Capt. C. T., 186
Women: adultery, 60–61,
  287n49; education for, 119–
  20, 297n8; official naming of,
  xx, 145; pregnancy and
  childbirth, 56–57; roles of,
  104–5
Women of the Apache Nation
  (Stockel), 6
Woodall, W. T., 218
Worcester, Donald, 13
Wotherspoon, Lt. William
  Wallace, 155, 158, 165, 166,
  168–69, 173–78
Wratten, George Medhurst, 96,
  129, 293n6; and Fort Pickens
  incarceration, 78–79, 97; and
  Fort Sill transfer, 186, 188,
  203–4, 205–6; and Mount
  Vernon incarceration, 152,
  153, 156, 157
Wright, Frank Hall, 221

Yanohza, 186

Zele, 186
Zi-yeh, 217
Zunis, 2, 277n1